POLITICAL
TERRAIN

Political Terrain

WASHINGTON, D.C.,

from Tidewater Town
to Global Metropolis

Carl Abbott

The University of
North Carolina Press
Chapel Hill &
London

The paper in this book meets the guidelines for permanence and durability of the Committee on Production Guidelines for Book Longevity of the Council on Library Resources.

Library of Congress Cataloging-in-Publication Data

Abbott, Carl.

  Political terrain: Washington, D.C., from Tidewater town to global metropolis / Carl Abbott.

     p. cm.

  Includes bibliographical references and index.

  ISBN 0-8078-2478-x (alk. paper).—ISBN 0-8078-4805-0 (pbk.: alk. paper)

     1. Washington (D.C.)—History. 2. Regionalism—Southern States. 3. Regionalism—Northeastern States. I. Title.

F194.A23   1999

975.3—dc21   98-41013

                                                                    CIP

03 02 01 00 99   5 4 3 2 1

Portions of this work have appeared previously in Carl Abbott, "Dimensions of Regional Change in Washington, D.C.," *American Historical Review* 90 (December 1990): 1367–93, used by permission of the American Historical Association; "Perspectives on Urban Economic Planning: The Case of Washington, D.C., since 1980," *Public Historian* 11 (Spring 1989): 5–21, used by permission of the Regents of the University of California, and "The Internationalization of Washington, D.C.," *Urban Affairs Review* 31 (May 1996): 571–94, used by permission of Sage Publications.

Excerpts from Karl Shapiro, "The Potomac" and "Washington Cathedral," © Karl Shapiro 1941, 1987 by arrangement with Wieser and Wieser, Inc., New York, N.Y.

Excerpts from Gary Snyder, "It Pleases," *Turtle Island* (New York: New Directions Publishing, 1974), by Gary Snyder; reprinted by permission of New Directions Publishing Company.

CONTENTS

ILLUSTRATIONS

—

MAPS

TABLES

—

PREFACE

This is a book about one of my favorite cities. I have been intrigued by Washington since a first brief visit at age seven. My mother and I had taken the Southern Railway from Knoxville to Washington on the way to visit an aunt, uncle, and cousins in Wilmington, Delaware. We arrived in the morning with time to spare before transferring to a second train, giving my mother the opportunity to grab a cab in front of Union Station to show me the capital city. The tour included quick glimpses of the Capitol and White House, mall and museums, Lincoln and Jefferson Memorials. The morning was gray and drizzling, but the buildings and spaces were unlike anything I had seen in my first hometown.

Since 1951 I have visited Washington more times than I can count and have lived there twice as one of those sojourners whose home is elsewhere. In the summer of 1966 I lived on Capitol Hill and took the bus to the State Department, where a team of recent college graduates read and coded Foreign Service personnel files for a study aimed at identifying the traits of a successful diplomat (courage under fire, great patience, and a passion for self-sacrificing socializing). Evenings and weekends allowed time to explore both the city's monumental core and the variety of its neighborhoods.

More than two decades later, in the winter and spring of 1987, I returned as Banneker Professor at the Center for Washington Area Studies at George Washington University and visiting member of the university's Department of Urban and Regional Planning. This time I lived in Bethesda and took the Metro into the city center. The generous support of George Washington University, sabbatical support from Portland State University, and a later summer research grant from the National Endowment for the Humanities allowed me to plunge into libraries and archives.

If the State Department job introduced me to Washington as a global control point, the association with George Washington University offered me a chance to explore the multiple neighborhoods and communities of the metropolitan area. On other visits to join in political demonstrations and marches I have experienced Washington as the stage on which Americans project their ideas about the good nation, and I have been challenged to think about Washington's persisting southern connections by arguing politics with my brother-in-law, an attorney and political activist in Fairfax County via the Eastern Shore of Maryland and the College of William and Mary.

My approach to Washington is rooted in a fascination with American regions and the ways that cities shape and express those regions. This interest derives, in part, from thinking about the contrast of early years in Tennessee and then in Ohio, from college in Philadelphia and graduate school in Chicago, and from teaching in Denver, Norfolk, and Portland—three cities that serve as commercial and financial nuclei for multistate regions. City and region have been a central theme of previous writing on the early hinterlands of Cincinnati and Chicago, the tension among Colorado's economic and cultural regions, the emergence of a set of Sunbelt cities, the differences between Seattle and Portland, and the character of an urbanized West. I am taken by the complex answers to apparently simple questions: Where does the West begin? Is wheat farming or automobile manufacturing the defining trait of the Middle West? Which novelists or scriptwriters best capture the distinctive feel of Oregon, Mississippi, or Montana, Los Angeles, Baltimore, or Boston?

This book is an answer to a similarly innocuous question that I have been raising at parties and faculty gatherings since 1987. "Where's Washington?" I ask. "How does it fit into America's regional mosaic?" The following pages are my own response, an attempt to understand how the capital city has grown and changed in relation to its neighbors and its nation.

A number of acknowledgments are in order. I am indebted to the special collections department of Gelman Library at George Washington University, to the multiple departments of the Library of Congress, to the Historical Society of Washington, D.C., and to the Washingtoniana Collection of the Martin Luther King Jr. Public Library, which very effectively serves the full range of persons interested in Washington history. I have learned much from Howard Gillette Jr., the leading historian of Washington planning and politics, and have benefited greatly from the opportunity to interact with other scholars of Washington such as Steven Diner, Dennis Gale, Jeffrey Henig, Kathryn Allamong Jacob, Alan Lessoff, Richard Longstreth, and Brett Williams. From outside the academy, I learned as well from such Washington experts as planner John Fondersmith, demographers Eunice Grier and George Grier, and the editorial team at the *Washingtonian* magazine.

POLITICAL
TERRAIN

One

PLACING
WASHINGTON

Americans sort out their cities with nicknames and slogans. Faced with dozens of major metropolitan centers and scores of aspiring cities, we simplify the task of distinguishing Kalamazoo from Kokomo and Topeka from Tulsa by attaching shorthand characterizations. We traffic in common nicknames whether or not we have ever visited the Motor City, Baghdad by the Bay, the Emerald City (that's Seattle, not Oz), the Big Apple, or Big D. We look for truth in appellations and catchphrases that take on a life of their own. Perhaps the West really begins at Fort Worth. Could Boston truly be the hub of the American intellectual universe? Did Atlanta grow so fast because its white residents really were too busy to hate?

Nicknames and slogans are the products of self-conscious image making by civic elites and professional promoters. But they also catch the popular imagination when they appear to give plausible answers to common questions.[1] What is life like there? Is it fast-paced, laid-back, artsy, businesslike? What does the place look like? Is it bathed in sunshine, washed by a mighty river, or crowded with bustling factories? What assumptions and values do residents share and emphasize? Are they tolerant, acquisitive, civic-minded, self-interested?

Sloganizing often ties a community specifically to its region. I grew up in Dayton, the Gem City of Ohio's Miami River Valley. For big events, like the first films photographed in Cinerama, we piled into the family Studebaker and drove fifty miles down the Dixie Highway (U.S. 25—the great connection between southern workers and middle western automobile factories) to the Queen City of the West, aka Cincinnati. Other names and slogans have tried and sometimes succeeded in identifying cities as the heart of Dixie, the capital of more than one inland empire, or the buckle of the Sunbelt.

In the midst of the urban babble, Washington, D.C., has been hard to pin down. As if the city is like one of its proverbial two-faced politicians, observers have struggled to capture its character in a single satisfying phrase or paragraph. John F. Kennedy reflected this difficulty with his often-quoted aphorism that Washington is a city of "southern efficiency and northern charm."[2] Novelist Willie Morris reflected the same ambiguity in *The Last of the Southern Girls* (1973) when he created a Washington dinner party that seated Arkansas-bred Carol Templeton Hollywell next to a famous middle western writer:

"Have you ever written about Washington?" [she asks amid the clatter of china and silver].

"No" [is the writer's reply]. "Everybody's too native to somewhere else."

"Northerners consider it Southern and Southerners think it Northern."

"That's why it's here."[3]

Morris's carefully crafted conversation is sharp writing but flawed analysis. It conflates two distinct approaches to understanding the essential Washington and blurs the fact that Americans tell two different stories about the character of their national capital. Aspects of these stories can be tested objectively, as I hope to do, but they have lives of their own. They are themselves cultural facts that help people make sense of an unusual place and give us entry points for thinking about cities, regions, and networks in the development of the nation.

The first story about Washington is a narrative of regional change. Washington used to be southern until . . . , or Washington is still southern despite. . . . This is the story that locals tell—journalists with Washington connections, congressmen with decades of Washington experience. It centers attention on the influx of outsiders and the influence of outside values that have supposedly changed the character of the city, but its timing is slippery. The turning point is sometimes put as far back as the Civil War or the Gilded Age. Others date the big change to World War I, or the New Deal, or World War II, or racial integration in the 1950s, or the New Frontier, or home rule in the 1970s, or globalization in the 1980s: "The sleepy Southern town that continued well into the 1970s has been replaced by a big-time city," said a 1994 edition of a slick hotel room sights-and-shopping guide.[4] Washington through this lens is regional but hard to focus, a southern city whose character seems to melt in the glare of television lights.

Gore Vidal's novel *Washington, D.C.* (1967), for example, describes such a process of regional change during the New Deal, when New York brain trusters and middle western graduate students arrived in numbers to rescue a ravaged economy through federal intervention. Vidal's spokesperson is a fictional society columnist with Potomac Valley roots. Hosting a genteel party at a northern Virginia estate, she remarks that "our lovely, gracious Southern city has been engulfed by all these . . . [she casts around for a tactful phrase] . . . charmin' people who've opened our poor eyes to so many things undreamed of in our philosophy."[5] Vidal's character would have had a sympathetic ear in Mississippi senator John Stennis, who lamented in the 1970s about the slow erosion of Washington's traditionally "southern attitudes in the social realm—neighborliness, friendliness, conviviality."[6] Nevertheless, his colleague Mark Hatfield, arriving in Washington from Oregon in the late 1960s, was struck by the city's continuing southernness. Why, he wondered, did Washington's short-order cooks serve up his breakfast eggs and toast with what seemed to be a puddle of Cream of Wheat on the side of the plate?[7]

This story of southern retreat and staying power as retold by Vidal, Stennis, and scores of other observers is a direct attack on an essential truth. Washington was born in a regional borderland that was itself pulled among alternative futures at the start of the nineteenth century. For two hundred years the growing city has balanced between Tidewater and Piedmont, between East and West, and most obviously between North and South. Perceptions and images of its character have changed as the meanings ascribed to the nation's dominant regions have developed and changed. In the process of these larger changes, Washington has been enlisted on behalf of different groups, different agendas, and the different needs of South and North.

A second and very different understanding of Washington comes easily to many Americans who look at the city from the outside. This is a moral tale of sin and fall without redemption, telling of a community that has purchased power at the price of its soul and character. Its communities of bureaucrats and lobbyists are thought to make the city into an aberration that lacks the regional identification and loyalties that might be expected in more ordinary communities ("everybody's too native to somewhere else," says Hollywell's dinner partner). Perhaps pandering to national prejudice, political leaders have frequently criticized Washington as a city of outsiders and temporaries. "There are a number of things wrong with Washington," said Dwight Eisenhower, himself the product of a peripatetic career; "one of them is that everyone has been too long away from home." Richard Nixon, an extremely self-conscious outsider, agreed that "Washington is a city without identity. Everybody comes from someplace else. . . . Deep down, they still think they're back home."[8]

The assumption of rootless residents implies that Washington cannot be understood as an identifiable place, but only as a collection of place seekers. To a newcomer like President Jimmy Carter, Washington was thus an "island" with few bridges to the American mainland. To journalist Joel Garreau, it is an aberration. Says one of the characters in Larry McMurtry's Washington-based novel *Cadillac Jack* (1982), "It's fine for spies and newspapermen, but it ain't everybody's cup of tea. Maybe you ought to move to Minnesota."9

This second story is also true. Washington has been extraregional even as its society and politics have been intensely regionalized. The city originated as a platform for the federal government that would be outside the direct administrative control of a single state or set of states (although the choice and development of the site was never apolitical). Efforts to base economic growth on a local hinterland repeatedly failed. Instead, the seat of govern-

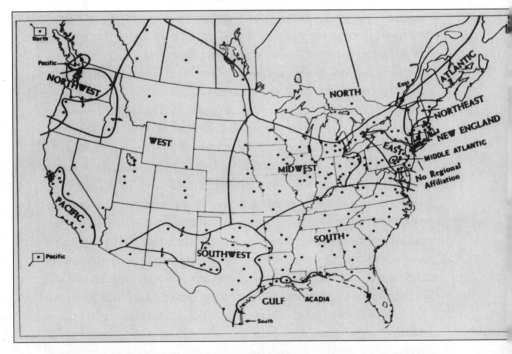

Washington and the zone of regional indifference. Geographer Wilbur Zelinsky found in the 1970s that Washington lay between areas of distinct regional identity but had no widely recognized regional identity of its own. (From Wilbur Zelinsky, "North America's Vernacular Regions," *Annals of the Association of American Geographers*, 1980)

ment slowly attracted national institutions and organizations—many of which now locate in Washington because of each other's presence, not because of the city's character as a special and specific place. The experts who operate these organizations come from a national pool of talent, not from the regional hinterland that supplies most middle managers in "real" cities like Milwaukee and Cleveland. Late-twentieth-century Washington is thus a node in national and global networks of power and communication.

These contrasting ideas about Washington's character as a metropolitan community are the starting point for this essay in urban history. I want to remain close to the case—to the experience of Washington and Washingtonians—but also to use this fascinating city to explore the historical processes that have been involved in the construction and interaction of American regions and networks. As I have considered Washington's history, I have come to believe that it provides a valuable arena for analyzing the tensions between local or regional allegiances and global change. Rather than allowing theorists of the local and the general to talk past each other, we can benefit from research that uses a specific community to examine the tension between the local and the general, between horizontal and vertical pulls.

Washington, of course, is an extraordinary rather than a typical city, but it is unusual in ways that illuminate the interplay between place and network. Because it has had such an ambiguous and contested regional identity, its local character has been an item of open discussion rather than an unspoken assumption. Because it is embedded in national politics, its fitness for federal, national, and international activities has likewise been a subject of frequent debate. In Washington, in short, the social and political construction of place has been a public process.

First, to put the question in its most unsophisticated form, I want to know what regions Washington has "really" belonged to. If we slice the American map into North, South, East, West, and a myriad of smaller regions, where should we put Washington? How have regional influences worked themselves out in Washington over two centuries? Which regional characteristics and connections have faded, which have persisted, and which have been reconstituted?

Second, I want to know how *extraregional* connections have functioned in one of the nation's most intensely networked cities. Have they supplanted or supplemented regional ties? When and how did the "federal city" become a "national city," and how have its national roles competed with those of other cities? How deeply can we trace the roots of its prominence as an international metropolis? And have these networked functions turned it into one of those artificially sustained "nonplaces" that critics of postmodernism so gleefully assail?[10]

A slightly different way to formulate the same questions is to ask where Washington has fit within a changing system of cities in the United States. What roles and functions have the city's leadership and the nation at large defined at different periods? How successfully has the city performed these roles? How have these roles differentiated it from neighboring or competing cities—first Alexandria and Georgetown, then Baltimore and Richmond, then New York and Atlanta? What have these developing roles meant for Washington's sense of itself as a community?

The pursuit of these specific historical questions inevitably engages theoretical discussions about the changing meaning and character of "place" or places in the modern and postmodern worlds. In developing this framework for analysis, we can think of Washington, and any other city, as pulled both "horizontally" among its neighboring regions and "vertically" from the local landscape to national and international roles.

An emphasis on regional connections and change raises empirical questions about the relative dynamism of different parts of the American nation. Because Washington is located in the border zone between two of the country's great cultural regions, much of its history is "mappable." It can be represented in terms of competing pulls and influences among geographic regions that are spatially articulated and involve a "horizontal" dimension in urban development. The idea of Washington as a border or frontier city is a way to conceptualize this horizontal dimension.

The second formulation introduces a "vertical" dimension involving tensions between locally based connections and character and the influence of wide-ranging networks. It embeds Washington in the dialogue about the impacts of modernization and the changing scale of formal and informal institutions in industrial and postindustrial society. Modernization has involved the incorporation of specific places into national and international economic and social systems. It involves the triumph of bureaucracy over personal connections, long-distance affiliations over next-door neighbors, generalizability over particularity. In detail, Washington's modernization thus demonstrates the rise of large-scale institutions and challenges the assumption that local allegiances can persist in a globalizing world.

Involved in both horizontal and vertical dimensions is a tension between past and future, for a sense of history is embedded in our reading of regional character as well as our understanding of modernization. For the century from the 1860s to the 1960s, Americans usually read South as "old" and

North as "new," with Washington as a mediator between systems of values rooted in time as well as place. As well as anyone, Baltimore-born Karl Shapiro summarized this understanding in the opening lines of his 1942 poem "The Potomac":

> The thin Potomac scarcely moves
> But to divide Virginia from today.[11]

As these lines suggest, to talk about Washington's regional character is also to contribute to debates about the character of the American South. In different versions and understandings, the South is disappearing, enduring, or even extending its influence. To the degree that Washington has permanently shifted from "southern" to "northern," its history suggests the inevitable erosion of a distinctively southern culture and society in face of national institutions and power. If Washington is best understood as an island and aberration, in contrast, the South by implication may be unaffected as a social and cultural region by the vast growth of a border metropolis. And if Washington is an arena in which southern connections are repeatedly revitalized, that experience offers evidence that the South itself remains a dynamic and lively region coequal with the North.

I assumed at the start of this project that I would be looking at nonpolitical Washington, paying little attention to the dynamics of federal power or to local government decisions. Instead, I find that everything about Washington is "political" in either a narrow or broad sense. Indeed, because of Washington's special symbolic and functional roles as the national metropolis, its identity repeatedly has been contested and redefined. Groups and factions within the United States have tried to use Washington to express and represent their own interests and values and to equate those values with the national interest. Regional claims on Washington have also been claims about the character of the nation.

At times these efforts have involved explicit contests for control of the institutions of government. Most obvious was the Civil War, which filled the city with Union soldiers and brought a Confederate army within the District of Columbia in 1864. Other explicitly political contests that used Washington as an arena for sectional agendas included the debate over the District of Columbia slave trade and the Compromise of 1850, the creation and abolition of territorial government after the Civil War, civil rights campaigns after 1945, and the battle for home rule for the District of Columbia in the 1970s.

At other times the contest has involved symbolic statements. A southernized social scene in the 1850s that revolved around political figures such as Clement and Virginia Clay implied that southern values were national values. A Republicanized city after 1865 sent the contrary message that the national values were northern. Attention to the inclusive symbolism of federal buildings and the rise of the Washington pilgrimage implied a nationalism that transcended region. The rise of a black middle class in Washington in the late nineteenth century was a way to assert symbolic (and real) claims to a full role in American society.

Washington as town, city, and metropolitan area has thus been political terrain—a place freighted with symbolic meanings. We can understand facets of Washington history as the product of tensions among places and regions, between cultural origins and economic functions. Washington's identity has been contested between South and North, white and black, native daughters and newcomers, local business interests and congressional committees. It has also balanced among local people, national aspirations, and international roles. The outcomes of these contests reveal much about what we have been as a nation. Fraught with symbolism at every step, these tensions have been manifested in the political process of making choices between competing interests and claims.

The remainder of this chapter explores how the two dynamics of regionalization and modernization have structured the developing nation and set a context for the growth of Washington. How do we understand the past geographies of American development? How have Americans been differentiated by regions, and how have they understood the resulting spatial patterns? How have national institutions and networks grown and overridden local interests and allegiances? What do these understandings suggest that we might discover about Washington, and what might Washington's growth tell us about models of national development?

Regional Dynamics: Culture, Connections, Claims

Cities are obvious enough. We usually know one when we see it: a vertical accent of skyscrapers, smokestacks, church spires, and grain elevators rising out of the horizontal landscape of North America. Regions are harder to find. They are abstractions defined at some times by shared heritage, at others by intermittent flows of people, objects, and information. They can be large or small, cultural, economic, or political. Regional boundaries vary with the purpose of the discussion and the perspectives of its participants.

Human beings construct their regional patterns through commonalities of culture, through social and economic connections, and through explicit claims. The literature of geography contains long-standing and lively discussions about the origins and spread of cultural regions, about the spatial patterning of economic activity, and about the codification of cultural and economic regions through the definition of political boundaries. These are the standard categories of regional types—vernacular, functional, and formal.

In each realm, regional patterns are most easily understood in terms of centers and peripheries. Systems of regions normally consist of strong, identifiable cores, each surrounded by zones of gradually decreasing influence. Toward the outer edges of such zones are "soft" borderlands where the multiple influences of one center overlap and gradually give way to those of another. Head south-southwest from Chicago through the valley of the Illinois River. Someplace in the corn belt of Illinois, small-town residents lose interest in the *Chicago Tribune* and opt for the *St. Louis Post-Dispatch*. Along the same gradient, more and more baseball fans root for the Cardinals and fewer for the Cubs. At some other point, the owners of Main Street stores find it easier to deal with St. Louis suppliers than with Chicago wholesalers.[12]

One of the basic conditions of American development was the early establishment of a set of cultural regions arrayed from north to south along the Atlantic coast and their consequent westward expansion along roughly parallel corridors of settlement. The analysis of such cultural regions emphasizes long continuities in the spatial distribution of values, customs, and other cultural information. English, French, and Spanish settlers brought sets of values and patterns of behavior to the New World. They responded to particular resource endowments by adapting this cultural heritage within the limits set by the world economy of the seventeenth and eighteenth centuries. In the British continental colonies, the result was distinct cultural areas around cores in New England, the Delaware Valley, the Chesapeake Tidewater, and South Carolina.[13] Expansion of settlement in the eighteenth and nineteenth centuries carried New England ways into the basin of the Great Lakes, Mid-Atlantic society into the Ohio and central Mississippi Valleys, and intensive plantation society across the Gulf states. The Chesapeake region contributed to the southwestward expansion of slave society and interacted with Mid-Atlantic traditions to create an "upland South" or "southern Midlands" in Kentucky and Tennessee.[14] Beyond the ninety-sixth meridian, the historic cultural regions have overlapped and mingled even more extensively with each other, with distinct Hispanic and Native American culture areas, and with separately established Anglo-American settlement systems spreading from Utah and California.[15]

The elucidation of cultural regions has been the province of a wide range of disciplines that emphasize the determining role of shared values. Specialists in American studies, anthropology, architectural history, cultural geography, linguistics, material and folk culture, political history, and sociology have offered important definitions of cultural regions.[16] Such writers emphasize the early definition or spread of cultural regions, with secondary attention to current expressions of the heritage of early settlement in contemporary regional patterns. Their methods tend to center on the examination of homogeneity in the spatial distribution of traits and behaviors that express common heritage or values. The detailed and influential descriptions of modern cultural regions by Wilbur Zelinsky and Raymond Gastil follow what the latter has called the "doctrine of first effective settlement." Gastil's work divides the United States into cultural regions defined by "variations in the cultures of the peoples that dominated the first settlement and . . . secondarily by variations in the cultures of peoples that dominated later settlements."[17]

The spread of research on popular culture in the last two decades has added twentieth-century examples to the extensive literature on folk culture in earlier centuries. Much of this work was summarized in the 387 maps published in This Remarkable Continent, a compilation organized by the Society for a North American Cultural Survey, an informal consortium of geographers, anthropologists, folklorists, and related specialists.[18] Many of the newer expressions fit within the framework of traditional cultural regions. Country and western music has evolved and flourished within the upland South. Political support for environmental protection and participation in high school soccer have been concentrated within the northeastern core and its westward extension along the New England settlement corridor. Other cultural choices, such as membership in Christian Science churches, popularity of different Americanized ethnic cuisines, and participation in high school football, appear to reflect new regional dynamics that ignore traditional cultural boundaries.[19]

Cultural regions are an inescapable part of popular culture. Americans continue to traffic in regional stereotypes. We gleefully tell jokes that target Iowans or Texans whereas we will no longer generalize about race or class. Advertisers play on the popular imagery of a wide-open West. Television and movies trade in regional stereotypes (or regional character)—The Dukes of Hazard and Baywatch, Annie Hall, and Fargo. Radio announcers read out state "residency tests" that retail regional stereotypes: Do you own or rent your mobile home? Do you own ten, fifteen, or twenty gold chains?

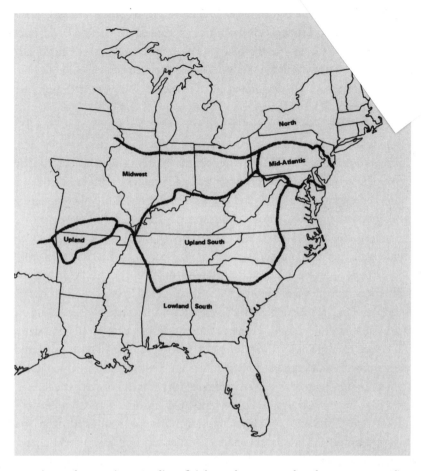

American culture regions. Studies of eighteenth-century cultural patterns agree that the middle and upper Potomac lay between the centers of colonial Chesapeake and "Pennsylvanian" culture. (From Henry Glassie, *Patterns in the Material Folk Culture of the Eastern United States* [1968])

On a theoretical rather than popular level, it is easy for description of preindustrial cultural adaptations and their persistence to nudge into advocacy of a simpler life—sometimes a special temptation for scholars of the South. Americans have avoided a culturally essentialist exultation of *Der Volk*, but many apologists and advocates for American regionalism in the twentieth century have explicitly argued for place as an alternative to modernity. So contended the regional communitarians and southern agrarians of the 1920s, western regionalists of the 1930s, and many neoregionalists of the 1980s and 1990s.[20] The latter are often political progressives looking for lo-

cal centers of resistance to global capitalism and its large-scale organizations. They are sometimes cultural critics who assert the need to reconstruct
social connections to specific places and applaud the vigor of regionally
rooted art and literature. But they can also be deep conservatives looking for
bastions from which to defend the untrammeled development of natural resources or the free exercise of racial bigotry.

Both progressive and conservative efforts to reromanticize region are
likely to find only limited success, however, because of the power of trade,
immigration, and investment to alter cultural patterns. People and property
in market economies flow to economic and social opportunities. Connections and communication do not necessarily trump culture, but they place
conditions on the persistence of old patterns.

Indeed, the articulation of cultural regions in the seventeenth and eighteenth centuries was a prelude to the emergence of a second inclusive regional pattern in the nineteenth century through the definition and development of a northeastern industrial core that centralized economic control
over peripheral resource regions. The result is a dual regional patterning on
a continental scale. Stages in the evolution of the economically dominant
American core include (1) the differential growth of the Atlantic ports and
the emergence of New York, Philadelphia, and Boston as national economic
centers in the eighteenth and early nineteenth centuries, (2) the attachment
of a growing system of middle western cities to these eastern centers between 1820 and 1870, (3) the concentration of American industry in the core
states through the reciprocal growth of markets and manufacturing between 1850 and 1920, and (4) the twentieth-century concentration of control
functions in the cities of the Northeast and Old Northwest.[21] By 1950 the industrialized corridor that extended from Baltimore and Boston to Milwaukee and St. Louis contained 7 percent of the nation's land area but 43 percent of its population, 50 percent of its income, and 70 percent of its
manufacturing employment. Flows of investment, trade, and business and
scientific information and the expanding reach of national institutions have
allowed the values and behaviors of the core to permeate the entire United
States as its "national" culture.[22] Within the same model, the American
South and West have filled a complementary role as the nation's economic
periphery.

Analysis of changing relations between core and periphery has been the
province of disciplines and scholars who stress the economic base of human activities and institutions. An older tradition of economic geography
defines regions in terms of homogeneity of economic base and nodal organ-

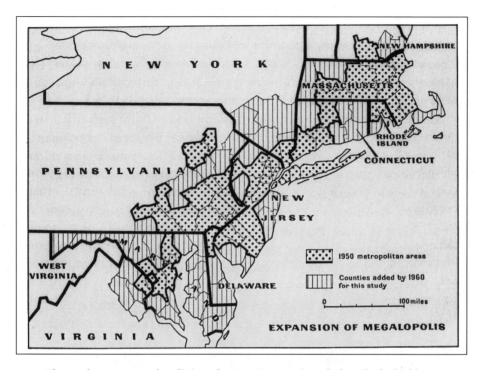

The northeastern megalopolis in 1960. Jean Gottman in 1961 described a highly urbanized and interconnected megalopolis that included Atlantic coastal metropolitan
areas from Boston to Washington. (From Jean Gottman, *Megalopolis: The Urbanized Northeastern Seaboard of the United States* [1961]; reprinted with permission from the Twentieth Century
Fund/Century Foundation, New York)

ization of trade and communication. The description of the northeastern
megalopolis by French geographer Jean Gottman is the climax of the traditional approach.[23] The shared economic characteristic of the urbanized
northeastern seaboard is the concentration of tertiary activities. At the same
time, northeastern cities are the "hinges" that control and connect the resources of the United States to the Atlantic world. *Megalopolis* is thus an up-
dated version of the "metropolitan thesis" with which Canadian historians
have interpreted continental growth in terms of the interactions of successive resource regions and metropolitan gateways.[24]

    More recently, writers working within the fields of historical sociology,
regional planning, and political economy have approached the core in terms
of the changing international division of labor and its impact on regional
functioning over the last two decades. They draw on world systems theory in

which the "metropolis" is expanded from a commercial capital to a dominant economic macroregion controlled by one or several nations. Regional patterning is seen as an expression of economic power or control-dependency relations. National regions rest within and frequently mirror a bifurcated world economy whose division between core and periphery explains the spatial unevenness of economic development and its exploitative consequences. The historical experience of the northeastern United States illustrates the evolution of a European colonial periphery into a new core region with its own periphery, followed by the rise of competing cores in the American Southwest and western Pacific.[25]

In the third part of the trio of regionalizing forces, cultural and economic patterns are also challenged or reinforced by direct political action. Governments create regional patterns by staking claims and drawing boundaries. The action may be as simple as the decision of the Bureau of the Census to place Oklahoma in the statistical South and to group Missouri with the North Central states or, for our own case, to place Maryland, Delaware, and West Virginia in the South. Formal claiming may also be as absolute as the drawing of formal national boundaries—dividing the natural economic region of the northern Pacific coast in 1845 or splitting the cultural region of northern Mexico in 1848.

Within the United States, however, political claims have most often involved sectional political alliances and sectional battles for the control of federal policy. Early national politics pitted commercial states against agricultural states. Over the next two centuries, Americans have divided along sectional lines over the extension of slavery, the annexation of Texas, the proper level of tariffs on imported manufactures, the coinage of silver and the gold standard, the need for farm subsidies, the acceptability of de jure racial segregation, and the proper management of federal lands. Analysis of these conflicts has been a staple of American history from Charles Paullin's *Atlas of the Historical Geography of the United States* to Richard Bensel's detailed work on political sectionalism.[26]

In these overlapping processes of cultural, economic, and political differentiation, cities are often senior partners, organizing hinterlands through the exchange of goods, people, and ideas. City people and urban institutions spearheaded the settlement and development of successive North American frontiers. They establish and manage routes of trade and travel, link local economic systems to their national and international counterparts, and draw raw materials and new residents more heavily from nearby districts than from distant places. They serve clients and customers in surrounding territories. They have channeled flows of information and provided focal points for regional culture and identity.

Residents of metropolitan hinterlands also share cultural traits that make themselves seen, heard, and felt in the metropolis. Migrants, business clients, and visitors from the surrounding territories bring languages, food-ways, behaviors, and expectations to the city—making San Antonio far different from Houston and Miami unlike Jacksonville. Through these flows of people and ideas, the city itself becomes an arena in which those specific traits are manifested, and its institutions support and nourish that regional culture in the same way that they provide support structures for ethnicity.

If you were an ambitious young person in rural New England in the early nineteenth century, for example, you felt most strongly the magnetic pull of Boston and helped to turn that city into a hub of business and letters at mid-century. Two generations later, middle western men and women with similar ambitions felt the same power of Chicago. You might be Jane Addams (from Cedarville, Illinois, and Rockford College), Theodore Dreiser (from Terre Haute, Indiana), Frank Lloyd Wright (from Richland Center, Wisconsin), Hamlin Garland (from West Salem, Wisconsin), or Carl Sandburg (from Galesburg, Illinois).

When a city lies in the heart of a cultural region, as the Boston and Chicago examples try to suggest, economic connections and culture reinforce each other. Such cities are regionally secure and unambiguous. They are easy to "center." Their location and relationships with their hinterland give them lasting character and sometimes even names such as Indianapolis or Oklahoma City.

Denver, for instance, is indubitably western and has been so since its founding in 1858–59. Its first generations built a city on the resources of the dry plains and high mountains. Denverites sallied forth to pan gold, dig silver, kill Indians, build railroads, dam rivers, route irrigation canals, agitate for national parks, and otherwise lay physical and institutional networks over a Rocky Mountain empire. Denver's present inhabitants take their sense of place from sweeping plains and high mountains that stretch hundreds of miles in all directions. The city houses organizations that claim to speak for western interests and needs—Mountain States Defense Fund, Center for the New West, and many others.

But other cities cut across, straddle, merge, and integrate disparate cultural and economic regions. They are market frontiers, centers of immigration and exchange that draw together different peoples and regions. Los Angeles pulls together Latin America, Asia, and Middle America; it is the "capital of MexAmerica," the "WorldPort" gateway to the Pacific Rim, and the seacoast of Iowa. Miami is simultaneously a suburb of New York, an outpost of the Caribbean, an extension of the American South, and a node in international business exchanges. Such cities are arenas that test and display the relative power of regional cultures and economies.

When national borders add a political dimension, these economic and cultural ambiguities can make cities prizes in contests for national power. The more San Diego and Tijuana grow into a single transborder metropolis, the more strongly American and Mexican laws, institutions, and national values come into tension. Despite claims from Seattle and Vancouver about the emergence of a transnational "Cascadia," even the low-keyed Canadian-U.S. border makes a big difference. On a more violent continent, European border cities are passed back and forth between nation-states and change their names in the process. Strasbourg turned into Strassburg in 1871 and regained its "o" in 1919; Helsingfors became Helsinki with the independence of Finland after World War I; Breslau became Wroclaw in 1945 and Koenigsberg became Kaliningrad, losing its name along with most other traces of its Prussian past.

As these examples suggest, political frontiers force decisive choices of regional identity. Within a continental nation such as the United States, cities faced the same forced choice only in 1861—when a quasi-national frontier ran along Washington's doorstep. More often, U.S. cities straddle internal divides of culture and economy. Competing strategies of economic growth and development may look to very different cultural regions, drawing in new residents with different backgrounds and values. Pittsburgh is eastern and middle western at the same time. Dallas–Fort Worth is western and middle western. Cincinnati and St. Louis are northern and southern.

The ambiguity of cultural and spatial borderlands had strong intellectual appeal in the late twentieth century. Postmodern theory directs attention to people and societies that are poised, pushed, and pulled between competing influences. For many social scientists, these frontiers are where the intellectual excitement lies. "Centers" are often fixed and unchanging, but edges are where dominant ideas may be weakest and where regional cultures can coexist and interact. Edges are places of conflict, change, and creativity, churning local expectations about culture and behavior, forcing the repeated renegotiation of a dominant local identity. Frontiers are thus redefined from border lines to borderlands where cultures overlap and interact, middle grounds for the creation of creole and mestizo societies. Frontiers become the spatialized expression of anthropologist Victor Turner's influential concept of liminality, expanded from a tool for understanding positions within a culture to understanding relationships among them.

Nodes, Networks, and
Modern Times

Modernization is a shorthand term for the complex of forces that transformed the relatively stable society and economy of eighteenth-century Europe into the constantly changing global polity of the twentieth century, bringing "a system of life constituted on a wholly new principle." As early as 1832 the *Manchester Guardian* wrote that "the manufacturing system as it exists in Great Britain, and the inconceivably immense towns under it, are without parallel in the history of the world." Karl Marx and Frederick Engels agreed in *The Communist Manifesto* (1848) that "the constant revolutionizing of production, uninterrupted disturbance of all social relations, [and] everlasting uncertainty and agitation" meant that "all ancient and venerable prejudices and opinions are swept away, all new-formed ones become antiquated before they can ossify. All that is solid melts into air, all that is holy is profaned."[27]

With Marx as one of its grandfathers, theoretical social science developed as a conscious effort to understand these changes. Henry Maine, William Graham Sumner, Ferdinand Tonnies, Georg Simmel, Emile Durkheim, Max Weber, Robert Park, Robert Redfield, Talcott Parsons, and dozens of other thinkers tried to develop theories of contrast. Their goal was to elucidate and explain the essential differences between the old days and today. By the early decades of this century, common discourse assumed that the big change had happened, giving Americans modern art, modern architecture, and Charlie Chaplin's movie *Modern Times*.[28]

Those who see the central force that created the world of the twentieth century as the rise of industrial capitalism emphasize the continual remaking of the economy through cycles of innovation. The process, as Joseph Schumpeter called it, is one of creative destruction. New products and industries, new centers of production, and new patterns of trade repeatedly shoulder aside the old. In these cycles of change, burgeoning cities take center stage as the points from which innovations spread to national and regional economies.

An alternative take on modernization has been to focus on the cultural and social consequences of urbanization. As rural societies become urban, the common model predicts the erosion of social connections and the triumph of individualism. The cash nexus replaces traditional values, and impersonal organizations leave no place for face-to-face contact. The generative cities of economic modernization thus become as well the alienating cities of Louis Wirth's 1938 essay on "Urbanism as a Way of Life."

In a third, "political" view, modernization has brought vast growth in the scale at which human activities are organized. We trace the revolution of modernization in the size of business corporations, the reach of communications and information sharing, the ubiquity and scope of government programs, and the ability to coordinate life in settlements that embrace 10 million people and thousands of square miles. Kenneth Boulding in the 1950s called attention to the "organizational revolution" of the twentieth century.[29] From the time of Max Weber to the present, much of social science has been devoted to describing and understanding the progress and implications of bigness.

Associated with this revolution of scale has been a vast expansion of wealth in the forms of productive capital and consumer goods. To know the modern era we must understand the systems of production and the cultures of consumption (the ways in which societies have adjusted to increasing abundance, longer life expectancy, and increased leisure). The changing division of labor, nationally and internationally, has been another staple of social science from Marx to the present. The rise of multinational corporations, global trade, and world cities is the latest stage in the multicentury process by which economic institutions have grown in size and reach.

American history since the Civil War invites this modernist narrative of scale. It is the story of increasing scope and scale of activity and organization in business, government, and daily life leading to a world of multinational corporations and Medicare, mass-market transoceanic tourism and the Internal Revenue Service. The so-called organizational synthesis of American history points to the increasing size and complexity of organization during the last century as a common theme that links the often disparate experiences of government, corporations, labor unions, and professions. The interpretation draws on theoretical work by institutional economists such as Boulding and John Kenneth Galbraith and on Robert Wiebe's argument that the United States has moved from a federation of "island communities" in the nineteenth century to a fully integrated national society in the twentieth century. The approach provides avenues for understanding the development of particular areas of activity, from medicine to the defense industry, as well as broad changes in the structure of American society.[30]

The corollary of organizational expansion is cultural homogenization. Regional cultures are presumed to have been eroded and submerged under

the nationwide marketing of goods and entertainment, with culprits ranging from radio and World War II army food to chain stores, television, fast-
food franchises, and easy travel. Cultural critics of the 1990s who decry the
homogenization of American spaces into manipulated theme parks are
complaining about the same process.[31] The nationalization of markets and
economic networks simultaneously weakens the social and economic foundations for local identities as local business is absorbed by conglomerates
and local leadership supplanted by outside managers.

The result for theories of modernization is an assumption about differentiated place. *Place*—locality and region as an amalgam of localities with
things in common—has been treated as a residual. The stronger the local
attachments or the regional identification, the less the place is thought to
have been influenced by modernization and incorporated within modern institutions. The South has been understood as the nation's most identifiable
region because it resisted incorporation and then trailed behind. The pre-
dominant theme in southern social science from the 1930s to the 1970s was
a catch-up thesis in which scholars analyzed social indicators to measure
southern convergence on national norms. As John Shelton Reed argues
(half seriously and half skeptically), the South may have "rejoined the Union" in the 1940s (when per capita income passed the level that the World
Bank uses to define lesser-developed countries), in the mid-1950s (when the
southern birthrate dropped below the national average), in 1960 (when
more than half the southern population lived in cities), or in the mid-1960s
(when the Voting Rights Act altered local politics and when southern states
ceased to defend de jure school segregation).[32]

Similarly, the West remains most identifiably "regional" in the outback,
where it lies beyond the reach of sprawling metropolitan centers and new
economic functions. Western aficionados (and historians) seek the essential
West in its landscape and wide-open spaces and the relationships between
people and environment. They sometimes try to define away California and
other urbanized parts of the region as no longer western. Colorado historian Robert Athearn, for example, is remembered for saying, "I wouldn't let
California into the West with a search warrant."[33]

A spatial manifestation of large-scale institutions is thus the subsump-
tion and incorporation of the periphery by the core. Rather than emphasizing the differentiation of core and fringe, we see both embraced in a single
system. Whereas residents of the periphery may still identify themselves in
regional terms, the core need not, for it is the norm rather than the variant.
The Prairie Provinces, British Columbia, Quebec, and the Maritime Prov-

inces all think of themselves as Canadian regions, but Ontario is simply "Canada." As a middle westerner who went east to college, I discovered that friends from New Mexico and Georgia also knew that they came from regions, but that friends from New York and Philadelphia did not.

The triumph of the core can thus mean the erosion of all place identity and affiliation in favor of network connections. What matters is not where a city is, but what other places it interacts with; not where a person is in coordinate space, but who she is internetworking with. Scholarship thus becomes a challenge of understanding change, as opposed to identifying and articulating the persistent traits of a cultural region.

Cities in the modern economy fit smoothly into a modern world picture as nodes in networks rather than "places." The essential managers of big business and big government are city-based executives and their bureaucracies. The global cities that cap the urban hierarchy of the late twentieth century are criticized for being interchangeable. Real estate markets and careers in Manhattan are connected more closely to the same in Tokyo and London than in Pittsfield, Massachusetts. A jet-set and executive culture becomes a homogenized layer in the world economy. William Sharpe and Leonard Wallock have remarked on a wave of global New York novels of the 1980s, "hip, streetwise" books such as Jay McInerney's Bright Lights, Big City (1984) and Tama Janowitz's Slaves of New York (1986). Their setting is a delocalized city where bars and boardrooms have taken the place of neighborhoods and street corners, where the interiors of fashionable nightclubs are described in great detail but daylit exteriors are ignored. "As the city recedes in contemporary urban fiction," they argue, "its deracinated inhabitants lose their ability to interpret themselves or the world around them."[34]

Some cities are intentionally developed as network nodes. International organizations, for example, often work best in neutral headquarter locations that are not linked to powerful nations and cultural blocs. Geneva—a multilingual city in a neutral nation—has been a prime site for international functions since the nineteenth century. Vienna, politically neutralized after World War II and centrally located between the European Community and the Council for Mutual Economic Assistance, emerged as another choice for world organizations. Brussels has been a conveniently central and nonthreatening site for the bureaucracies of the European Union.

Also at the heart of networks of information exchange are deliberately created capital cities. Artificial capitals have usually been intended to symbolize the future of a modern state or nation and to mediate or stand above regional divisions. Within the new United States, for instance, Indianans deliberately sited a new capital at the unsettled geographic center of their state as a statement about its agricultural and industrial future. Next door, Ohioans chose Columbus as a state capital to balance Cincinnati and Cleveland. Canberra accomplished the same balancing act between Melbourne and Sydney after six separate colonies consolidated into the Commonwealth of Australia in 1901.

The later twentieth century brought another set of new capitals. Islamabad, officially occupied as the capital of Pakistan in 1967, represents the national future in contrast to a recent colonial past. Abaja, which replaced Lagos as the capital of Nigeria in 1991, is geographically central and ethnically neutral, offering common ground for the multiple religions and ethnic groupings that have fueled political tension and triggered bitter civil war in the 1960s. Brasilia, the best known of the contemporary artificial capitals, serves several roles, turning attention to the Brazilian interior and away from the rival claims of coastal cities and regions.

Washington poses the same sorts of questions as Brasilia or Abaja. How has it balanced regional claims and mediated regional rivalries? As an intentional city, how has it symbolized a new government and an emerging nation? How have its institutions and residents interacted with other Americans through their roles as sources and transmitters of information? And how have these roles promoted or hindered the development of distinct local and regional identities among the residents of the networked city?

Coming Attractions

When I started this project, I thought I knew what I was going to find. Remembering Bruce Catton's trilogy on the Army of the Potomac—among the first serious adult histories that I consumed—I thought of Washington as a border city that had entered the crisis of 1861 with strong southern connections. I also knew that Jean Gottman's widely acclaimed book *Megalopolis*, published a century after the great sectional crisis in 1961, matched Washington with Philadelphia, New York, and Boston as anchors of a northeastern metropolitan corridor. With these two interpretations as guideposts in a process of regional change, I expected to assess Washington's initial southern character as a sort of Charleston-on-the-Potomac and then explore its complex and gradual transformation through two centuries of planning and growth into something newer—northern city, national city, global city.

Instead, I have discovered a more complicated pattern in which successive generations of Washingtonians have added new characteristics and connections to the city without obliterating the old. Over two centuries, the national city has expanded in scope and reach without losing its original purpose. The regional city has been repeatedly undermined, redefined, and reinforced.

The research behind these conclusions has been eclectic and revealing. The information base for this study includes census data and business organization newsletters, novels of limited literary value and personal correspondence of notable Washingtonians. The study also draws on visual texts in addition to written materials. The growth of the city has involved the creation of buildings and spaces with direct and indirect symbolic functions. An example of the former is the Kennedy Center, of the latter the Pension Building of the 1880s. These symbolic places have been parts of larger spatial systems that have supported Washington's various functions and activities. A national city, for example, needs spaces for public assembly and ceremony, stages for enacting the rituals of nationhood. An international city needs intense communication networks and arenas for sophisticated consumption.

Scholarly writing about urban personality and the sense that we develop of metropolitan communities as distinctive entities is relatively rare in history and social science, despite pioneering work by sociologist Anselm Strauss and historians such as Richard Wade. In part, we are suspicious of claims about the character of a city because we see such statements as the self-serving comment of elites, as vacuous boosterism, or as fluffy journalism and sloganizing.

Although acknowledging this concern, I believe that a city IS a "place" that has an identifiable and changing character. People recognize urban and metropolitan communities as entities, assess their strengths and weaknesses, offer or withhold loyalty. In everyday life we think and act as if cities (or metropolitan communities) are entities with distinct character and distinct modes of action. Cities are black dots or yellow splotches on the map. They are names in the NFL and NBA standings, whose successful teams elicit community pride.[35] We rate and rank cities and talk about their character. We recognize metropolitan areas as labor sheds, retail markets, and focused communication systems and make investment and business decisions accordingly. We establish citywide and metrowide institutions of formal governance and service delivery. We persist stubbornly in using the metaphor of vitality, talking about cities as living things that grow, flourish, decline. In this context, my study is an exploration of Washington as a socially constructed entity with which residents have identified and to which visitors have responded.

An interest in Washington as a civic entity has to be balanced by attention to multiple Washingtons and Washingtonians. A large and complex city means different things to different of its members. It means different things to people with varied economic interests, professions, and ethnic backgrounds. Washington's peculiar history has assured in particular that it has served different social and symbolic needs for southern blacks and southern whites—two groups for whom it has had special importance.

I have worked under the assumption that cultural and economic sources of regional patterning are complementary rather than exclusive, as both patterns are manifested by shared behaviors that work to structure the perceptions and orientations of individuals. I have therefore focused much attention midway between individual Washingtonians and the metropolitan community taken as a whole. The strategy is to supplement the explicit commentary left by a minority of residents and observers by examining a variety of patterns and structures of social, economic, and political behavior that have conditioned or impinged on the activities of everyday life. I assume that such mediating structures have influenced the ways in which Washingtonians have understood and responded to the regional character of their city by helping to form predispositions, orientations, and habits of mind. To try to describe such structures, I ask a series of questions about individual perceptions, expectations, and experiences. What regional magazines are Washingtonians most likely to page through in their dentist's office? What sorts of neighbors have residents been most likely to encounter? Where have local business owners expected to find out-of-town customers? The answers help us to understand the formation of habits of mind and to construct a history of regional orientation in which incorporation in national systems ironically has reinforced connectivity and identification with both the North and the South.

My first cut through the material aimed to analyze and categorize. I accumulated long lists of ideas under headings such as "How Has Washington Been Southern?" and "Variety of National Roles." From this starting point, I then tried to write historically, pulling apart the analysis and reordering the evidence in a series of chapters that follow Washington's development as a complex metropolis in rough (and overlapping) chronological order. Each chapter explores empirical questions of community character and identity; each tries to use that evidence to illuminate broader issues of American history and social theory around the interacting themes of place, region, and network.

The study therefore presents Washington as historically layered, a city where earlier cultural and social patterns are overlaid but not erased by characteristics expressing new sources of growth. In simplest form, the southern city has been successively northernized, nationalized, and internationalized. There is a succession from a southern town to a northern city and then to a networked metropolis with greater impact on the nation and world than on its regional hinterlands.

But first generalizations tell only part of the story. Neither the "before" nor the "after" in this straight-line model is as simple as a casual observer might expect. Modernization and globalization have coexisted with vitality of local and regional identities, and national and international roles and connections have been central to Washington from its beginning.

On the one hand, Washington was a networked city from the very start. Residents of the modern metropolis may be more self-conscious about their position in information space than were earlier generations, but 1820s congressmen in their little boardinghouse cliques and breakfast clubs were also "symbolic analysts," to use the 1990s term for brokers and traders in information.[36] They energetically worked to build far-flung networks in support of abstract ideas. They were also as isolated from a regional Washington as are today's short-term association executives and jet-setting think tank gurus. For both, Washington has been an address rather than a community.

On the other hand, older layers of identity were submerged but not lost. Earlier facets of the city's character have changed and reformed as the city has changed. Relationships with the Tidewater and Piedmont landscapes have been rediscovered and rethought. "Northernness" has coexisted with repeated resouthernization as old allegiances and orientations have been renewed and redefined. A useful metaphor might be a two-hundred-year-old desk or kitchen table covered with multiple coats of paint. On some parts the newest coat gleams brightly; on the back side the new paint was never completely applied; on other parts the top layers have worn through to reveal the color preferences of previous generations.

Poets, not surprisingly, are often better than historians at reducing complexity to a few clear words. Here is how Gary Snyder saw Washington's multiple character as government center, national symbol, and Tidewater town during a protest demonstration on the Mall ("It Pleases," from *Turtle Island*):[37]

> Far above the dome
> Of the capitol—
> It's true!

A large bird soars
Against white cloud,
Wings arched,
Sailing easy in the
humid Southern sun-blurred
    breeze—
        the dark-suited policeman
        watches tourist cars

The poem opens with the seat of national government set against the symbolic aspirations of the nation. But the poet, with a careful sense of place, follows by setting the evocative bird and its white cloud in the muggy air of a specific Tidewater city. Then, it dips down to earth and back to the functional city of practical pilgrimage, the political terrain on which tourists and protesters alike act out the meaning of the nation.

THE GRAND
COLUMBIAN
FEDERAL
CITY

Washington, D.C., was George Washington's city on George Washington's river. The city gained its name in September 1791, when the three commissioners who had been appointed to manage the construction of a federal capital announced that the new federal district would be "Columbia" and the federal city within that district would be "Washington."

The choice of names was one step in a protracted and politically sensitive process of capital making. The Constitution mandated that the permanent seat of the new national government be a district of up to ten miles square, at a location designated by Congress and ceded to congressional control by the appropriate state or states. In July 1790 the lawmakers had responded to dozens of suggested sites and several serious contenders by picking an eighty-mile stretch along the middle reach of the Potomac from its juncture with the Eastern Branch (Anacostia River) northwestward to the confluence of the Connogocheague River. They also gave the new president the job of picking the most suitable spot for the United States to raise its grand Columbian federal metropolis from among the marshes and wooded bluffs that lined the river.[1]

George Washington used the responsibility as the occasion for a triumphal tour through what was very familiar territory. Before narrowing the possibilities to a single location, he visited the towns and hamlets along the Maryland side of the river. He received petitions, heard presentations of local advantages, enjoyed banquets and festivities. The citizens of Hagerstown met him three miles out of town and conducted him down the main street to the pealing of church bells. The cheers gave way in the evening to lanterns and bonfires to illuminate the aspiring city.[2]

Washington did not need his ceremonial junket to make up his mind, for the Potomac was very much his river. He knew its direction, course, and resources, its behavior in winter and summer. He had grown up along the Potomac and Rappahannock Rivers. In 1752 he inherited Mount Vernon with its view down to the wide tidal river and after 1758 made his home there. Until the revolution of 1775, he had tried to make ends meet by supplementing tobacco and wheat with harvests of Potomac fish.[3] The upper river he knew from work as a surveyor in 1749 and from campaigns against the French from 1754 to 1758, returning with an excited vision of the way in which the headwaters of the Potomac interwove with the sources of the Ohio. The Potomac, he wrote in 1754, was "the more convenient, least expensive, and I may further say by much the most expeditious way to the [western] country."[4] With Virginia's independence secured as a participant in a new confederation, he organized the Potomac Company in 1784 to clear rocks from the river and build canals around its falls with the object of opening "a channel of commerce" for the "trade of a rising empire." His personal estate by 1794 would include an estimated 20,000 acres adjacent or accessible to the Potomac.

Everyone in the know expected the president to fix the federal district below the falls and rapids, at the head of navigation for oceangoing ships. In the larger debate over the location of a capital, for example, the Potomac alternative had often been shortened to "Georgetown"—the young Maryland port town with a thriving local trade and high ambitions. Washington's report to Congress in January 1791 therefore surprised no one. The federal district would center on the point of land between the Maryland shore of the Potomac and Eastern Branch, with the corners of the ten-mile square oriented to the points of the compass. The bulk of federal territory would lie northward from that core, but one fringe would extend along the southern side of the Eastern Branch (the Anacostia Heights) and a second fringe along the Virginia shore of the Potomac (including the thriving port of Alexandria and the future Arlington County).[5]

The end product of Washington's decision making was a *Potomac* city as well as a national city. The capital would be as close to Mount Vernon as possible, on rolling riverside terrain that looked much like Mount Vernon and on old tobacco fields reminiscent of Mount Vernon and other Fairfax County farms. Both President Washington and Secretary of State Thomas Jefferson assumed that the capital would face toward its rivers and fill the lands between them before growing toward the hills to the north. The president acquired the national townsite within the District of Columbia in March 1791 after playing off rival landowners from Georgetown and the Anacostia to get a decent price. The tract he chose promised a riverside town: "all the land from Rock-creek along the river to the eastern-branch and so upwards to or above the ferry including a breadth of about a mile and a half, the whole containing three to five thousand acres."[6] As Washington supervised the surveys and sketches of planner Pierre L'Enfant he again emphasized the importance of Potomac views and Anacostia docks. The federal city was intended to be no ceremonial campus of secular temples topping green hills. It was to be an eminently practical gateway to the new nation and its new empire—an improved Philadelphia, a republican London.

George Washington's role makes the larger point that Washington City was not planned and built as an abstraction. For its first half century it was deeply rooted in a particular part of North America. It was a waterfront town at a key site on a strategically located river. Its social patterns grew out of the society of Tidewater Virginia and Maryland, and its economic ambitions reflected the geopolitical ambitions of Virginia's patriot generation.

A Capital for Middle America

The transcontinental trek of Meriwether Lewis, William Clark, and their Corps of Discovery in 1804–6 is one of the great adventures and hero tales of U.S. history and a story normally told as part of the history of the American West. But from a different vantage, the planning and preparation for the expedition illustrate some of the ways in which the new federal city was an organizing center for guiding America's movement westward and a platform for linking the ambitions of Virginia, Pennsylvania, and the Ohio country into a national core.

The expedition was the brainchild of Thomas Jefferson and the practical responsibility of Meriwether Lewis. The older Jefferson and the younger Lewis were neighbors from Albemarle County on Virginia's northern Piedmont. Lewis's second in command was William Clark, son of an Albemarle family that had moved to Kentucky and younger brother of Virginia general George Rogers Clark, who had taken the lands northwest of the Ohio River for Virginia and the nation during the American War of Independence. Jefferson and Lewis talked through initial plans in Washington, where Lewis was personal secretary to the new president. Lewis drew his weapons from the Harper's Ferry armory and most of his supplies from Philadelphia. He learned celestial reckoning from Andrew Ellicott in Lancaster, Pennsylvania, and the basics of medicine and natural science from Benjamin Rush, Caspar Wistar, and Benjamin Smith Barton in Philadelphia. Lewis and his supplies traveled west from the Virginia and Pennsylvania seaboard through Frederick, Maryland, to Pittsburgh, where the expedition embarked down the Ohio River for St. Louis and its rendezvous with destiny.[7]

This brief summary offers an occasion to think twice about the origins of the city of Washington and to reconstruct the framework of regional thinking and politics that provided the context for Washington's creation myth. That origin story, of course, involves one of the first great deals of the new nation—the dinner table discussion between Thomas Jefferson and Alexander Hamilton that broke two deadlocks in Congress in 1790. As Jefferson reported, the secretary of the treasury buttonholed the secretary of state in front of the president's house in New York and walked him "backwards & forwards before the President's door for half an hour" of earnest conversation about the key issues dividing the first Congress. The two statesmen consulted further over the next day's dinner, where they rolled some big logs and scratched some regional backs. Jefferson agreed to persuade three members of Congress to drop their opposition to federal assumption of state debts contracted during the war against England. Assumption favored heavily indebted northern states but seemed a burden without benefit to more solvent southern states. To sweeten this pill "peculiarly bitter to the Southern States," Hamilton delivered northern support for a Potomac River capital. Under the Residence Bill passed on July 16 (formally titled "An Act for Establishing a Temporary and Permanent Seat of the Government of the United States"), Congress would meet in Philadelphia from December 1790 through November 1800 and in a new capital on the Potomac beginning on the first Monday in December 1800. The Residence Bill ended the aspirations of New Jersey and Pennsylvania and seemed to give a southern tilt to the nation's political system.

As the introduction of George Washington as well as Thomas Jefferson suggests, a national capital below the falls of the Potomac was not a sudden creative idea that came to Hamilton and Jefferson with a second bottle of wine. A Potomac location was a strong candidate from the start, with specific implications about the larger process of nation making and its many acts of politics, war, diplomacy, and cultural chauvinism. Americans in the 1780s had a multitude of expectations about the ways that a federal city might contribute to the national project. Virginians and Marylanders had their own thoughts about the regional and national benefits of a Potomac location and its superiority to a location in Philadelphia or New York, in the Pennsylvania mountains, or on a seacoast in New Jersey.

Indeed, Jefferson and Hamilton's deal and George Washington's selection of the specific site capped fifty years of ambitious thinking about the Potomac corridor and a decade of vigorous debate about a national capital. To retrace the arguments and aspirations is to see American regionalism through eighteenth-century eyes.

The decision to place a capital on the Potomac River was certainly a plum for the South. Eighteenth-century Americans understood a divide around the head of the Chesapeake Bay and along the Mason-Dixon line. The fierce contest between Potomac and Pennsylvania locations was a battle of South and North. Indeed, southern states threatened secession if the prize went to the North. From the viewpoint of the 1860s or the 1990s, with the con-sequences of the North-South split graven into national history, this seems *the* regional issue in the location of the federal district.

In the context of the 1790s, however, there was also a second regional view in which the new city also recognized the power of the "center" and the prospects of the West. For Virginia's revolutionary generation, in particular, the development of a Potomac metropolis was part of the sweeping vision of an expansive homeland. If Americans in the 1790s frequently tried out the term "empire" to describe their coastal republic and its western extensions, it was Virginians and their "nation" that had the most practice with imperial visions.[8] These visions framed decisions about an American capital, *focusing* attention on the Potomac and *broadening* Virginia's identity as the heart of the American heartland.

Virginia was the colony that had acted most vigorously on its western in-terests before 1775. Making claim to land that would eventually constitute eight American states, members of Virginia's elite in the first half of the eighteenth century used their positions in the Governor's Council and the House of Burgesses to reward themselves with grants of western land for their children or for resale to new immigrants. Land speculation schemes such as the Ohio Company (1747) and Loyal Company (1749) promised to extend the model of Proprietary colonies across the mountains. Tighter Crown controls and war with France in 1754 curtailed the land grant system, but declining prices for tobacco in the 1760s animated a younger generation of Virginians with the same conviction that the most promising future for their families lay westward. The chief rivals were Pennsylvanians who devel-oped trading networks into the Ohio Valley, organized their own western land companies, and strongly contested Virginia's claim to the mountains and valleys south of Fort Pitt.[9]

Especially in northern Virginia was the West on everyone's mind. Marc Egnal has identified an expansionist party that coalesced in the 1750s and

1760s in the Northern Neck between the Rappahannock and Potomac Rivers and in the counties at the base of the Blue Ridge Mountains.[10] Here were the homes of men who were deeply disturbed by the Proclamation of 1763, which interdicted settlement beyond the crest of the Appalachians. Thomas Jefferson, James Madison, James Mason, Henry Lee, Patrick Henry, Robert Carter, and George Washington were simultaneously Virginia expansionists and American patriots. In the short run in the 1760s they shared opinions like that of Robert Beverly: "I assure you I think seriously of taking Advantage of procuring lands upon the first Establishment of this new Colony on our Frontier . . . 20 years hence our sons will think a Tract of suitable land on the Waters of the Ohio no Contemptible Possession."[11] By the mid-1770s they saw independence from England as the key to economic survival and the continental empire. When Virginia opened a western theater in the ensuing war in 1778, George Rogers Clark kept his eye on Virginia's future settlements, targeting Indian towns at Piqua and Chillicothe (both in the future state of Ohio) as much as British garrisons.

The terms of Virginia's empire changed after 1783 but not the goal. Virginia ceded its claims to land north of the Ohio River to Congress in 1784, but it did not cede its economic ambitions. The creation of a national domain in the West was a tool to promote national unity and confirm national interest in securing the Mississippi Valley against Britain and Spain. Meanwhile, Virginia remained the largest state with its territories south of the Ohio River and its reserved lands for military veterans north of the Ohio between the Scioto and Little Miami Rivers. The widely shared expectation that the tide of settlement was running southwestward meant that Virginia was holding its most promising lands athwart the path of migration.[12]

The Potomac corridor was the essential link in this imperial vision. Early in the eighteenth century, the lower Potomac had been a near frontier, distant from the center of Virginia on the James and York Rivers and the Maryland heartland along the margins of Chesapeake Bay. As tobacco farming moved into the Piedmont, however, the Potomac looked increasingly central to the Chesapeake colonies. A set of riverside trading towns appeared in the 1740s and early 1750s: Alexandria (1749) and Georgetown (1751) most importantly, but also Bladensburg, Occoquan, and Port Tobacco.[13]

The river entered popular discussion as the best avenue for continental commerce—we have already heard from George Washington—and took on an additional political role in the 1780s as "one of the grandest Chains for preserving the federal Union" as free commerce would make easterners and westerners "one and the same People."[14] Thomas Jefferson made the commercial argument in *Notes on Virginia* (1785) with claims that the Potomac offered by far the most convenient access not only to the Ohio River but also to the Great Lakes via the Cuyahoga River; he wrote to Madison that the proper public works would "spread the field of our commerce Westwardly and Southwardly beyond any thing ever yet done by man."[15] Both statesmen might have been familiar with John Ballandine's 1772 manuscript "Map of Potomack and James Rivers," which emphasized the Potomac as a corridor to the Ohio.[16]

Potomac property owners acted as well as dreamed. Maryland investors from Winchester, Annapolis, Georgetown, and Frederick joined Virginians such as James Madison and George Washington in the Potomac Company as an enterprise that promised to please equally "Friends to American Commerce and American Happiness."[17] If all went well, Georgetown, Alexandria, or some nearby point on the river would be the great gateway that knit the worlds of ocean trade and river trade into a prosperous whole. Henry Lee, another ambitious Virginian from Westmoreland County, joined the Potomac Company, invested in western lands, and laid out a town on 500 acres near the Great Falls. He expected Matildaville to intercept the vast stream of Potomac trade before it reached Georgetown and to grow into the metropolis of the river.[18]

In the same decades that Virginia was looking so optimistically westward, the Chesapeake settlements were also tilting northward, beginning to draw away from the Lower South and closer to the middle colonies of Pennsylvania and New Jersey. From the 1760s, the long valleys of western Maryland and Virginia were increasingly settled by way of Pennsylvania. Falling tobacco prices were meanwhile turning many Virginia and Maryland tobacco planters—George Washington not the least of them—into wheat farmers.[19] Grain trading vessels out of Philadelphia controlled the commerce of the Eastern Shore and competed with the booming town of Baltimore for grain from the western Chesapeake and Potomac; when the Revolution cut off the British market for tobacco, Philadelphians rushed to export the Chesapeake staple directly to Europe.[20] In a larger view, Virginia, Maryland, Delaware, Pennsylvania, New Jersey, and New York seemed to some observers to be developing in the 1780s and 1790s into a Middle American wheat belt whose family farms could feed both American and European cities and whose common interests blurred and outweighed the divisions of slave and free states or agricultural and commercial states.

Economic connections underwrote political similarities. Regional alliances in Congress in the early 1780s were fluid. Votes sometimes divided be-

tween North and South, but congressional alliances also showed the out-
lines of a dominant core reflecting the economic and political nationalism
of New York, Pennsylvania, New Jersey, Maryland, and Virginia.[21] Congressional delegates James Monroe and Patrick Henry in 1786–87 worked deliberately to draw Pennsylvania and New Jersey away from New Englanders in
order to kill the Jay-Gardoqui Agreement with its twenty-five-year prohibi-
tion on American navigation of the Mississippi.[22] In the constitutional debates of 1787–89, Virginia aligned with more northerly states in opposition
to continuation of the slave trade—repugnant to republican values and un-
necessary for an emerging economy of grain farmers.[23]

These northern connections of Virginia and Maryland are reminders that
sectional identities and divisions in the new nation were malleable and
uncertain. The coastal extremes were firmly identified. New England was a
distinct "East" or "North" and Georgia and the Carolinas a distinct "South."
In between was less certainty. When observers divided the nation in two,
they usually used the Mason-Dixon line, but they might sometimes include
Pennsylvania and even New York with the South. Less frequent descriptions
of a third, "middle" section went as far east as Connecticut and as far south
as Virginia.[24]

In political terms, the late 1780s and 1790s saw the emergence of a potent
"central interest" represented by the alliance of Virginia and Pennsylvania.
George Washington spoke for many of his state's leaders who set apart the
Carolinas and Georgia as southern states and grouped Virginia with the
"middle states." At the Constitutional Convention, middle states delegates
such as William Paterson (New Jersey) and George Mason (Virginia) spoke
of the "distant" and "central" states.[25] Voting in the convention showed a regional distinction between a nationalistic and an expansive core that included Virginia and Maryland and the parochial interests of eastern and
southern peripheries, a reaffirmation of the nascent political core of the early
1780s.[26] Constituting this core were the states that were entering three
decades of balanced agricultural prosperity and urban growth from the expanding wheat belt,[27] that looked forward to improvements in internal transportation, and that would dominate national politics from 1787 to the
1820s—Virginians and Pennsylvanians as the chief architects of the Constitution, Virginians in the White House, Pennsylvanians such as Albert Gallatin and Mahlon Dickerson in the cabinet, and Democratic-Republican voters
in Pennsylvania and New York assuring governing majorities in Congress.

Only in this complex and shifting environment of economic and political
regions can we understand the advantages that a Potomac capital held over

fifty or so other sites from the Hudson River to Chesapeake Bay whose merits were proposed and argued between 1782 and 1790.[28]

Everyone agreed that the federal government should be located centrally. After being driven from Philadelphia by disorderly soldiers in 1783, Congress received offers to meet as far south as Williamsburg, Virginia, and as far east as Newport, Rhode Island. It tried out only the more central places—Annapolis, Trenton, New York.[29] As James Madison argued at the Philadelphia convention, the seat of government had to be "in that position from which it could contemplate with the most equal eye, and sympathize most equally with, every part of the nation."[30] A few years later, an anonymous essay praised L'Enfant's plan by arguing that "to found a City in the center of the United States, for the purpose of making it the depository of the acts of the Union . . . which will one day rule all North-America . . . is a grand and comprehensive idea. . . . Here [the Capitol] he fixed the center of the city, as the city is the center of the American Empire. . . . Each street is an emblem of the rays of light which, issueing from the Capitol, are directed toward every part of America, to enlighten its inhabitants respecting their true interests."[31]

But the interpretations of centrality varied. In 1784 Thomas Jefferson ticked off a comparison of Delaware River and Potomac River locations as a permanent seat of Congress under the Articles of Confederation. The former was central with regard to population and number of states and convenient for obtaining news by sea. The latter was geographically central, close to western territories already ceded to Congress, and likely to induce further land cessions from North Carolina, South Carolina, and Georgia.[32] Madison and other Virginians agreed vehemently that a "central residence" of the government had only to mean centrality to the West and Southwest via the Potomac River. Any site northeastward would alienate the western settlements and threaten fragile national unity.[33]

Jefferson's bargain with Hamilton, in this light, was a southern deal in general but a Virginia and Maryland bargain in particular, building on hard work by James Madison and the moral influence of George Washington. Two of the three congressmen who switched their votes represented northern Virginia and the other represented Maryland. The debate among Delaware River, Susquehanna River, and Potomac River sites was a compromise between North and South, but also a debate about leadership within the national core. Jefferson's deal made sure that Virginia would be Pennsylvania's senior partner in the articulation of the American empire.

To its advocates, a Potomac capital was thus essential for Virginia's prosperity and national unity. Centrality did not mean splitting the difference between North and South by locating in an ambiguous borderland. It meant finding a site that could support a great commercial city that would function as the economic and political heart of the national heartland. A Potomac capital would promote a new version of Virginia's imperial ambitions and meet the interests of Potomac landowners. It would be accessible to the growing population of the "New South" between the Appalachian Mountains and the Mississippi River. And it would also guarantee national unity by anchoring a "Middle America" that knit Virginia, Pennsylvania, and the Ohio Valley into one.

Centrality and Commerce

One way to appreciate the way that Jefferson, Madison, and their contemporaries understood their continental geography is to look at John Mitchell's 1755 map of North America, the standard depiction that was used in the peace negotiations of 1783. The map emphasizes the changing orientation of the eastern coast around the mouth of the Delaware River. To the south, Mitchell showed essentially a North-South coastline; to the north, the coast trends dramatically eastward toward Nova Scotia and Newfoundland. The Chesapeake Bay thus lies at the sharp angle of the coast, with the Potomac reaching westward toward both the Ohio River and the Great Lakes far more directly than either the Delaware or the Susquehanna. Americans of the 1780s would have been in no doubt that Georgetown and Alexandria were the closest possible ocean ports to the Ohio River, making Washington an early Brasilia located close to and accessible to the interior.[34]

Centrality remained a theme in descriptions of Washington through the city's first generation. Joseph Martin's detailed geography of Virginia and the District of Columbia was typical: "The situation of this metropolis, is upon the great line of communication, about equi-distant from the northern and southern extremities of the Union, and nearly so from the Atlantic and Pittsburgh."[35]

As is well known in Washington history, however, the grand commercial vision foundered with the failure of specific schemes of internal improvements—a failure that became clear in the 1830s. One failure was national. The politics of state and section made it nearly impossible to realize *national* schemes for internal improvements (which usually gave prominence to Washington as the national city). At the direction of Congress, Secretary of the Treasury Albert Gallatin in 1808 prepared a plan for national improvements that placed Washington on a nationally funded Maine-to-Georgia turnpike and linked the upper Potomac to a U.S. turnpike to the Ohio River.

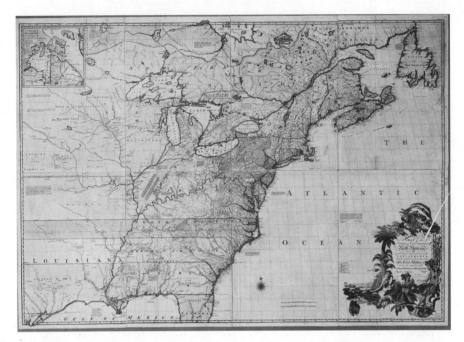

John Mitchell's map of North America, 1755. John Mitchell's map was used in the Paris peace negotiations that recognized the independence of the United States and set its boundaries. It remained a standard reference to the end of the 1700s, visually emphasizing the Potomac River as a central feature of the new nation. (Geography and Map Division, Library of Congress)

The latter was haltingly realized as the Cumberland or National Road, but the rest of Gallatin's scheme languished.[36]

The military disasters of 1812–15 incited new interest in a set of highways radiating outward from Washington to Buffalo, St. Louis, and New Orleans. Still an ardent nationalist, Secretary of War John C. Calhoun offered several versions. A bill in 1830 bundled the roads together in a single package for a "great interior artery" from the northern to the southern frontier by way of the "heart" of the "body politic." The proposal ran headlong into rivalries among alternative routes, confusing proposals for additions, and jealousy from bypassed states. The scheme was also too late. The sense of military insecurity was fading, steamboats were more efficient than wagons, and the smart money was beginning to think about railroads. The federal government got out of the road-building business with Andrew Jackson's veto of the Maysville Road in Kentucky in 1830 and congressional transfer of the National Road project to Ohio, Indiana, and Illinois in 1834.[37]

Washington's other hope for commercial greatness was the Chesapeake and Ohio (C&O) Canal, designed to connect District of Columbia cities with the Ohio River in a practical realization of Washington's cartographic centrality. President John Quincy Adams's advocacy of the canal as a national project helped convince Congress to get the effort started with an appropriation of $1 million in 1825. The canal also attracted public investment from Washington City, Alexandria, Georgetown, and the state of Maryland. Washington purchased the City Canal from Congress to make sure that barges could get from the C&O terminus at Georgetown to the harbor on the Eastern Branch, making the connection in 1831. Alexandria built its own canal up the right bank of the Potomac and across to Georgetown on the Aqueduct Bridge, completed in 1846.

Even before work on the C&O Canal began in 1828, however, the enterprise faced problems. Engineering challenges and a dearth of private funds soon forced promoters to scale back the western terminus to Cumberland, Maryland. Into the 1830s, Virginia congressmen tried to muster support for an essentially local improvement by claiming its national character and its route "through the center of the Republic," but transportation improvements were now considered thoroughly local concerns. Congress ignored a request for more funds in 1830 and rejected another plea in 1835.[38]

The shortening of the C&O Canal showed that Washington's lack was not so much a geopolitical vision as ready cash. Established commercial cities such as New York, Philadelphia, and even Baltimore had local sources of financial capital and influence in state legislatures. Washington had little wealth of its own, small pools of funds in rival Alexandria and Georgetown, and an increasingly jealous regard from Maryland. Indeed, once the Baltimore and Ohio Railroad was under way, Maryland increasingly favored the railroad over the canal. The best thing for Washington's commercial future would have been for the British fleet in 1814 to have ignored the Potomac and sailed directly to the Patapsco, blasted past Fort McHenry, and leveled Baltimore. Short of such outside help, Washington found itself constantly behind its wealthier competitors. The canal itself ended up a local supplier of coal, timber, and building stone, not an avenue to riches.

Washington was conceived as a city that would link Tidewater and Piedmont, coast and interior. It was expected to anchor and create a center of gravity that would draw Virginia, Maryland, and their Ohio Valley offspring into the dominant core region of the new nation. New England merchants and Carolina rice kings would bob along in its wake. In so doing, Washington-on-Potomac was to transcend the incipient division of political

South and political North and meet the political and commercial needs of a new nation.

Instead, the antebellum District of Columbia remained local rather than national in its economy and in the character of everyday life. The tidal river dominated the feel of the *place*. Tidewater towns and plantations set much of the tone for Washington society. The result, despite the ambitions of its founders, was a city in the decades of Monroe, Jackson, and Polk that reflected the Upper South more than the ambitious nation.

Riverside Settlement

In the 1990s Washingtonians enjoyed a cosmopolitan cuisine. Cuban, Ethiopian, and Vietnamese restaurants reflected the city's role as a refuge from socialist revolutions during the Cold War. Japanese sushi bars and northern Italian cafés spoke to the high-powered economy of the Group of Seven. Russian, Thai, Romanian, Indonesian, and other national restaurants demonstrated the increasing mobility of jet-age populations.

A century and a half earlier, good eating in Washington meant local abundance, not worldly sophistication. Early guidebooks and gazetteers dealt in loving detail on the abundant Tidewater wildlife—deer in the hills, vast runs of herring and shad, oysters, rock fish, sturgeon taken just below the Little Falls of the Potomac, canvasback ducks from the margins of the Potomac and from Analostan Island across from Georgetown. Even Tiber Creek, running roughly along the route of the present Constitution Avenue, was at the city's beginning "overspread in spring and autumn with wild ducks, and often penetrated as far as the present Railroad depot [Seventh Street NW] by multitudes of shad, herring, pike, perch, &c."[39] Visitors heaped the local ducks on their plates and then heaped praise on one of the greatest luxuries that could grace a table. Formal descriptions of the city and its vicinity devoted page after page to the fisheries. Shad by the millions and herring by the hundred millions were taken around Alexandria and the Eastern Branch, salted and packed by the barrelful, and sent by the wagonload to Pennsylvania and by the shipload to the West Indies.[40]

Such detailed attention to local foods was one of the many ways in which the Americans of the early nineteenth century understood Washington as a Tidewater town, with its character and expectations shaped by the Potomac River. Its founders planned a riverfront city that visitors would enter and leave by water. In turn, visitors mapped and drew and described a city held firmly in the grasp of its two rivers.

Site planning as well as site made the federal city river-centered. Thomas

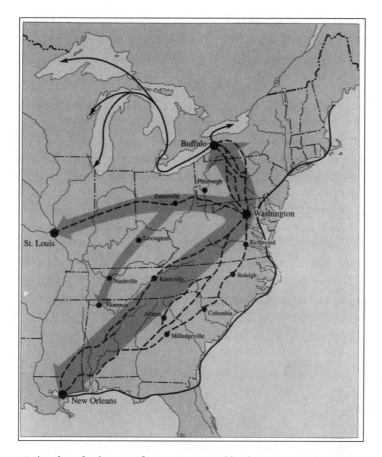

National road schemes, 1815–30. Prompted by the nation's vulnerability in the War of 1812, a series of national road proposals placed Washington at the center of improved communication to the western frontiers. (From Donald W. Meinig, *The Shaping of America*, vol. 2, *Continental America, 1800–1867* [1993])

Jefferson in March 1791 drew up a quick sketch that anticipated the plats of hundreds of new towns that would dot the lakes and rivers of the West, proposing to locate the first blocks of the national city along Tiber Creek. Along the water would run public walks and parkways. The sketch called for expansion southeastward to fill in the cleared lands toward the Eastern Branch, designating that area as land "to be laid off in future."[41]

George Washington shared many of Jefferson's expectations. He thought that the best site for a new city was the plateau between Jenkins Hill (Capitol Hill) and the Eastern Branch. A great commercial city would need a fine harbor, and the Eastern Branch offered deep water free from the winter ice that crashed over the Great Falls and Little Falls to slow trade at Georgetown.[42] Tobias Lear, Washington's private secretary from 1786 to 1793, described what was certainly the president's evaluation:

> The eastern branch affords one of the finest harbors imaginable. . . . The channel is generally so near the city, that a wharf, extended forty or fifty feet from the bank, will have water enough for the largest ships to come up, and discharge or receive their cargoes. The land on each side of the branch is sufficiently high to secure shipping from any wind that blows . . . and, while vessels in the main river, if they should happen to be caught there by ice, are liable to receive great injury, and are sometimes totally lost by it, those in the branch lay in perfect security.[43]

Pierre L'Enfant's plan of 1791 conformed in large measure to the Virginian vision. He located the itinerary post, or zero mileage marker, directly east of the Capitol site. Massachusetts, Pennsylvania, and Virginia Avenues, named for the key states in shaping the new independent republic, took pride of place in connecting the Anacostia and Potomac shores.

With few fine buildings or bustling crowds to take their attention, early visitors described a city that sprawled over a rising benchland between the tidal margins and a romantic ring of hills and heights.[44] To the west were the heights of Arlington, to the east the abrupt ridge of Anacostia Heights, and to the north a line of hills from Georgetown Heights to Meridian Hill to Prospect Hill. A frequent image of the new city took the view from the road northwest of Georgetown: a foreground of verdant hills and gnarled trees framed a distant town and Capitol.[45] Working over the hills and along the stream beds, early naturalists carefully cataloged the District's natural vegetation and compiled long lists that D. B. Warden and William Elliot published in their descriptions of Washington as *Florula columbiana*.[46] The official boundaries of Washington City extended to the foot of these northern hills, whose summits the army engineers in 1861–62 transformed into Fort Reno, Fort Stevens, Fort Totten, Fort Lincoln, and other strong points to protect against invasion.

Early descriptions of this riverside city usually treated the two rivers as equals. Washington was "watered by the Potomac and Anacostia rivers," said Jonathan Elliot; George Watterston used nearly identical words. It was built along "the left bank of the Potomac and the right of the Anacostia," according to William Force. The city extended equal distances along the Potomac and Eastern Branch, commented early travelers such as John Davis and the Duke de la Rochefoucault-Liancourt. It was at the "junction" of the two rivers in a 1793 description by George Walker, at the "angle" between the rivers in John Hayward's 1853 gazetteer.[47]

Early mapmakers confirmed the sense of Washington as a water-bounded city perched between the main stem and the Eastern Branch of the Potomac. Each of the three standard depictions of Washington and its environs drew the eye immediately to the two rivers.

First was the plan of the city itself. L'Enfant's drawings and the official map of streets and squares engraved and printed by James Thackara and John Vallance in 1792 showed the city cupped within the wide "Vee" of the two rivers. One reason for a delay in publication was George Washington's desire to include soundings of the rivers. The dominant axis is the line formed by the lower Potomac below the confluence of the rivers and continued by Delaware Avenue from Greenleaf's Point through Capitol Hill. For the next three quarters of a century—until Washington neighborhoods began to outgrow the original street layout—this depiction of a city embraced by rivers was the standard city map.[48]

Cartographers who wanted to show the entire District of Columbia had a problem of orientation. On a standard map with north at the top, the District looks like a diamond. To show the entire federal territory without wasting marginal space, most early mapmakers tilted it forty-five degrees to the right or the left. The tilt to the right turned the Potomac into a dominant vertical element on the left-hand side of the map and made the Eastern Branch into a horizontal element along the lower margin. This orientation implied a city founded on the Eastern Branch and growing inland from its harbor.[49] The alternative tilt to the left put the Potomac along the map's lower margin with the Eastern Branch rising vertically along the right-hand edge. Again, the first impression was a city framed and held by its rivers and stitched together by the main avenues that ran from one to the other.[50]

A third option took a step back to place the entire District of Columbia in relation to its rivers. In these maps the broad lower reach of the Potomac rises vertically from the center of the lower margin and then forks to the left and right for the main stem and Eastern Branch. The District sits like a diamond over the junction with its northwestern corner pointing to the top of the map. The message is clear: here is a river town with its widening estuary drawing it toward salt water.[51]

Like Washington's mapmakers, artists and engravers until roughly the 1840s emphasized the rivers as well as the built environment. One example showed the city as approached upriver from Alexandria or the Chesapeake. The Capitol tops its hill in the center background. Dominating the view are

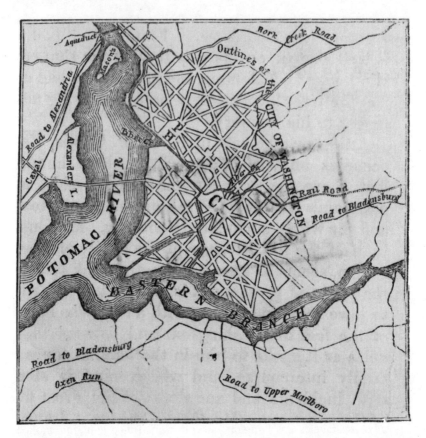

Washington City, from *Harper's Magazine*, 1852. Many antebellum maps showed Washington oriented to the Eastern Branch, with its key streets carrying business from the river into the city. (Geography and Map Division, Library of Congress)

the Potomac below Greenleaf's Point, with steamboats and sailing vessels, and its northeastern shore below the Anacostia.[52] Another showed the city from Arlington behind a broad and busy Potomac.[53] Even more striking was a popular and frequently copied view of the city from what is now the Anacostia district. William Bennett in 1834 turned a painting by George Cooke into the "City of Washington from Beyond the Navy Yard." From the bucolic Anacostia Heights we look across the broad Eastern Branch to an active waterfront with the governmental city in the background. In 1848 William Q. Force's *Picture of Washington* included a similar "Washington: View from Giesborough," again looking northward across the Eastern Branch. The dome of the Capitol centers the horizon, but the dominant feature is the river running in front of the city, and the dominant action is river-related:

the buildings of the Navy Yard, a sailboat, a fisherman pulling nets to the southern shore.[54]

Washington's rivers, in short, were central not only to the vision of an emerging Middle America from the Atlantic to the Mississippi but also to the ways in which people saw the city. Visitors arrived by land from Baltimore and Annapolis via Bladensburg and the upper reaches of the Anacostia. The water route brought travelers up the Potomac past Alexandria to land along the Eastern Branch or perhaps to continue upstream to George-

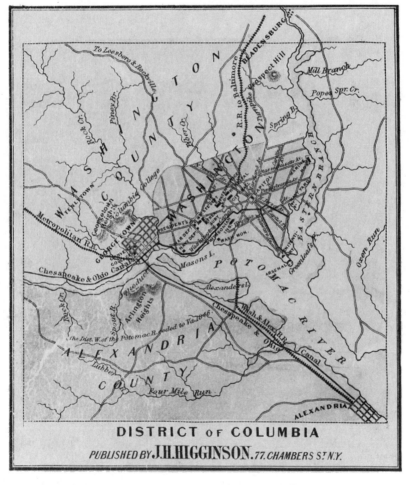

District of Columbia, by J. H. Higginson, 1860. The most common depiction of antebellum Washington emphasized the prominence of the tidal Potomac. (Geography and Map Division, Library of Congress)

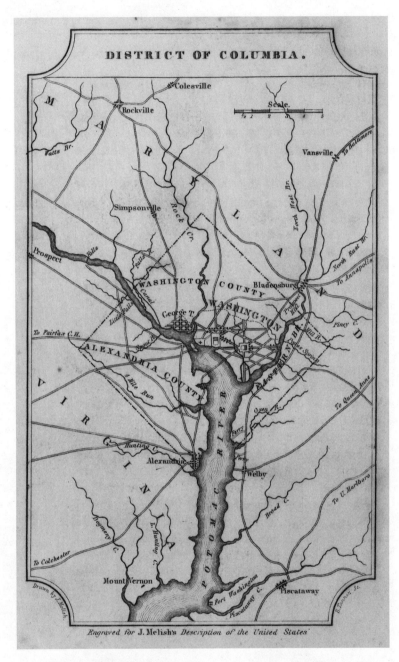

District of Columbia, by J. Melish, ca. 1820–30. A number of early maps of the District of Columbia perched Washington like a flower on the stem of the tidal Potomac. (Geography and Map Division, Library of Congress)

town. The literature and iconography of early Washington complemented the typical itinerary and framed the way that outsiders visualized the new capital. Even those who never visited the city were left with no doubt that it was as much a riverside city as Philadelphia and London.

Tidewater Town

In the waning years of the twentieth century, congressional golf tournaments and the Paris Air Show exerted powerful attractions on the members of the American Senate and House of Representatives. Leaders of the two houses were well advised to work around key dates that drew their members out of town.

City of Washington from beyond the Navy Yard, 1834. Beautifully drawn by William Bennett, this view from the Anacostia Hills shows the Navy Yard and the early city rising from the Eastern Branch to Capitol Hill, with the White House in the far distance. (Prints and Photographs Division, Library of Congress)

General view of Washington, ca. 1840. Far cruder than the Bennett view and confused in its geography, this depiction of Washington superimposed the young city on a clichéd riverside landscape; the artist turned the Eastern Branch into a cascade. (Machen Print Collection, View 302, Historical Society of Washington, D.C.)

At the start of the nineteenth century, fast horses had much the same power to shape the congressional schedule. Continuing a Georgetown tradition, an annual session of races took place each fall. On Tuesday, November 8, 1803, both houses, tired of debating the purchase of Louisiana, adjourned their sessions in order to attend the first races of the season, despite threatening weather that turned to rain and left dozens of politicians with a cold trudge back to Capitol Hill boardinghouses. By the following Saturday the sky had cleared and 3,000 to 4,000 people came out. Elegant ladies and their servants watched from high ground to the west of the mile-long circle. A knob of high land in the middle held bleachers for spectators who arrived on foot. "While the horses were running," recalled Dr. Manasseh Cutler, "the whole ground within the circus was spread over with people on horseback stretching round full speed . . . to see the race." Money changed hands with the sale of fine horses and by wagers among congressmen, Georgetown merchants, and Virginia and Maryland farmers. The event was still going strong a decade later, when Mr. and Mrs. Madison led the parade of "grand equipages" to the track.[55]

The prominence of the race track is one of many ways in which early Washington reflected the society and habits of agricultural Maryland and Virginia. The affluent planter-farmers of Prince Georges County and Fairfax County and the merchants of Alexandria and Georgetown were already on the scene when the first clerks and bundles of records of the twelve-year-old federal government arrived in December 1800. The Keys, Calverts, Tayloes, Laws, and other families with land and political connections built the first big houses, founded the first churches, organized the dancing schools, threw the parties. Their social institutions and cultural systems instantly colored the new federal city (as did the fact that Thomas Jefferson and James Madison came from closely associated backgrounds).[56]

Set against these local roots were metropolitan aspirations. As a new city, Washington had to construct an identity from a permanent local population, a changing set of transient politicians and politicos, and great expectations about the character of a world capital. During its early decades, community making therefore started with local materials of Tidewater society and gradually added the self-conscious forms of a national city that hoped to please big-city people from both sides of the Atlantic.

Planter society meant horse racing and horse trading. It meant a prominent role for lawyers (the major intellectual training of the Virginia elite) and regard for social caste. It also meant lavish but informal entertaining, drinking and cock fighting to entertain the gentlemen, dancing and card playing for both sexes.[57] "Cards were a great resource of an evening," noted English attaché Augustus Foster, "and gaming was all the fashion, at brag, especially, for the men who frequented society were chiefly from Virginia, or the Western States, and were fond of this, the most gambling of all games. . . . Loo was the innocent diversion of the ladies."[58] Brag—an early form of poker—identified the new city with the rough-and-tumble society of Virginia, Kentucky, and Tennessee. For the ladies, loo looked eastward to London and Bath.

Nearby towns offered a slightly different model for blending local and cosmopolitan orientations. Washington in 1800 was encircled by Alexandria and Georgetown with a few thousand residents each and Bladensburg with a few hundred residents.[59] The merchants and men of affairs in these towns were the offspring of Potomac planter families, Scots traders, and ambitious northerners who followed the national government after 1800. Their aspirations were set by Atlantic commercial cities, especially the great upriver port of Philadelphia, the very model of a proper town. So, too, did Washington itself aspire to be like Norfolk and Alexandria at the least, to emulate Philadelphia, London, and other centers of Atlantic commerce at the best.

Atlantic ambitions were manifested in the design of Washington's early town houses. Terraces and rows of red brick town houses were the standard dwelling for the merchants and middle classes of commercial cities on both sides of the ocean. Early building regulations for the new city anticipated the reproduction of the same cityscape, calling for high stone or brick structures built parallel to the street. Indeed, many individual Washington property owners imitated the upscale brick dwellings of Alexandria and Georgetown. Ambitious speculative builders grouped several houses behind single symmetrical facades as did their counterparts in Charleston and London. As Bernard Herman argues, "the most ambitious projects clearly looked beyond the Chesapeake world. The town house terrace quickly assumed the status of the most modern and urban building option in the new city."[60]

But behind many of the brick facades was an architectural tradition adapted from the southern plantation. Rural plantations in Virginia and Maryland surrounded the main house with storehouses, cook houses, barns, stables, and quarters for slaves. As elsewhere in the South, slaveowners who relocated to Washington or added a town dwelling squeezed domestic outbuildings and housing for servants or slaves onto back lots. Unifying the complex were brick walls or board fences that created miniature urban plantations. Off on the side streets in poorer parts of the city were small frame houses that copied the dwellings of small Chesapeake farmers.[61]

The adaptation of plantation architecture was a concrete reminder that early Washington was a black city as well as a white city.[62] From 1800 to 1850 blacks constituted roughly one quarter of the people of Washington City (Table 2.1). The balance between slave and free, however, fluctuated substantially. In the surrounding countryside, a shift from tobacco to grain production, with its intermittent demand for labor, made slavery economically inefficient. Manumitted slaves often moved to the cities of the District, pushed by the Virginia law that required freed blacks to leave the state within six months. City life itself undermined slavery. Householders found that free blacks were just as good as slaves in performing the tasks of domestic service. Slaves who were hired out as laborers could sometimes use a portion of their wages to purchase freedom, and the higher earning power of free blacks allowed them to buy the freedom of family members.

The changing legal status of Washington's black workers brought legal restrictions as a form of racial management. Initial regulations were relatively permissive, resembling those in northern cities more than southern cities. Washington's 1820 charter required free blacks to register with the city and post a bond to ensure that they would not become public charges. Increasing numbers of free blacks, however, prompted new restrictions. Ordinances in 1827 required residence permits and placed limits on assembly. Nat Turner's rebellion in southern Virginia persuaded Georgetown to adopt its first black code, and the antiblack "Snow Riot" in Washington in 1835 (which targeted successful black property owners) caused the city to exclude blacks from a number of occupations. The overwhelming majority cooked meals, cleaned houses, dug foundations, and shifted piles of goods and building materials as servants and laborers.

At the other end of the social spectrum, the rise of a formal or "court" society carried some of the same ambiguities as domestic architecture. Jefferson treated the White House informally as another Virginia country house open to visiting friends. Entertainment at Jefferson's house meant drinking tea, conversing casually around the dinner table, trying out new Italian recipes, or viewing the "mammoth cheese," a 1,600-pound wheel that had been curdled and pressed from the milk of Democratic cows and carted from Connecticut to honor the president—who bemusedly stored it in a spare room of the presidential house.

Washington manners grew steadily more formal with the Madisons and their White House successors. To visit Jefferson was to go to dinner; to visit the Madisons was to attend a reception. Postwar Washington (post-1815) developed a winter social season that started with rounds of New Year's calls and extended through balls and receptions. The social scene was fully enough developed in the early 1820s for Librarian of Congress George Watterston to publish a satirical novel The L——— Family at Washington: or, A Winter in the Metropolis, which tracked members of a Hartford, Connecticut, family as they tried to make their way through Washington's political and social scene. Margaret Bayard Smith followed with another fictional view of drawing room society and politics in A Winter in Washington; or, Memoirs of the Seymour Family.[63]

Beginning in the 1830s, Washington directories published complete lists of government officials, members of Congress, diplomats, officers of the army and navy, clerks, and even assistant messengers employed in the executive departments (along with their salaries). Taxpayers presumably wished to know if they were getting their money's worth; hostesses wanted to make sure not to miss someone important or to get precedents out of order.[64] Washington's new sophistication by the 1840s could be painted in contrast to Alexandria, presented as a quaint repository of historic Tidewater culture whose residents retained the simple manners of colonial times.[65]

Table 2.1. Slaves and Free Blacks as a Percentage of the Washington City Population, 1800–1860

	Slaves	Free Blacks
1800	19.4	3.8
1810	17.5	10.6
1820	14.7	12.8
1830	12.3	16.6
1840	7.3	20.6
1850	5.3	20.4
1860	2.9	15.1

Source: Constance McLaughlin Green, The Secret City: A History of Race Relations in the Nation's Capital (Princeton, N.J.: Princeton University Press, 1967), 63.

Nevertheless, the city remained deeply embedded in its Tidewater/fall line location and the cultural systems and economic expectations that accompanied that location. The Washington elite hoped to be worldly enough to impress British visitors. Britons remained deliberately unimpressed, bad-mouthing the capital out of principle and passing their time in the far more agreeable Philadelphia "until Congress is fairly in action."[66]

Potomac River Community

Since 1860 the Potomac River has been an internal border. It was a military frontier during the Civil War and a physical barrier to the North-South communication system of the railroad and automobile eras—an interruption to be bridged or crossed. In Washington City's first generation, in contrast, the idea of the Potomac as a barrier would have been curious at best. The early Potomac was George Washington's river and Thomas Jefferson's—a potential connection between East and West, a zipper between Maryland and Virginia and the three fragments of the District of Columbia. It was the front pathway for visitors and a dominant element in representations of the city.

Early Washington, in short, was deeply embedded in its place. To understand the ideas and aspirations of the founding generations, we need to know how they thought about the specific tract of landscape on which it was built and about its situation relative to the various parts of the new nation. Place was physical, social, and economic, involving relationships to hinterlands, competitors, and continental settings. The specifics of that place—wildlife, neighbors, potential position within an emerging and fluid system of cities and regional trade—substantially determined the sort of city that emerged, affecting the rhythms of daily and yearly life in the context of rural society.

On both the local and continental scales, the dominant feature of that place was the Potomac River. No mere backdrop for marble monuments and site for recreation, the early Potomac affected dinner tables and commercial possibilities, the city plan and the city's role in a new republic. U.S. regional patterns were not firmly established in 1800. Regions were in flux and formation as Americans moved westward, competed to build transportation systems, and looked for political advantage in different alliances of states. In the minds of its creators, Washington was posed between East and West as well as between North and South. It is commonly described as the "southern" element in the great compromise. But as it developed in its first decades, it was not only "southern" (a political abstraction that was still in process of formation) but also "Tidewater," "Virginian," "western," and "central," the hoped-for anchor of an emerging national core that might overshadow differences between North and South.

After a few mutterings about removal to Philadelphia between 1800 and 1815, proposals to replace Washington always argued for a more western location that would represent the extension of the Pennsylvania-Virginia core: thus Cincinnati in the 1830s, St. Louis in the Gilded Age, Denver in the 1930s and 1950s.

In effect, a national middle region did arise with the blending of Middle Atlantic and Chesapeake cultural regions in the first half of the nineteenth century. The farmers and town makers who moved westward from Pennsylvania and the Upper South mingled in the Ohio and Missouri Valleys to create a Middle America marked by courthouse squares, Methodists, Disciples of Christ, and corn-hog agriculture. It was a heartland that was deeply strained by sectional tension and civil war. It was also a region whose states ultimately chose the Union—not only Ohio, Indiana, Illinois, and Iowa but also West Virginia, Kentucky, Missouri, and Kansas. But for Washington the regional outcome was ironic, for the personal and commercial ties that helped to bind Middle America to the Northeast and preserved a national government for Washington to house ran to Baltimore, Philadelphia, and New York rather than to the metropolis of the Potomac.

TRANSITIONS

From Town to
Metropolis

*M*ARGARET HALL was not impressed by Washington in the winter of 1828. Like many other visitors from Britain, she found the physical city dreary and its social life sorely lacking. The chief daytime amusement was visiting the Capitol to listen to rival politicians "abuse each other in a most gross way." Evenings meant early dinner at five o'clock, to allow national leaders and hangers-on to attend evening parties at seven-thirty and get home by eleven. Parties meant whist tables in "small, ill lighted rooms," dancing to "defective" music, and "dirty-looking refreshments" on old japanned trays. All in all, she thought, Washington resembled an English watering place—perhaps Tunbridge Wells in the rustic uplands of Kent.[1]

Looking back from 1844, Ohioan Caleb Atwater remarked on changes that would have pleased Margaret Hall. In the first Jackson administration, he remembered, Washington had indeed been "a long straggling village." Now in the mid-1840s, the capital was assuming "more of a city-like aspect." There were improvements to public spaces, new buildings (the grandly imposing Treasury Building began to rise in 1836), and fewer drunks staggering in and out of barrooms and hotels.[2]

The question of public dissipation aside, Atwater understood that Washington was growing gradually into a city. First-generation Washingtonians lived in a loosely knit Tidewater town whose buildings grouped in distinct clusters around its riverside knolls—the source of the repeated complaint that it was nothing more than a collection of villages. As its population rose from 13,000 in 1820 to 19,000 in 1830, however, Washington acquired some of the first signs of urban status. In 1820 the second city charter divided the small community into six wards. Two years later, Judah Delano compiled Washington's first directory "showing the Name, Occupation and Residence of each Head of a Family and Person in Business." Other locally compiled and published directories followed in 1827, 1830, and 1834.[3]

Washington residents in the 1830s began to popularize new terminology to describe the city where civilian federal employment was rising from the hundreds to the low thousands (reaching 1,014 in 1841 and 1,533 in 1851). Few Washingtonians in the thirties and forties continued to refer to their home in constitutional language as the "seat of government" or as the "federal city."[4] They wrote instead about "our rising metropolis," the "proud metropolis," "the metropolis of the union," or "the metropolitan site for this great and growing empire."[5] R. S. Fisher's *Gazetteer of the State of Maryland* called Washington the "national metropolis of the United States." Joseph Martin's *Comprehensive Description of Virginia* offered "metropolis of this great empire of Confederated Republics."[6]

Metropolis was a word of multiple meanings. In part, it was a technical claim to be the location not only of Congress and president but also of other federal offices—a grand way to say "seat of government." By extension, the term also claimed that Washington was the right and proper location for any and all activities with national rather than statewide scope, such as universities and museums. In this light, to be the metropolis of the republic was to bypass the commercial competition in which Washington was losing hope of catching Baltimore and New York.

Metropolitan status implied grand ambitions. The "great metropolis" to which Americans still compared themselves, and from which they still learned lessons in urban management and government, was London. To be the metropolis of the Union was thus to be bustling and self-confident like Philadelphia, to be another grand and powerful London, not another Tunbridge Wells.

Around midcentury, artists and their publishers began to reflect Washington's growth as a city in their preferred depictions. They ceased to foreground Washington's bucolic setting of Anacostia hills and Eastern Branch, Georgetown's hills, or Arlington heights and Potomac River. In place of G. I. Parkyn's bucolic landscape of 1795 or George Cooke's "City of Washington from Beyond the Naval Yard" from 1834, the new emblematic picture was an anonymously drawn "View of Washington City and Georgetown," published by Casimir Bohn in 1849 and included with his guidebook to

Washington. Bohn's view looked west and northwest from the west portico of the Capitol, and it showed Washington as a sprawling and expansive city. The Mall and Pennsylvania Avenue draw the eye to the new Washington Monument, the new Naval Observatory, the Treasury Building, and the growing districts that were finally linking Capitol and White House. The Potomac and the Virginia hills blend with the horizon as framing elements rather than prominent parts of the composition.[7] Over the next generation, variations and elaborations on Bohn's view were standard in the work of other engravers such as Robert Smith, George A. Morrison, and Edward Sachse. The implied message was cityhood. Washington as a built environment now dominated its site.

Whether Washington was a real city depended on viewpoint. British travelers tended to dislike what they *saw* and continued to make disparagement a cottage industry, cribbing complaints from each other and looking for new insults. As fast as it was developing, after all, Washington could scarcely keep pace with Europe. Even a relatively sympathetic visitor such as Alexander Mackay commented that "Washington so violates one's preconceived notions of a capital, and is, in its general features, so much at variance with the estimate which one forms of the metropolitan proprieties, that it is difficult, in dealing with it as a capital, to avoid caricaturing a respectable country town." The more acerbic George Sala, a correspondent for the *London Telegraph*, denied head-on that Washington in any way looked like the metropolis of a powerful nation.[8]

American writers shared some of the same impulse. New Yorkers and Bostonians on quick visits, made cranky by dust and heat and confused by the angled intersections and diagonal avenues, ranted about the flawed street plan and loose-jointed pattern of development. Even so, a writer for *Harper's New Monthly Magazine* in 1859 noted "amazing strides toward permanent grandeur" in the last half decade. An *Atlantic Monthly* correspondent on the very eve of the Civil War had to admit that "notwithstanding all these impediments and disadvantages, Washington is progressing rapidly. It is fast becoming a large city. . . . Its destiny is that of the Union."[9]

John Silva Meehan had an entirely different perspective. A longtime Washingtonian and Librarian of Congress from 1829 to 1861, Meehan depicted both the old and the new city in his diary. "The frogs are singing merrily tonight in the marshes to the north of my dwelling," he wrote on July 2, 1846, describing the lowlands between the present-day Senate office buildings and Union Station. But that same spring had brought throngs of strangers to visit the city's National Fair (officially the National Exhibition of

American Manufacturers and Products of Mechanical Art) and "some of the thousand attractions for which Washington City is so renowned." His whole family was amused at the contrast between the bustling, noisy city of the present and the nascent metropolis that traveler John Davis had described at the beginning of the century.[10]

In the context of the antebellum United States, Washington *was* a city by the 1840s, reaching 40,000 residents in 1850 and 61,000 on the eve of war in 1860. It hovered just below the top ten cities in population. Well behind the great ports of Boston, New York, Brooklyn, Philadelphia, and New Orleans, it traded ranks back and forth with second-tier centers such as Providence, Albany, Rochester, and Pittsburgh. Slowly but surely, the bullfrogs were on the way out, the throngs of admiring visitors on the way in.

Three

A Two-Sided
Mirror

On a trip from Washington to Philadelphia in May 1877, Frederick Douglass stopped in Baltimore to deliver a lyceum address on "Our National Capital." For nearly two hours Douglass offered detailed reflections on the capital city, where he had lived since 1870. In a talk that ranged widely over history, present conditions, and future prospects, he tried to sum up Washington's distinctive character and qualities. He recalled its faltering origins, pointed to its public monuments, and praised recent improvements to streets and public services. Echoing the national Republican agenda, he argued that the triumph of "centralization" over sectionalism was now building a great city. Never had Washington "been so truly as now, the capital of the whole nation."[1]

Thus far the speech offered no controversy. But Douglass proceeded to analyze the effects of Washington's Potomac location. The city before the great war had been "southern in all its sympathies and national only in name." It had been "a garden . . . choked with poisonous weeds and infested by twisting serpents." Even after the suppression of rebellion, the southern influence still rankled. The city's "white trash" ignored common economic interests out of bias against black citizens. The old Tidewater elite had lost power but still haunted the city. They were now "masters without slaves, lords without land, Honorables without honors, idols without worshipers. . . . The old Virginia stock, once so powerful in Washington and in the counsels of the nation, is now a thing of the past, an anachronism, a superstition, a dim and flickering light on the distant and hazy horizon of a fast-declining day."[2]

Reports and excerpts from the talk in the *Baltimore American* and *Baltimore Sun* and then in the *Washington Evening Star* set off an explosion of indignant criticism. Two years earlier, Douglass had given the same talk in Washington to no attention whatever. Now many members of the local establishment clamored that his aspersions on southernized Washington and Washingtonians made him unfit to serve as marshal for the District of Columbia, a position to which he had just been appointed by President Rutherford B. Hayes and confirmed by the Senate. Anti-Douglass petitions reportedly gained twenty thousand signatures. In turn, northern newspapers such as the *New York Times* and *New York Tribune* rose to his defense. So did supporters such as James Fishback, who wrote to offer moral support against Washington's "old Rebs" and "fogies." Douglass himself tried to calm the situation by claiming simultaneously to have been telling the undeniable truth about racial relations while being misunderstood in detail.[3]

Douglass held on to his federal job and remained one of Washington's most distinguished residents, but the tempest was a nasty reminder that Washington after the Civil War was an explicit prize in a battle for the nation's soul. The capital had recently been on the front lines of sectional warfare. Douglass was claiming and celebrating what he thought was the undeniable sectional victory of North over South, but he learned in 1877 that he was defending a tenuous triumph. In 1875, when he first delivered "Our National Capital," U.S. policy on region and race was still guided by Radical Republican ideas. In 1877, after the great compromise that linked reunion and reaction, many white Washingtonians and sympathizers outside the city were far less willing to hear criticism of Washington's southern character and were eager for an opportunity to undermine a prominent black leader.

Frederick Douglass's Washington speech was thus one small episode—at a pivotal moment—in a hundred-year contest over the character and identity of Washington. Specifically, the reaction to Douglass showed how temporary and arbitrary had been the process of northernizing Washington in the 1860s. More broadly, it was one more episode in the long competition to define the balance between North and South. It demonstrated how fully the growth of the nineteenth-century capital was deeply enmeshed in the national politics of drawing sectional borders.

North and South did not exist as finally formed categories when Washington was founded. They were emerging ideas that had to be more fully developed and constructed—there were boundaries to identify, defining traits to emphasize, histories to devise. For Washington, the first stage in the process was the implicit debate between "middle" and "southern" identities for the Potomac Basin. As sectional tensions increasingly controlled national politics from the 1830s through the 1860s, Washington found itself on a progressively sharper regional divide. Over the longer period from the

1830s to the 1930s, we can trace a repeated ebb and flow between "south-ernization" and "northernization" that saw the strong southern claims of the 1840s and 1850s challenged and overridden during the Civil War and Reconstruction, only to enjoy a comeback early in the new century. The result of these changes was to set in motion a dynamic of "reconstruction" and "redemption" that left Washington in the early twentieth century a persistently southern city in culture and in the mores and values of local government despite its new northern connections and its growing role as the symbol of a reunited nation.

This chapter is about that dynamic. It explores a variety of ways in which North and South laid claims on the border city. Some of the claims were explicit and political, calling for particular actions and policies by Congress, city council, or short-lived territorial government. Others were implicit, involving choices of trading partners, sources of residents and their family connections, and orientations of cultural institutions. Some were made by Washington residents, some by national politicians, and some by outside observers happy to assign the capital to a regional location and identity.

The interpretation of this Washington experience is a contribution to a larger debate over the relative power of change and continuity in the history of the postbellum South. For southern economic boosters since the proclamation of a New South in the 1880s and for southern social scientists from the 1930s to the 1970s, the dominant theme was catch-up and convergence. Having been held back by slavery, war, and agrarian institutions, the South was now ready to become "American" in economy and social patterns. "Now" might variously be defined as the 1880s, the 1920s, the 1940s, the 1960s, or the 1970s, but the common narrative was one of rapid change through which a laggard South was narrowing measurable differences from the northern norm.

Within the framework of social theory, the problem was to explain (and promote) the transformation from backwardness to modernity. Although the degree to which manufacturing development and other economic changes actually disturbed the status quo was limited, industrialization was commonly presumed to be a transforming cause that would bring large cities, a cosmopolitan middle class, modernization of values, and a more open society. Dozens of sociologists, historians, and economists stated the theory of convergence, analyzed its implications, discussed political nationalization, and mined each decennial census for data on urbanization, occupational structure, health, income, and education that might confirm the "national incorporation" of the region.[4]

For students of culture rather than cash flow, in contrast, the South appears as a historically stable region rooted in its resource base and ethnic composition. Because more people left the South than moved into it from 1860 to 1960, southerners did not have to accommodate large new populations that might challenge regional character (the major exception being fringe cities such as immigrant Tampa, seaport New Orleans, navy town Norfolk, and federal Washington). Except perhaps for Baltimore, even these peripheral places absorbed newcomers into communities that remained predominantly southern in tradition and culture, even if perceptibly different from Richmond or Jackson.

An important school of recent southern scholarship argues long continuities in regional traits. Titles like *The Enduring South, Why the South Will Survive, The Lasting South,* and *Place over Time: The Continuity of Southern Distinctiveness* state the theme. So does the exemplary *Encyclopedia of Southern Culture.* Civil war, industrialization, urban growth, and national mass communication may have added new elements to the experience of the South, but its boundaries and essential character as defined by religion, language, rurality, and accommodation to racial variety have remained remarkably stable.[5]

As a popular consequence, the image of the South as an alternative to modern mass society has shown its own staying power. The idea takes us from Virginia "cavaliers" to the "Dukes of Hazard," from rich and proud to poor but proud. A consistent image of the South remains one of passion. The popular myth of hot heads and hot bodies in a hot climate brings us wild Celts in butternut uniforms charging Union trenches, Scarlett O'Hara at Tara, the characters of Erskine Caldwell, Tennessee Williams, and William Faulkner. Jack Temple Kirby has traced the evolution from sharecropper and neo-Gothic novels and documentary photography in the 1920s and 1930s to the "tribal, passionate, and neurotic South" of the 1940s and 1950s. Civil rights movements and reactive violence in the 1960s brought neoabolitionist dramas that confronted the evils of a "devilish South."[6] The contrasting "southern chic" of the 1970s, which ranged from the television series *The Waltons* to the popularity of country music, offered an upbeat version of the same emotive South of pastoral simplicity and honest feelings.

My analysis is an argument not for direct survival but for re-created and reformulated continuity. "Southernness" in Washington has possessed the staying power to survive two regional invasions. It outlasted economic carpetbaggers and political reconstruction in a northeastern image between the 1860s and the 1880s—the central material of this chapter. It survived an even larger invasion of attaché case toters and national bureaucratization since the 1930s—one of the subjects of Chapter 4. What emerged each time was certainly not the old city, for northernization and nationalization changed the character of the city and its people. But each "new" Washington was also a city that was southern in important and sometimes new ways.

Border Politics

At the beginning of the 1840s, the U.S. Capitol was the occasion as well as the site for sectional politics. Senators and representatives had considered the sectional implications of legislative and executive action in the building's meeting halls since 1801. But now, half a century after the adoption of the Constitution, the building itself was a focus of regional rivalry.

The question was art—specifically the four new paintings that were to adorn the Capitol rotunda, supplementing four relief panels and four historical renderings of the Revolution by John Trumbull.[7] At issue were conflicting regional versions of the national creation story. In 1836 New York artist Robert Weir received the commission for the first of the paintings. After initially proposing the storming of Stony Point, Weir settled on *The Embarkation of the Pilgrims at Delft Haven, Holland*. The painting, completed in 1843, spoke to Yankee pride in New England as the hearth of a new nation and the Pilgrims as the "germ" of the great republic. The idea that the American nation grew from a Massachusetts seed sat poorly with Virginian Henry Wise. For a second picture he pushed the story of Pocahontas as a way to remind the nation that its true beginnings were along the banks of the James River. In 1840 Virginian John Chapman painted *The Baptism of Pocahontas* to represent a national countermyth to the Pilgrims.[8]

The politicization of the Capitol's art program was new. Previous decoration had included reliefs of William Penn's treaty with the Indians, Daniel Boone, Pocahontas and John Smith, and the Landing of the Pilgrims but had avoided explicit political controversy. Now, as the 1830s gave way to the 1840s, Americans no longer seemed willing to accept a plural view of their nation. Instead, they felt the need to claim pride of place for a New England or a Chesapeake origin. And in that drive to promulgate a northern or southern version of national birth, federal institutions and the federal city were newly important trophies.

As the rotunda debate suggests, the fluidity of American regions collapsed after 1835 into a fundamental division between North and South. The engines of the division were the rise of radical abolitionists and the regional targeting of antislavery agitation in the 1830s, followed by the reemergence of the issue of slavery expansion in the 1840s. Both the moral rhetoric of abolition and the economic agendas of sectional expansion created stronger and stronger sectional self-consciousness. Americans began to understand North and South as political sections and distinctive cultures as well as economic regions or loose groupings of states. Mediating institutions begin to split under the pressure—even the open-doored churches of Baptists and Methodists in 1844–45, for example.

The new sectionalism had specific impacts and implications for the Chesapeake subregion. The old Virginia vision of anchoring a Middle America that stretched from the Potomac and Delaware Rivers to the Mississippi was squeezed between the claims of North and South. In the wake of Nat Turner's rebellion, Virginia explicitly debated and chose a southern identity as it considered and rejected the gradual abolition of slavery in 1831–32. Caught between changing visions of nation and section, the old Chesapeake region became steadily more southern than "middle."

In the midst of these changes, Washington's tattered hopes of being the nation's great central city evaporated as well. Washington in the 1840s and 1850s became what it had not been before—a border city balanced between

Robert Weir, *The Embarkation of the Pilgrims*. New England's version of the American foundation myth for the Capitol. In a nation with few artists and fewer museums, the public art of the Capitol held far greater importance in the antebellum decades than in the twentieth century. (Architect of the Capitol)

John Gadsby Chapman, *The Baptism of Pocahontas*. Virginia's counterversion of the national foundation myth as sectional tension mounted in the 1840s. (Architect of the Capitol)

an increasingly self-conscious South and an increasingly self-assertive North. The newly substantial city that was gradually replacing the small Tidewater town became both a player and a symbol in the contest between northern and southern versions of the United States. It was still common ground, but it was also a place that was available to be conscripted for regional agendas.

To observers who visited or resided in Washington in the Polk, Pierce, and Buchanan years, the city "felt" more southern than northern. To be sure, there were more northerners from Pennsylvania and New York on the streets and in the workplaces than there were deep southerners, and more immigrants from England, Germany, and Ireland than either.[9] But none of these groups compared to the black and white Marylanders, Virginians, and D.C. natives from whom antebellum Washington drew both its white business class and its white and black working class.

The *Seventh Census* gives a clear picture of the regional origins of white Washington in 1850. More than half (52 percent) of the white residents of the District of Columbia had been born in the federal district. Another 19 percent were Virginia natives and 10 percent Marylanders. With 80 percent of the white residents drawn from the margins of Chesapeake Bay, the remaining 20 percent divided equally among European immigrants and migrants from elsewhere in the United States.[10]

Black Washingtonians, of course, were even more heavily from the federal district, northern Virginia, or Tidewater Maryland. Already substantial, the free black population increased rapidly after Alexandria's retrocession to Virginia in 1846, as Virginia law prohibited free blacks from living in the state for more than six months. Outnumbering European immigrants two to one in 1850, blacks served the meals in Washington homes and hotels, made the beds for the gentry and forked the straw for their horses, wielded the picks and shovels on road work and construction projects, and left visitors an indelible impression of a southern town.[11]

The large black population, both slave and free, was the backdrop for a long and bitter political battle over the slave trade in the District of Columbia. The right to buy and sell slaves represented continuity with the origins of the federal district, but it came as well to symbolize—to antislavery activists—the hold of the South on the national government. In the 1830s abolitionists began to petition Congress to abolish slavery and prohibit the slave trade within the District. Moved by an expedient desire to avoid a contentious issue and by the South's growing tendency to make slavery its badge of honor, Congress in 1836 adopted the "gag rule" by which it automatically tabled all petitions relating to slavery in the federal district without consideration.[12]

With the annexation of northern Mexico in 1848, slavery abolition mixed with the problem of the status of slavery in the new territories. As a package of proposals moved toward adoption in the Compromise of 1850, abolition of the District slave trade returned to official attention as a modest and acceptable southern concession to northern opinion. Inclusion of the measure in the compromise was made easier by the recent return of Alexandria to Virginia sovereignty. Alexandria was a much more important slave trading center than Washington or Georgetown, and its 1846 separation removed economic pressures for maintaining the trade in the federal district.[13]

In turn, population and politics were the twin underpinnings for antebellum Washington's southernized social and political elite. As in the previous generation, southerners held a firm grip on the national government through the 1840s and effectively controlled the Democratic administrations of Franklin Pierce and James Buchanan.[14] Southerners seemed to observers from other places to be born for politics, naturals for its mix of posturing and deal making. Visitor Alfred Bunn had exactly this impression, populating his description of Washington in the early 1850s with a series of colorful characters who were nearly all southerners—cotton planter, slave owner from Richmond, New Orleans merchant, Kentuckian, Tennessee congressman, Arkansas planter . . . leavened with a lonely abolitionist.[15] Other observers described the way that the touchy southern sense of honor entwined itself around political issues. Congressmen sometimes went armed, took insult and tussled on the House or Senate floor, and faced each other in the early morning on the dueling grounds at Bladensburg.[16] In the context of southernized politics, the notorious assault by South Carolina's Preston Brooks on Massachusetts Senator Charles Sumner in 1856 was shocking but not surprising.

Reinforcing the southern tone of official politics was an easy social alliance of Tidewater families and southern politicians. Southern congressmen were much more likely than northerners to bring their families to Washington and to mingle with local business leaders such as the Riggs, Corcoran, and Tayloe families. In the 1850s the "Southern queens of society" were Mrs. Jefferson Davis of Mississippi, Mrs. John Slidell of Louisiana, and Mrs. John Crittenden of Kentucky.[17] For a sympathetic observer, it was lively and light-hearted society that inspired the envy of dour outsiders. "There was, on the part of the North," remembered Virginia Clay, the young wife of an Alabama senator, "a palpable envy of the hold the South had retained so long upon the federal city, whether in politics or society." For the unsympathetic, it was narrow and unchallenging: "It was a pleasant sort of life, if one would steer clear of the humanities and be a philosopher of the Southern make; that is, to have more egotism than charity. It was not a very cultivated condition. People did not talk books, and had no pretension to artistic taste or scientific achievements. We dealt largely in politics and little social chit-chat."[18]

North and South both knew who managed the social connections and political gossip. In J. B. Jones's novel *The Rival Belles*, the Tingle family descends on Washington in the mid-1850s for father to pursue a cabinet post and daughters to snag husbands. When Anne and Emily meet the Honorable Charles Edward Dudley of ———— Carolina, they try to ensure acceptance into local society by making absolutely clear that their home may be Philadelphia but their sympathies are fully southern.[19] Proper Washingtonians developed a habit of embarking to Virginia Springs, White Sulphur Springs, and other southern mountain spas to continue the social whirl through the summer. A novel of 1853 described the departure and return: "The long, bright, sunny, sultry summer days have passed, and the elite of Washington, who, to avoid the heat and dust of August, went to Shannondale, Warrenton, Piney Point, or some other place where the votaries of fashion do assemble, have returned to their city homes, and are busy making preparations for the enjoyments of the gayeties of the coming winter."[20]

By the 1850s both northerners and southerners saw Washington as the first *southern* city on the road southward from New York and Philadelphia, the last southern city on the way north. Georgetown College drew most of its students from southern Catholic families; Columbian College filled its halls with southern Baptists until the University of Richmond began to cut into its market in the 1850s. For Henry Adams, first impressions in 1850 were of "low wooden houses . . . scattered along the streets, as in other Southern villages" and slavery: "Slavery struck him in the face; it was a horror; a crime; the sum of all wickedness. . . . Slave states were dirty, unkempt, poverty-stricken, ignorant, vicious."[21] For Mary Jane Windle, the judgment was altogether different, equating southernness with genteel society and soft climate, tulip trees, clematis, and lilacs rustling in the spring breeze. A transplanted Pennsylvanian writing for a South Carolina newspaper during the Buchanan administration, she found that "our southern home [Washington] has gained astonishingly" by a peep at "money-loving, money-grasping" New York. "Pleasant was it, after the dust and drought of Broadway . . . to inhale the fragrance of the sweet-brier and honeysuckle of the Capitol grounds, listen to its birds, and set foot on its elastic turf once more."[22]

Allen Tate's fictional portrait of the Washington region on the eve of the Civil War in The Fathers captures the southward tilt.[23] By contrasting the ambitions and fears of a younger generation born after 1830 with the ideas of their fathers and uncles born at the opening of the century, Tate depicts the tension within a society that was naturally "tidewater" for "the fathers" but is viewed as southern by their children. Tate's characters are members and relatives of the landed elite of Tidewater Maryland and Fairfax County. They are grain farmers, horse breeders, men of commerce, politicians, and army officers posted to the War Department. They circulate easily among Virginia manor houses, Georgetown mansions, Alexandria taverns, and Washington ballrooms; they use and abuse slaves as a matter of course; and they help to keep Washington comfortably southern in the tone of daily life.

The great divide in the novel is between middle-aged Major Buchan, the Virginia farmer, and George Posey, a young and ambitious Georgetown businessman. As Tate sets up the conflict, it is one more round in the great nineteenth-century battle of tradition against modernity, family responsibility against individualism, manners against amorality. But there is also a tension between old and new views of regional identity and affiliation. Major Buchan's world is the Northern Neck, and his horizons stretch no farther than the boundaries of Virginia. He cannot imagine his Virginia, his northern Virginia, joining forces with such alien places as Alabama and Arkansas. George Posey and the major's son Lacy Buchan, in contrast, have a strong sense of the South as a distinct section and nascent nation. They and the other younger men in the novel go with the southern cause, as did many of their real-life counterparts from Alexandria and Georgetown.[24]

Reconstructing Washington

Before the great war between the states, wrote Mary Clemmer Ames in 1875, "Washington was nothing but a place in which Congress could meet and politicians carry on their games at high stakes for power and place." Americans focused their pride and ambition on regional centers—New York, Boston, Chicago, New Orleans—rather than looking to a single rallying point for patriotism. But then war changed it all as Americans rallied to defend the nation and its capital:

> Thus from the holocaust of war, from the ashes of our sires and sons arose newborn the holy love of country, and veneration for its Capital. The zeal of nationality, the passion of patriotism awoke above the bodies of our slain. . . . Never, till that hour, did the federal city—the city of George Washington, the first-born child of the Union, born to live or to perish with it,—become to the heart of the American people that which it had so long been in the eyes of the world—truly the CAPITAL OF THE NATION.[25]

Mary Ames's rhapsody to the new Washington certainly rang false to many southern Americans, but Washingtonians loved her sentiments. As postbellum Washington fought off proposals to move the federal functions to St. Louis or other points west, boosters hammered the idea that blood and treasure given in Washington's defense had sanctified it as a shrine as well as a capital, "far dearer to the nation's heart now than it was before the breaking out of the war of the Rebellion."[26]

During the Civil War Washington stood just behind the front lines. In the war's first months, secessionist mobs in Baltimore nearly cut the city's railroad connection to Philadelphia and New York and remained a threat through the spring, while secession sentiment was especially strong in the Maryland counties east of Washington.[27] On July 21, 1861, Pierre Beauregard and Irvin McDowell tested out their new armies near Manassas, Virginia, thirty miles west of Washington; the belching and rumble of the guns carried across the Potomac to the hills around the city.[28] Northern and southern forces shattered the ensuing fall calm with a firefight at Ball's Bluff, thirty miles up the Potomac, in November 1861. In the next three and a half years, tens of thousands of recruits passed through Washington. In hospitals, offices, forts, and camps on both sides of the Potomac, they waited and recuperated in the shadow of the Capitol and half-finished Washington monument.[29]

Washington was a strategic pivot as well as an activity center. As the fortified command post of the Union, the capital was the strong point around which the war in the East revolved. The winds of war swirled around the city in vast clockwise turns as if it were the eye of a great storm system. George McClellan roused himself to action in 1862 to launch the Army of the Potomac southeastward by steamer in search of the back door to Richmond. From their camps along the Potomac, John Pope, Ambrose Burnside, and Joe Hooker followed in search of the decisive engagement with the Army of Northern Virginia, sending their troops rashly southward and then rebounding in defeat.

Robert E. Lee and his lieutenants, in turn, tried great wheeling turns to loop around Washington from the west. One campaign ended along Antietam Creek. The next year's attack culminated at Gettysburg. Jubal Early's audacious raid in July 1864 brought an army of the Confederate States within the boundaries of the District of Columbia. Sweeping up the Shenandoah Valley and turning across Maryland, Early's men reached the ring of forts on the heights north of Washington just as federal reinforcements arrived from the Virginia front. As President Abraham Lincoln poked his head dangerously over the parapet of Fort Stevens to stare down the rebels, the defense of Washington became a symbol of the northern/national cause.

Whether the battles were close or distant, the war steadily altered the private city. Substantial capital fled south in 1861 along with Georgetown militia members and businessmen with southern affiliations. Merchants with long-range business faced interrupted access to many of their usual southern customers but found new markets within a growing city and federal establishment. The booming city was newly open for ambitious entrepreneurs and new wealth. "For every traitor who has deserted," said the *Washington Chronicle* in 1864, "ten honest people come here to settle down and occupy ten times his former space."[30]

The newspaper was not far off about the trends in migration, as northern newcomers crowded the city. A rapidly rotating population of soldiers and war contractors raised the District of Columbia from 75,000 to 132,000 residents. Crowding the lobby of the Willard Hotel and the dining rooms of boardinghouses were contractors and inventors, officials and office seekers, petitioners and poets, foreign journalists and American railroad promoters. There were strange faces in the barrooms and restaurants and visitors from Ohio or New York who wanted to be close to the action. New men puffed their cigars as they strolled across Lafayette Park or sought out the brothels south of Pennsylvania Avenue. By the winter of 1863–64, Washington was attracting northern "society" as well as business. "From what I hear of west End Gossip," wrote Elizabeth Blair Lee in September 1863, "the North is coming down to Washington in fashionable force—& it is that fact that makes houses rent so high."[31]

If contractors and journalists were "new people" by the hundreds, refugee and emancipated blacks from Virginia and Maryland were "new people" by the tens of thousands. In 1861–62 escaped slaves from Virginia were defined as "contraband of war" and taken under federal supervision. Slaves from Maryland were officially to be returned to their owners, but congressional abolition of slavery in the District of Columbia in May 1862 made that regulation impossible to enforce. Approximately 40,000 blacks moved to or through Washington during the war years for an aggregate increase of 20,00–25,000 by the end of the decade. A census of 1866 by the Freedmen's Bureau found an increase of 16,000 over 1860, a special census of the District in 1867 found an increase of 22,000, and the 1870 federal census fixed the increase at 25,000. The local census of 1867 found that more than two-thirds of black Washingtonians and half of all white residents had arrived since 1860.[32]

The changes of 1861–65 opened Washington to both political and social reconstruction. The former involved the explicit clash between alternative versions of an American future as played out in the national city. The second involved an implicit tug-of-war between the economic influence of the North and the cultural staying power of the South.

Washington at the close of the war was not only a symbol of the Union, but also a location for Radical Republicans to advance their complex agenda for a reconstituted nation in which moral progress advanced in hand with prosperity. James Wilson of Iowa spoke to Congress in January 1866 of both economic and social goals. "Where in all the country," he asked, "was there to be found such evidences of thriftless dependence as in this city before the cold breath of the North swept down here and imparted a little of 'Yankee' vigor to its business and population?" But Wilson valued personal freedom as well as prosperity, calling for black suffrage so that "the example of the nation may induce the States to aid in hastening the development of a perfect Republic."[33]

Voting rights for black men in the District of Columbia—the proposition to which Wilson was speaking—was the pivotal issue for shaping a model city for an emancipated nation. For Radical Republicans such as Charles Sumner and George Julian, Washington was a testing ground for an integrated society. During the course of the war, Congress had funded black schools, integrated street railways, and opened local courts to blacks. In 1865–66 Sumner and others turned to the extension of voting rights. The District's white residents were outraged, voting overwhelmingly against the proposal in an advisory referendum in December 1865; the tallies were 712 to 1 in Georgetown and 6,591 to 35 in Washington. Such "southern" resistance strengthened the resolve of voting rights advocates, who passed their measure in December 1866 and repassed it over President Andrew Johnson's veto in January 1867.[34]

For the next two years Washington experimented with a biracial political coalition. Blacks constituted 45 percent of the registered voters in the 1868 elections for mayor and board of aldermen. Winner of the mayor's office by a narrow margin was Sayles Bowen, a faithful Republican Party worker and immigrant to Washington from the North. Blacks won several city council seats. Against opposition Democratic aldermen, the tenuous radical-black alliance eliminated the word "white" from local ordinances, obtained increased funds for black schools, appointed blacks to city jobs, and enacted antidiscrimination laws.[35]

Washington's rainbow coalition was short-lived. Local white resistance and divisions among Republicans combined to undermine Bowen's reelection campaign. For conservative Republicans such as the editor of the Washington Star, racial justice was less important than economic improvement, and the best road to prosperity seemed to be territorial rather than municipal government. Over the objections of radicals, Congress in 1871 provided a new form of government for the federal district with a presidentially appointed governor and a Board of Public Works.[36]

Territorial Washington was thus an effort to tone down a Radical Republican city administration and find a more socially conservative but economically progressive Republican middle ground. In 1871–72 the new territorial leadership kept portions of the civil rights agenda alive with civil liberties legislation and continued attention to black education. But a reorientation to public works was unmistakable in the growing influence of Alexander Shepherd, a Washington-born businessman who hoped to restructure

Washington's economy and politics after the model of northeastern cities. Shepherd had become a part owner of the Star and helped to organize a short-lived Board of Trade (1865–71) that wanted to secure Washington's commercial future with direct rail links to New York and the Middle West.[37] He also dominated territorial government as president of the Board of Public Works (1871–73) and governor (1873–74). His program of public investment on roads, bridges, sewers, and water lines was intended to give Washington an up-to-date infrastructure comparable to that of New York or Philadelphia. The goal was clear to supporter George Townsend, who described the value of the public works projects and complained that Washington before Shepherd "had always been a Southernized city, little intent upon things of general value, and immethodical and slovenly as to its police, sanitary, and scientific regulations." Others shared the same judgment that only with substantial public works had Washington grown from a "struggling village into a well-built and well-paved emporium" and assured its permanence as a capital.[38]

Shepherd's regime offered an economic rather than a moral version of northernization. Although a native of the city, he came from the aspiring middle class rather than the Tidewater elite and spoke for newcomers. Alan Lessoff has found that three-quarters of Shepherd's inner circle were born in the North or abroad, and most had arrived in Washington since 1860; they were men on the make. In contrast, three-fourths of his active opponents were natives of Washington or nearby areas and had been active in business before the war. Sometimes working through a Citizens Association and neighborhood property owners associations, these "old citizens" objected to Shepherd's high-handed tactics, his focus on downtown, and the exorbitant costs of his projects. Behind the complaints were a dislike of fast change and new leadership and nostalgia for the more genteel antebellum city.

The program of creating a modern business-oriented city aimed to strike a middle ground between Radical Republicans who saw Washington as a testing ground for racial progress and wealthy, southern-oriented members of Washington's antebellum business community. By offering specific benefits to a ring of politicians and investors from the North, however, Shepherd's administration opened itself to damaging congressional investigations. In 1874 an increasingly conservative Congress listened to Shepherd's enemies, abolishing territorial government and substituting a system in which a three-member commission appointed by the president supervised the expenditure of carefully guarded congressional appropriations. Old-line white Washingtonians traded away self-government for federal money and the elimination of blacks as a political force. William Maury's conclusions summarize the conflicting regional agendas at issue in the early 1870s:

> Isolated from the left of their own party, and rebuffed by potent old-line Washingtonians, the Republicans, many of whom were relatively new to the city, sought to solidify their control. They used the techniques of northern machine politics, but like Republicans in other southern cities they were opposed by antebellum Democrats. The city government became an island of Grant Republicanism set about by a boiling sea of opposition. As the early shoots of Bourbon recovery were coming up in other parts of the South, its full flower became visible in Washington. By mid-1874, Reconstruction in Washington had ended.[39]

The short-circuiting of Shepherd's efforts to make Washington a part of the emerging national core was obscured in part by the economic success of a carpetbagger generation in the 1870s. Before and after 1874, Washington continued to attract northerners looking for new opportunities in a changing southern city. Political appointments were in the gift of a Republican Party with its base in the North. Businessmen arrived from the North during the 1860s and 1870s with an eye to opportunities in a rapidly changing economy.

These opportunities might be large or small. An advertising volume published in 1887, *Industrial and Commercial Resources of Washington*, listed professional men and retailers.[40] These were the lawyers, real estate agents, booksellers, awning makers, dry goods merchants, and eyeglass sellers who filled the growing downtown north of Pennsylvania Avenue. The business profiles included a previous place of residence or business for 111 firms. Fifty-six were from Maryland, Virginia, or the District of Columbia. Thirty-four were from the Northeast. Thirteen had come to Washington from abroad, eight from the Middle West, and none from other parts of the South.

Higher up the social scale, Shepherd's modernization had also made Washington at least minimally acceptable to social climbers and to members of east coast high society. The city's improvements, noted the *Nation* in 1874, were attracting "a respectable class of winter residents who formerly held it in great contempt." The Board of Public Works and its "reconstruction and renovation of the city upon a grand scale," echoed a local guidebook a decade later, had laid the foundations for "the present advantages of Washington as a residence city."[41]

The bankruptcy, retreat, or retirement of the southern-oriented elites of the antebellum decades had made room not only for ambitious entrepreneurs but also for a complex society of northern politicians, patricians, and parvenus. Kathryn Jacob has sketched several phases in this emerging

Washington society.[42] In the late 1860s and early 1870s, the capital saw a northern version of the political society that southerners had dominated before secession. There were more offices and officeholders in the executive departments and more members of Congress who brought along their families from Illinois and Connecticut. Rented houses and hotel suites for families replaced the communal boardinghouse culture of earlier congressional generations.

The scandals of the second Grant administration and the arrival of the teetotaling Hays household in the presidential mansion shifted the social focus from triumphant Republicans to an economic elite of wealthy sojourners. These newcomers of the late 1870s were often middle-aged couples with plenty of money and children to launch into marriages and careers. Many came year after year for the three- to six-month social season, entertaining each other in lavish mansions and apartments. They were nearly all northerners and frequently from middle western cities or smaller northeastern cities (Boston and Philadelphia had their own social seasons, thank you). Both the glamour of Washington's diplomatic corps and the city's social openness attracted families who wanted to break into a wider social circle than was available in Rochester, Scranton, Dayton, or even Cincinnati and Chicago.

The eighties and nineties, in turn, marked a high tide of reconciliation with the world of the northeastern social elite and its economic version of a northernized America. While Washington's southerners still summered in the Virginia mountains or coast, its northerners headed for Saratoga or New England. With an eye to this leisure society, one journalist in 1881 declared Washington to be an annex of New York, its "winter end . . . as Newport is the summer extension of the metropolis." Another noted that it was "as fashionable to have a winter house in Washington as it is to have a summer one at Newport or at Saratoga." White Washingtonians now claimed themselves as "cosmopolitans" and their city as a "winter resort for people of means and influence."[43] More than it had been since its founding, Washington was part of the circle of northern cities that dominated the United States.

A Negro National City

Paul Laurence Dunbar had come and gone by the time he described Washington's "Negro Society" for the *Saturday Evening Post* in 1901. But his celebration of the capital as a center for black America certainly fit briefly his own career. Dunbar left his home in Dayton, Ohio, in 1898 to work as a reading room assistant in the Library of Congress and rub shoulders with a sophisticated black elite. "Here come together the flower of colored citizenship from all parts of the country," he told the magazine's readers. "The breeziness of the West here meets the refinement of the East, the warmth and grace of the South, the culture and fine reserve of the North. . . . Here we are at the very gate of the South, in fact we have begun to feel that we are about in the centre of everything."[44]

What Dunbar described was one segment of a bifurcated black Washington. The disenfranchisement of District of Columbia residents in the 1870s, first with the switch from city council to territorial government and then with the transition to government by federal commission, ended the brief hope of building a black urban community around a comprehensive alliance of local business and local government. In the fully federalized city, white residents and a national government driven by the agendas of white voters and politicians set limits and opportunities for black Washington. After 1875, black residents could look either to specific roles in the local economy or to federal institutions.

For the majority of black Washingtonians, the postbellum city was a "Negro regional city" tied to local markets and rural communities around Chesapeake Bay. The men and women who had flooded Washington from Tidewater counties in the 1860s and follow-up migrants from Maryland and Virginia had close personal ties to surrounding counties. They earned their living by serving black customers as small retailers, artisans, and owners of service businesses; as servants in white households; and as laborers. These were people whose fortunes rose and fell with the local economy.[45] In the absence of a political voice or significant influence on the white community, their leadership came from the District of Columbia Chamber of Commerce, which represented black business operators such as insurance agents, undertakers, dry cleaners, beauticians, realtors, and others with purely local market interests.[46]

In sharp contrast was a small black elite that worked to differentiate itself from the mass of new black Washingtonians by emphasizing the capital's special attraction as a national center for black Americans. For selected residents, late-nineteenth-century Washington was a "Negro national city" where blacks could construct economic and cultural institutions and wield national influence. Supporting their ambitions was an important but ultimately flimsy scaffolding of federal jobs and federally assisted institutions. If Reconstruction had stalled within city politics, it still had support from the national Republican Party and its "northernizing" agenda to reshape the nation in the image of Indianapolis. At least until the end of the century, the nourishing of a Negro national city—symbolized by the handful of black congressmen from southern states—was part of the Republican agenda of reform and modernization.

Paul Dunbar thought it was obvious why Washington attracted so many blacks from around the country: "Young men come here to work in the departments." Republican presidents reserved a number of federal appointments for blacks and maintained the federal service as an available career route for a small but growing group of clerical workers (perhaps 250 or so at the end of the century) and a larger number of messengers, groundskeepers, and laborers. The number of blacks in federal jobs (most of which were in Washington) rose from 620 in 1883 to 2,393 in 1893.[47]

More important was the semifederal institution of Howard University.[48] Founded as a project of the Freedmen's Bureau in 1867, Howard began with a combination of remedial classes, liberal arts courses, and professional training in law, education, and medical fields. In 1879 the university convinced Congress to begin an annual grant in recognition of its national importance as a "Capstone of Negro Education." By the end of the century, Howard could claim with some accuracy to be the "national Negro university." In an era of regional colleges, it managed to draw one-fourth of its students from the North and Middle West.[49] For black intellectuals around the turn of the century, an appointment to the Howard faculty was often the climax of a career that included previous positions within the system of all-black southern colleges.[50]

The presence of the Howard faculty made Washington a significant center of literary and artistic work into the mid-1920s, when the allure of Harlem became nearly irresistible. Washington's national role also attracted the headquarters of scholarly organizations such as the American Negro Academy (1897) and the Association for the Study of Negro Life and History (1915). Association founder Carter G. Woodson began to publish the *Journal of Negro History* in 1916 and undertook research and documentation projects that employed young literati such as Langston Hughes. Literary circles such as the Saturday Nighters, who met at the home of Georgia Douglas Johnson, brought together native Washingtonians with aspiring writers from the South and Southwest.[51]

A third pillar of the black bourgeoisie was Washington's well-funded black school system. M Street High School (later Dunbar High School) was probably the most rigorous black preparatory school in the country around the turn of the century, with Armstrong High School a close rival. The separate school system allowed hundreds of men and women to earn good salaries as teachers. Strong schools also attracted families to Washington in the interest of opportunities for their children. Dr. Alonzo McClendon of Charleston, for example, relocated his family to Washington to secure his children an M Street education.[52]

Jobs in federal bureaus, Howard University lecture halls, public school administrative offices, and the Freedmen's Hospital were the basis for a small but very self-conscious social elite. Washington's black leaders were largely noncommercial in employment and interests. A brief profile of thirty-five leading black Washingtonians in 1898 counted four physicians, six educators, and fourteen current or former federal workers. The census of 1900 found more black clergymen, physicians, and teachers in Washington than in the much larger cities of Chicago and New York.[53]

Washington listings in national black *Who's Who* volumes for 1915, 1928, and 1950 confirm the construction of a cultured community of university faculty, high school teachers, government workers, lawyers, and clergy. Three-quarters of the persons listed for each year worked in education, the arts, or the learned professions. The other quarter consisted of an increasing proportion of civil servants and a decreasing proportion of small businessmen.[54]

The origins of this elite reflected both its southern and national origins. The upper circle had its roots in antebellum Washington's free black community and attracted members of free black families from elsewhere. Through the first half of the twentieth century, community leaders remained preponderantly local or southern in birth. The proportion of prominent civil servants, educators, clergymen, physicians, real estate dealers, and other business proprietors born in Maryland, Virginia, and the District of Columbia held at a steady 36–37 percent between 1915 and 1950; the proportion from the rest of the South ranged between 40 and 46 percent.

At the same time, northern connections were important. Blacks from the northern states constituted a stable minority of 15–17 percent among the early twentieth-century leaders. For blacks from all parts of the country, the route to a good Washington position often lay through northern colleges. Young African American men and women with degrees from Oberlin, Harvard, and Smith found the capital a relatively easy place in which to teach, or practice law, or build a medical practice.

What attracted other affluent blacks to Washington was the social life—society—dominated by perhaps one hundred intertwined families. Supporting many of its churches, theaters, and clubs were several hundred other families with steady white-collar incomes. For high-status black families as well as white, Washington offered opportunities for young women and men from the provinces to make good marriages. Josephine Beall Willson of Cleveland married Blanche K. Bruce, a former U.S. senator and federal official. Mary Church of Memphis married Robert H. Terrell, a teacher and then principal at H Street High School and later a District of Columbia judge. For members of established black families in New Orleans or Charleston, Washington was an attractive alternative to southern communities that were constricting long-recognized freedoms and opportunities.[55]

This national and northernized black Washington got attention in both the white and black press, but its success ironically demonstrated the "thinness" of Washington's reconstruction. To reach out nationally, the black professional community emphasized its difference—and distance—from the majority of African Americans in the District of Columbia. The power of education, the great engine of the capital elite, was not diffused throughout black Washington. Growing up poor on one of Washington's alleys, said Board of Education member John Francis, was unsatisfactory background for a schoolteacher.[56] Instead, members of the elite lived in socially acceptable neighborhoods near Howard University, frequented the proper summer resorts, quietly favored people with light skin tones, and focused on the brightness of the social whirl.[57] They also operated on the sufferance of white society. Day to day, whites could allow or take away access to good neighborhoods, theaters, and social organizations. On a broader canvas, the black elite depended on an inclusive federal government for steady jobs and for indirect support via funding for education. As new migrations and new ideologies of racism altered the relative position of the elite after 1900, the institutions and assumptions of the black aristocracy would prove fragile, like bright and brittle ornaments of glass.

A New York for the South

In 1906 the *Washington Evening Star* chartered a "Greater Washington train" that hauled a contingent of businessmen and exhibit cars to Lynchburg, Roanoke, Raleigh, and smaller towns in between. The purpose of the traveling trade show was to drum up business for Washington wholesalers and manufacturers. As they doled out cigars, liquor, and fancy talk, the Washingtonians hoped to convince South Atlantic merchants to place their orders close to home in Washington rather than far afield in Baltimore, Wilmington, or New York. The result of the "trade getting train," claimed one enthusiast, was to call into play "a new public opinion which has resulted in the cry for 'Greater Washington' that has not only thrilled the District of Columbia, but the whole South."[58]

Gradually in the 1880s and with increasing clarity toward the turn of the century, Washington's white business community formulated a new regional strategy for economic growth. It found Washington's future as a South Atlantic metropolis. The vision saw the capital as a manufacturing, distributing, and banking center for the Virginias, Carolinas, and points south. In a phrase, advocates of this view envisioned a New York of the South.

The forums for economic discussion were the nineteenth-century standards—newspapers such as the *Washington Star* and *Washington Post* and local commercial organizations. Leading business and civic leaders established the Washington Board of Trade in 1889. The first directors included the publishers of the *Star* and *Post*, prominent retailers, manufacturers, bankers, and attorneys. Washingtonians soon accepted that the Board of Trade spoke for the local market businesses and investors in areas ranging from economic development to government and public services. The Chamber of Commerce, appearing in 1908, defined its goal more narrowly as a "Greater Commercial Washington." Its membership overlapped the Board of Trade but with heavier representation of smaller retailers and wholesalers. As in other nineteenth-century cities, professional publicists and journalists filled out the roster of active participants.[59]

In many respects, the Washington Board of Trade functioned as a shadow government into the 1950s. The federally appointed commissioners who managed Washington after 1878 took care of basic urban services but offered District of Columbia residents little opportunity for direct participation in local affairs. In response, the Board of Trade assumed a quasi-governmental role, claiming to represent all sectors and interests of the city in relation to economic development, planning, and public service needs. Its claim was as valid as that of many formally representative business-reform governments of the 1910s and 1920s or the neoprogressive city administrations that worked the will of business coalitions in the decades after World War II. There is no reason to believe that strategic thinking proceeded any differently in Washington than in Dallas, Phoenix, Omaha, or other cities where nonbusiness interests were systematically disregarded.[60]

Washington as the business center for the New South was an idea that fell easily into the practiced rhetoric of American boosterism. Washingtonians phrased the city's southern strategy in the familiar language of inevitability. It had "great advantages" in the South, it was "destined" to utilize southern resources, it was a "natural," "proper," and "logical" center for southern business.[61] In one view of natural advantages, Washington was the "Gateway to the South from the North Atlantic States" for travelers and merchandise. Southerners seeking the summer resorts of the North and northerners looking to winter in the South would find Washington a natural stopover. To capture business travelers, Washington wholesalers needed only to expand their stocks of goods and intercept southern storekeepers before they reached Baltimore or New York. In a complementary emphasis, Washington was presumably the most convenient assembly and processing point for the raw materials of the South—coal, cotton, and lumber on every list, tobacco, iron, sulfur, and phosphates on one or another. Northern capital and local entrepreneurship could combine to turn the region's natural products into manufactured goods and ship them back to southern customers.[62]

Growing interest in southern markets was tied to the improvement of Washington's southward rail connections. J. P. Morgan built the Southern Railway system in the mid-1890s on the foundation of the Richmond and Danville Railroad, locating the executive offices in New York but the operating office in Washington. The Southern operated a main line through the Piedmont and secondary lines to southern Atlantic ports and the southern Ohio Valley. The new Atlantic Coast Line and Seaboard Air Line, railroads assembled from smaller companies by Richmond and Baltimore capitalists, linked Chesapeake Bay cities to the Tidewater and Florida. In 1909 Washingtonians enjoyed more frequent service to Georgia and Florida than to St. Louis or Chicago.[63]

The Southern Railway showed a special interest in promoting its headquarters city and northern terminus and in attracting settlers and investors into the South. Its managers claimed to be "not merely a carrier of the people and products of the South, but also a helpful factor in Southern development." Its Land and Industrial Department published the monthly *Southern Field* from 1895 to 1905. It boosted southern progress and opportunities in resource production and manufacturing, Washington's economy, and northern Virginia as a locale for country estates and winter homes. "As Washington is the gateway to the Southland," said an 1898 pamphlet, "there is sentimental as well as business justification for locating here the headquarters of this, the greatest and most comprehensive transportation company in the South."[64]

Interest in a southern strategy peaked during the national boom of 1905 to 1912. Washingtonians argued that their own city would rise in tandem with the "progress of the rejuvenated South."[65] Newspapers and booster literature cited Washington wholesale, business service, and construction

Southern Railway Building, 1910s. Formed in 1894, the Southern Railway Company consolidated several smaller lines that tied Washington to southeastern states. The new company took over the downtown Washington offices of the Richmond and Danville Railroad and enlarged the building in 1899. Standing at Pennsylvania Avenue and 13th Street NW, the headquarters gave visible expression to Washington's commercial ambitions. (Photograph furnished by Norfolk Southern Corporation, Atlanta, Georgia)

firms whose trade extended as far south as Tennessee and Alabama. A Southern Commercial Congress incorporated in Washington in 1911 to promote regional development.[66]

In diminished volume, Washington business continued to think southern through the 1920s. The Board of Trade, Chamber of Commerce, Merchants and Manufacturers Association, Real Estate Board, and Arlington Chamber of Commerce jointly sponsored an industrial survey that reiterated Washington's potential as a gateway to the South and reminded readers of its superior rail connections southward. Washington boosters were also pleased that Washington was a stop on the new airmail route from Boston and New York to Atlanta and New Orleans.[67]

The doctrine of southern resources was also restated in industrial surveys and economic planning documents. Washington as the portal to the South Atlantic states remained a standard theme into the 1950s, when the Board of Trade's economic research department mapped a hinterland that extended only 100 miles to the north but 400 miles southward.[68] Atlanta now appeared more often than Richmond as Washington's chief competitor and comparator, but a southward tilt remained.[69]

The Capital of Reconciliation

Behind the southern economic strategies was a remarkable resouthernizing of Washington society and culture. A striking characteristic of Washington from the 1890s through the 1920s was the reassertion of southern values and affiliations. Despite the continued presence of successive political generations of northerners and the expansion of national institutions, Washington in the Coolidge years was more closely tied to the South than in the years of Rutherford B. Hayes.

Starting points for understanding the resurgence are two novels, one published in 1880 and the other in 1900. The first is Henry Adams's acerbic *Democracy*. The second is Gertrude Atherton's melodramatic *Senator North*. The two authors express quite different messages about southern values through the medium of northern and southern heroines.

Democracy itself offers a preview of the thinness of Washington's northern reconstruction. Madeleine Lee of New York, the novel's protagonist and perceptual filter, is a visitor who descends on Washington out of boredom to observe the political scene and leaves after a few social seasons; she is an intellectual carpetbagger. One of the rivals for her attention is the sharply contrasting John Carrington, a lawyer from southside Virginia transplanted to Washington to repair his fortunes after the war. Carrington arrives in the capital before Madeleine Lee, fits in more easily with local manners, and stays after she has departed.

This being said, Adams is unambiguous about the merits of northern victory. The interesting issues for Adams are those of public life, and he is not in doubt that the North has the better hand. His Virginian is a social counterpoint, not a paragon. He charms Mrs. Lee but lacks the authority to sweep her away. Indeed, Carrington knows that the South has been passed by, realizing as early as 1861 that "whatever issue the war took, Virginia and he must be ruined." As Adams later wrote, the antebellum southern elite "had nothing to teach or to give, except warning. . . . No one learned a useful lesson from the Confederate school except to keep away from it. Thus at one sweep, the whole field of instruction south of the Potomac was shut off; it was overshadowed by the cotton-planters, from whom one could learn nothing but bad temper, bad manners, poker, and treason."[70]

Atherton also drives her plot through a young woman who has decided to learn about politics. Betty Madison has returned to Washington after several years in schools and Europe. She is a woman of an old Washington family, one of the cave dwellers pushed aside by the flood of postbellum newcomers such as Madeleine Lee. Betty is by far the most "modern" of her family, contrasting with a mother who eschews all attention to politics and a brother who cultivates the air of a professional southerner. But unlike Mrs. Lee, she is locally rooted, with no New York as an inviting fallback when Washington grows boring. In characters and plot, the world of *Senator North* shows the staying power of the South. Sojourning northerners are less prominent, as if the capital is losing its interest and allure. Southern family is stubbornly persistent. And the novel's action turns on the unhappy life of Betty's half sister, whose fate is sealed by the taint of a distant black ancestor.

For Atherton, southern values are the only appropriate model for white Washingtonians. It is fine to be up-to-date like Betty—to be New Southern—but tragedy ensues when generations of racial custom are thrown aside. A northerner and westerner with no direct experience of the South, Atherton found it easy to adopt the social attitudes of a reviving region. Racial mixture meant an inevitable flaw of character with tragic results—an idea that was profoundly central to the southern agenda of the 1890s.

Atherton's Madison family would have been happy with the resurgence of explicitly regional intellectual activity in-turn-of-century Washington. At the end of the nineteenth century, the capital began to host a series of narrowly regional intellectual endeavors. The genteel Virginian Thomas Nelson Page made his Washington home a social and literary center for southern writers in the 1890s and 1910s. Southerners residing in Washington founded a Southern History Association in 1896 and sponsored occasional publications and meetings until 1907.[71] The few (and mostly short-lived) Washington periodicals that claimed a regional rather than a national audience offered titles such as *Southern Churchman*, *South Atlantic*, *Southern Guide*, *Southern Literary Messenger*, and *Southern Commercial*.

In the same years, Washington was becoming more southern in its people. Census figures on the place of birth of the District of Columbia's

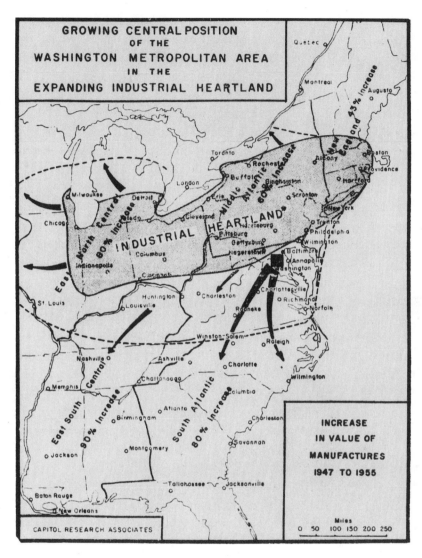

Washington as commercial gateway to the South, 1958. As demonstrated by this map submitted to a congressional hearing in 1958, the commercial vision of Washington as the intermediary between northern producers and southern consumers survived decades of practical disappointment. (From *Hearings before the Joint Committee on Washington Metropolitan Problems*, July 1958)

white residents are available for each decade through 1930. Native-born whites can be divided among those born in the North and the West, those born in the District of Columbia, Maryland, and Delaware, and those born in the remainder of the South. Between 1870 and 1930, the percentage of residents born in the District, Maryland, and Delaware declined from greater than two-thirds to just over one-half (Table 3.1). The proportion of southerners more than doubled, but that of northerners grew by only 28 percent. The ratio of northern-born to southern-born whites declined from a high of 1.91 in 1870 to 1.20 in 1930.

The composition of the white elite reflected the same fading of the "carpetbagger" generation. The founders of the Washington Board of Trade, the new spokesmen for the commercial city, included the publishers of the *Star* and *Post*, factory owners, merchants, and professional men.[72] Half of the founding directors in 1889 were northerners, whose median arrival date in Washington was 1872 (Table 3.2). By the 1910s, 1920s, and 1930s, however, native Washingtonians and southerners held an increasing edge as Board of Trade directors. The Chamber of Commerce (1908–34) focused more narrowly on the promotion of retailing and wholesaling. Its membership overlapped with the Board of Trade's, but with a heavier representation of smaller retailers and wholesalers. By the 1920s, its leadership too was weighted toward the South.[73]

The regional composition of Washington's black community underwent a similar tilt toward the South. Stability at the top of the social hierarchy masked the fact that a new wave of migrants from the rural South transformed the black community in aggregate. The economic depression of the 1890s renewed the migration from Virginia and Maryland. In turn, the Carolinas and Georgia began to supplant the Chesapeake states as the source of black migrants after 1910.[74] From 1880 to 1930, approximately 40 percent of the District's black residents were born within its boundaries (Table 3.1 above). However, the deeper South now replaced Virginia and Maryland as the dominant source area of new residents. Net black migration from the Carolinas, Georgia, and Florida was three times that from the North in the 1910s and more than ten times during the 1920s. The ratio of northern-born blacks to those born south of Virginia dropped from 0.68 in 1870 to 0.19 in 1930.

The new migration was deeply embedded within family memories and connections of twentieth-century Washington. Edward Jones's short story, "A New Man," centers on a Washingtonian who started in Georgia and worked his way north through the Carolinas and Virginia: "He also found in

Table 3.1. Place of Birth of District of Columbia Residents, 1870–1930

	Total	North	D.C.	Md.-Del.	Va.-W.Va.	Other South
Native Whites						
1870	72,091	20.8%	53.9%	14.3%	9.4%	1.5%
1880	101,024	20.4	55.4	12.5	9.3	2.5
1890	134,836	21.6	52.6	12.8	10.2	2.8
1900	175,040	24.3	47.7	12.6	11.5	3.9
1910	209,289	23.4	47.0	12.7	12.7	4.2
1920	295,299	30.6	38.4	11.0	12.8	7.1
1930	320,940	26.7	40.0	11.0	14.6	7.7
Native Blacks						
1870	43,324	1.3	31.0	27.1	38.7	1.9
1880	59,478	1.7	41.7	20.6	33.8	2.3
1890	74,883	1.9	42.3	20.1	32.3	3.2
1900	86,446	2.1	42.0	18.3	32.7	4.9
1910	93,517	2.7	43.3	16.8	30.5	6.7
1920	108,879	3.4	42.8	16.0	27.1	10.6
1930	130,450	3.8	40.2	12.6	23.7	19.7

Sources: Ninth Census of the United States, 1870, vol. 1: Statistics of Population, table 6; Tenth Census, 1880, vol. 1: Population, tables 11–12; Eleventh Census, 1890, vol. 1, pt. 1: Statistics of Population, tables 25, 28; Twelfth Census, 1900, vol. 1: Statistics of Population, tables 26, 29; Thirteenth Census, 1910, vol. 1: Population, tables 36–37; Fourteenth Census, 1920, vol. 2: Population, tables 18–19; Fifteenth Census, 1930, Population, vol. 2, tables 22–23.

the trunk some letters he wrote his father from the camps and from railroad yards and from the places he worked as he made his way up to Washington."[75] With expanding job opportunities, Washington was the most accessible "northern" city, but it was still much more homelike than a New York or a Pittsburgh. It was a place where Langston Hughes could appreciate the vibrancy of Seventh Street, "the long, old, dirty street, where the ordinary Negroes hang out, folks with practically no family tree at all, folks who draw no color line between mulattoes and deep dark-browns, folks who work

Table 3.2. Place of Birth of Washington Business Leaders, 1890–1940

	North	D.C.	South	Overseas	Unknown
Board of Trade Directors					
1890	11	3	5	3	9
1900	15	4	3	3	5
Board of Trade Directors and Committee Chairs					
1910	12	17	7	2	7
1920	12	21	7	1	5
1930	8	20	11	1	10
1940	13	13	10	1	5
Chamber of Commerce Directors					
1920	8	12	8	3	4
1930	10	9	9	3	9

hard for a living with their hands. On Seventh Street in 1924 they played the blues, ate watermelon, barbecue, and fish sandwiches, shot pool, told tall tales."[76]

If men dominated the Seventh Street sidewalks, women did much of the work of maintaining cultural links. They organized and nurtured church organizations that maintained Carolina social connections. They kept track of widespread families and supervised visits between country and city. They conserved down-home behaviors and household customs. This is a role that novelist Marita Golden tries to capture in the life of Naomi Reeves Johnson of North Carolina: "When I got settled good in the house, I sent for Mama and Daddy. . . . I'd planted a Carolina garden out in the backyard of squash, tomatoes, and peas, just like I'd done back home and Mama sat on the back porch when she saw it, shaking her head and smiling."[77]

What many of Washington's new black migrants found, however, was no longer the relatively open and "northern" community of the 1870s and 1880s. Instead, the city joined the developing southern system of race relations—gradually in the 1890s and more rapidly in the early twentieth century. De facto segregation appeared in hotels, restaurants, theaters, and hospitals in the early 1900s, at the same time that southern congressmen such as Thomas Heflin began to press for formal segregation of the public transit system. The *Elite List*, an early *Social Register*, had included several blacks to the end of the 1880s. The initially integrated Board of Trade excluded several blacks of significant economic standing, such as hotel owner and building contractor James T. Wormley. The Woman's Christian Temperance Union had no room for black women after 1908.

The Republican policy of cementing the allegiance of black voters by opening positions in the federal bureaucracy met its first setbacks under Grover Cleveland in 1885. Elizabeth Chapin, of Iowa, herself waving the bloody flag, complained that "the old rebel element drank in good bourbon toasts to the incoming Democratic administration" while Treasury Department clerks who had grown old in service to the Union feared for their jobs.[78] An early version of the Republican "Southern strategy" added a racial component after 1900. Soon after North Carolina's George H. White, the last Reconstruction-era black congressman, left office in 1901, Theodore Roosevelt (and his successor William Howard Taft) lost interest in finding jobs for black Republicans. By 1908 the number of black federal employees in Washington dropped to 1,450.[79]

The Carolina-Washington Connection. The program of a 1987 conference at American University encapsulates the place of Washington within the community networks of twentieth-century African Americans.

A troubling trend became a revolution with the inauguration of the southern segregationist Woodrow Wilson. The new president further curtailed the customary appointments of high-level black officials in the federal service after 1913. Cabinet and subcabinet officials followed his lead. New attitudes at the top of the executive branch set the tone for assaults on job security, often in the name of a "harmonious workplace," as when the director of the Bureau of Printing and Engraving hastened to replace a black supervisor with a white worker with less seniority.[80] Blacks found it harder to obtain entry-level jobs as well, especially after 1914, when the U.S. Civil Service Commission required photographs on all application forms. Accompanying the standard "rule of three" that allowed employers to pick from the top three names on Civil Service job lists, the photographs made racial discrimination easy. The only practical purpose, wrote Kelly Miller in 1923, was "to exclude the applicant whose face shows pigmentation."[81]

Wilson's officials also segregated federal workplaces with strong support from the president. The Wilsonian position was repeatedly to argue the advantages of separation: "My colleagues in the departments . . . were seeking, not to put the Negro employees at a disadvantage, but they were seeking to make arrangements which would prevent any kind of friction between white employees and the Negro employees."[82] The elimination of friction and the creation of "pleasant" working conditions required separate desks, separate cafeteria tables, separate lunchrooms. Behind the formal actions was the power of southern opinion as Wilson sought to entrench the Democratic Party in the federal government and to appease white racial radicals such as novelist Thomas Dixon, who wrote to Wilson that "the establishment of Negro men over white employees of the Treasury Department has in the minds of many thoughtful men and women long been a serious offense against the cleanliness of our social life."[83]

Despite campaign promises, a return to Republican presidents in the 1920s did not alter the progress of segregation. Cabinet secretaries under Warren G. Harding and Calvin Coolidge retained the segregated bureaus that they had inherited from the Wilson administration and often expanded racial separation in periodic office reorganizations. The argument of "efficiency" justified segregated lunchrooms, elevators, rest rooms, and offices—sometimes split by flimsy improvised partitions. Even the relatively progressive Herbert Hoover was only a temporary exception. Approaching a presidential campaign, Hoover as secretary of commerce ended segregation in the Bureau of the Census in 1928. Southern Democrats such as Cole Blease of South Carolina and Thomas Heflin of Alabama used the action for blistering attacks on Hoover's "systematic plan to humiliate white girls from whatever part of this Nation they may happen to come" and his disturbance of "the splendid segregation arrangements . . . by the Democratic Party, under which the negroes were working and getting along well in one section and the whites were working in another and pleased with the situation." After his election, Hoover ignored complaints from the NAACP and the National Equal Rights League and shied away from further steps toward workplace integration.[84]

In the nation's capital, federal officials set the tone. Washington by the 1920s was "a southern city as far as blacks are concerned."[85] Reflecting the influence of southern congressmen and the deep-seated assumptions of old-line white Washington, racial relations reached what Constance Green called the "new nadir" when "the national government took the tone of the Deep South, and white people as private persons now looked upon Negroes scarcely as citizens at all." Langston Hughes arrived in Washington in 1924 after growing up in the Middle West and exploring Europe. He discovered a city "like the South" with "all the prejudices and Jim Crow customs of any Southern town. . . . I could not get a cup of coffee on a cold day anywhere within sight of the Capitol, because no 'white' restaurant would serve a Negro."[86]

Economic crisis in the 1930s added massive unemployment to the problems of social segregation, while a new Democratic administration moved ever so cautiously on issues of job opportunity and discrimination. John Dos Passos in 1933 pointed at the continuing problem while trying his hand at dialect writing. He reported a conversation between two black men in the Union Station waiting room: "Jobs . . . man there ain't any use to think about it. . . . I doan know where yu come from, but you better tun roun' an' go back there while the goin's good. A man of color ain't got no more chance to git a job widde democrats than he has to . . . to . . . to git to be president."[87]

Mary Church Terrell had little in common with the discouraged job seekers in frayed overcoats, but she too knew that Washington had changed for the worse in her fifty years of residence. In her 1940 autobiography, *A Colored Woman in a White World*, she titled her chapter on the Jim Crow capital "The Colored Man's Paradise." "I have lived in Washington for fifty years," she noted, "and while it was far from being 'a paradise' for colored people when I first touched these shores, it has done a great deal since then to make conditions for them intolerable." In effect, the black elite had survived the inundation of the 1860s and redefined itself as a national African American aristocracy with big help from the federal government. In the early twentieth century, however, it took the double hit of eroding federal support and a new influx of unsophisticated rural southerners. And Terrell had no question that Washington was thoroughly southern: "If it [the capital] had been located in the North, East or West the status of colored people would be far better than it is."[88]

White observers agreed that Washington was (again) part of the South, but how they read "southernness" varied from genteel hospitality to fierce racism. A Chicago-based banking magazine, reflecting on the pleasures of a Washington convention, noted that "the people of Washington are largely Southern by birth and training. Indeed the Capital may well be accounted a Southern City." Other observers liked the continuity of southern history—a depiction very different from the national city of the Reconstruction years. The capital was on the list of historic southern towns in one book, "a Southern city geographically" in another. Harrison Rhodes in 1920 found Washington "pleasant . . . in a warm, well-fed, Southern way."[89] But others noticed a downside, commenting on the way in which northern newcomers to Washington moved quickly to take on southern values in race relations: "the great majority of white people here hold the Southern view of the negro, and as for the Northerners here, it takes but a little while for them to become infinitely more anti-negro than any Southerner."[90]

The Persistent South

Washington by 1900 had changed irrevocably from the city of 1860. Residents understood the change with a set of parallel dichotomies: southern/northern, sleepy/wakeful, passive/active, old-fashioned/modern. Here is how one resident summed up the changes at the turn of the century: "The old-time, dreamy Southern do-nothing dynasty had passed forever; the bustling energetic city-builders of the North and West poured in, and at once proceeded to make a wide-awake modern city out of a sleepy town."[91]

The contrast was certainly true—and conveniently compatible with twentieth-century social science ideas about the dynamics of modernization—but it was also overstated. In many ways the Washington of 1900 reflected not a permanent glacial advance of northernization but a high tide that receded in following decades, shifting economic ambitions and opportunities and stranding the progressive social goals of the postbellum decade in a politically inhospitable environment.

Evidence on business orientation, population, public values, and public image suggests that Washington's first great transformation during and af-

ter the Civil War triggered a two-way process of regional change. As Henry
James put the situation so allusively after a journey southward in 1906,
Washington lay in that zone where "the North ceases to insist, [and] the
South may begin to presume."[92] James was contrasting the northern mode
of explicit political and economic influence (insistence) with a southern
mode of implicit cultural influence (presumption). Both were *active* or expansive, but they operated in different fashions in different realms.

Descriptions of metropolitan regions often emphasize their role as pur-
veyors and exporters of culture and information that is presumed to diffuse
outward from a center of origin and down the urban hierarchy.[93] Because
postbellum Washington was located near the edge of a politically assertive
North and its expanding economic core, the capital city provided a gateway
through which new ways and people entered the South from the national
economic and intellectual core in the Northeast and Upper Middle West.
The northernization of national institutions from 1860 to 1900 was perhaps
the most important way that Washington became an agent for regional
change, but even its southern commercial strategy remained dependent on
capital from the larger northeastern cities.

Gateways work two ways, however. Although Washington certainly represented and transmitted a dominant northern culture and interest, it had a
reciprocal function in attracting and concentrating southerners and central-
izing institutions oriented to the South. The assembly of small railroad
companies into the Southern, Atlantic Coast Line, and Seaboard Air Line rail
systems during the 1890s, for example, may have opened southern markets
to penetration by northern manufacturers, but the railroads also made
Washington an easy destination for southerners looking for urban opportunities. Networks for professional recruitment and the dissemination of
ideas spread south as well as north. The same economic processes that tied
the city to Philadelphia and New York thus stabilized its southern cultural
affiliations in an ironic balance of regional relations. The city in 1930 was
linked to national networks focused on the Northeast, but it was equally at-
tached to the South in the character of everyday life. It was restructured but
not reconstructed.

In another view, the reverse of reconstruction was reconciliation—the
conscious effort to blend the traditions of South and North rather than to
supplant the one with the other. This is what Woodrow Wilson thought he
was doing, reaffirming American nationality by sandpapering down differences. But "reconciliation," of course, meant different things to different
Washingtonians. As an economic strategy to help Washington benefit from

a "New South," it was morally neutral. As a way to span cultural distance and heal personal wounds, it might be a positive process. Washington was thus an appropriate setting for formal gestures of reconciliation, as when the Daughters of the Confederacy met in the capital in 1912 and Confederate veterans in 1917.[94] And as a political program embedded in racial reaction, reconciliation steadily made Washington an uncomfortable home for many residents who could not claim a Confederate connection.

TRANSITIONS

———

Women, Work,
and Region

*T*UCKED AWAY on the shelves of the Washingtoniana Collection in the Martin Luther King Jr. Memorial Library is the story of *Rhoda Roland: A Woman from the West in Washington*.[1] As told in a plump 1902 novel by H. S. Sutton, Rhoda Roland is a plucky young widow from Iowa who spends a year in the capital. While living in a boardinghouse and supporting herself with a variety of private office work, Rhoda flirts with the edges of "fast" society and offers a series of astute observations about the growing city.

Rhoda Roland's adventure in Washington was possible because of a sweeping transformation in the gender division of white-collar work that marked the last decades of the nineteenth century. It was a change that started in the capital in 1862, when U.S. treasurer general Francis Spinner responded to a shortage of male clerks by hiring women to sort and package bonds and currency. Despite concerns about the sexual implications of mixing men and women in the same offices ("Treasury courtesans" was one phrase), Spinner found his new employees to be cheap and reliable. By 1870 the number of women in clerical positions in Washington's federal offices was probably in the low hundreds. They were numerous enough for a character in *Through One Administration*, Frances Hodgson Burnett's novel of the Hayes administration, to learn to "recognize many a face that passed him, and comprehend something of what it typified. He could single out the young woman who supported her family upon her salary, and the young woman who bought her ribbons with it; the widow whose pay fed half-a-dozen children."[2]

In antebellum America women were often domestic servants, sometimes mill operatives, and increasingly schoolteachers, but they were not office staff. Clerks were men—sometimes settled into lower-middle-class careers and sometimes learning a business from the inside before rising into management. Their jobs were copying letters and documents, maintaining files, tracking orders and correspondence, and keeping financial records.[3]

The last third of the century, however, brought an information explosion in American business and government. Improved postal service, dropping telegraph rates, and the spread of the telephone around the turn of the century facilitated communication at a distance and allowed absentee management. Increasingly large organizations with activities in multiple locations needed quick, accurate, and manageable information. In the aggregate, for example, the information revolution meant that the sales of ordinary postage stamps roughly doubled in every decade from 1866 to 1916.[4]

Within the office, the information revolution meant increasing demand for clerks, telephone operators, stenographers, and "typewriters" (as the operators of the new machine were called in the 1880s and 1890s). Large organizations learned to turn information processing into a set of routinized tasks. Filling the demand for desk workers were increasing numbers of middle-class women with high literacy, often guaranteed by the high school diplomas that went disproportionately to women in the later nineteenth century.[5] By 1900 women comprised 76 percent of all stenographers and typists and 29 percent of bookkeepers, cashiers, and accountants.[6] Men still determined what was to be said, but women transcribed, transmitted, recorded, and archived their messages.

As an information city without peer, and the headquarters for an organization with a continental system of branches and offices, Washington continued to lead the gender transformation of the American office at least until World War I. In the early 1890s Washington offices and bureaus employed perhaps four thousand women in clerical positions. Among them were Mrs. S. F. Fitzgerald, a forty-year employee of the Treasury who knew "more about National Bank notes than any other living person," and Mrs. Patti Lyle Collins, "the greatest living expert on deciphering illegible and defective letter addresses."[7] By 1910 the total of female clerical workers was 8,443. Sixteen percent of all women employed in the District of Columbia then held clerical positions, compared to 7 percent of all women nationwide. The District had more women working as clerks, typists, bookkeepers, and in similar occupations than entire states such as Maryland (four times the population), Virginia (six times the population), or Texas (twelve times the population).[8]

Women clerks at Treasury Department. (Still Photographs Department, National Archives)

As *Rhoda Roland* suggests, the woman-centered Washington novel changed character to reflect the reality of a city where one-third of all workers were women by 1910, compared to 21 percent of workers nationwide. Antebellum novelists had typically been aspiring (and often incompetent) Jane Austens, spinning domestic tales of husband searching and personal hardship against the background of political gossip.[9] Postbellum authors added the plucky heroine on her own, striving to support herself and her widowed mother, find romance, *and* retain respectability. In such new novels, office jobs are integral to the action. James Edwards's *The Court Circle: A Tale of Washington Life* is a tearful counterpart to *Rhoda Roland*.[10] The central character is Bertha Raymond, who has come to Washington from New York to seek government employment to support an ailing mother after the family fortunes fail. She lands a job in a federal bureau, suffers harassment by a martinet supervisor, loses her job because she lacks patronage, and regains it through fortunate connections.

In many of these same tales of late-nineteenth-century Washington, gender roles also took on a regional dimension. It was northern women from Iowa or New York who applied for office jobs when they needed to support themselves or an invalid relative. White southern women in the same situation took in roomers or opened a boardinghouse, extending the domestic sphere in a way familiar to previous generations. Rhoda Roland lived in a boardinghouse run by a southerner. So do several characters in William Franklin Johnson's *Poco A Poco* (1902), where Mrs. Bailey is described as "a descendant of one of the first families of Virginia . . . [who] kept a few select boarders, the purpose being a livelihood. She called them guests." The novelists mirror Mrs. Logan's comment that "the southern women maintain their strong hold upon the boarding houses, whose numbers are legion. Many of them are cultured women of proud extraction, daughters or descendants of old families ruined by the Civil War."[11]

Fiction, it turns out, reflected reality. Cindy Aron's study of Washington's early female clerks examined the 229 women who applied for work in the Treasury Department in 1862–63 and 1870 and the 1,410 who applied to the Interior Department in 1880 and 1890. She found several hundred women who had moved from northern states to take Washington jobs but only fifty women from southern states other than Virginia and Maryland.

A much larger group of southern women filled domestic rather than office roles. A small handful of black women secured tenuous positions in federal agencies, and Washington-born blacks often found work as cleaning staff for businesses and government agencies. But thousands of other blacks moved from southern farms to domestic service in the national capital, a migration that grew rapidly in numbers after the turn of the century. Often arriving in Washington in their teens and early twenties, many such migrants worked first for their own kin and then took newly learned domestic skills into white households as personal maids, house maids, cooks, and nurses. By World War I, remembered Mathilene Anderson, "nobody in Georgetown hired a girl unless she came from down South. They knew that as these jobs got open up them girls from here was going to be gone. They had better training, and when they could do cleaning at the army hospital or anyplace they'd leave a family and never look back. Pretty soon people'd only hire someone born and trained-up in the South."[12]

Through "old" and "new" women, values were regionalized. In *The Court Circle*, a sense of social propriety keeps the very southern Miss Georgia Myrtle a stay-at-home while Bertha Raymond is valiantly earning a living. In the novel of politics, too, northern women challenged tradition whereas southern women ultimately upheld it. *Democracy*'s Madeleine Lee of New York is a bit of a goad and gadfly. Adelaide Harrison in Adam Badeau's *Conspiracy: A Cuban Romance* (1885) is a Madeleine Lee imitation—a tall, blond, brilliant New Yorker "whose realm was the world, her role to rule in a real society."[13] Bertha Herrick Amory (*Through One Administration*) has been educated in a large eastern city, clearly has eastern family connections, and is "certainly cleverer than the majority of her acquaintance."[14] In *Senator North*, in contrast, the equally capable Betty Madison articulates and preserves southern values of family and race. Whether in the world of formal society or the economic marketplace, in short, to be a northern woman was to be associated with social and economic change. To be a southern woman was to fill traditional roles and preserve traditional values.

MRS. REV. STEPHEN BROWN.
Over thirty years in service of the United States Treasury. The greatest living expert in identifying burned, mutilated, and unrecognizable money sent for redemption.

MRS. PATTI LYLE COLLINS.
Twenty-five years in the Dead Letter Office. The greatest living expert in deciphering illegible and defective letter addresses.

The eminently proper appearance of Mrs. Rev. Stephen Brown and Mrs. Patti Lyle Collins tacitly refuted rumors about the promiscuity of women office workers as well as showing the importance of women for government operation. (From Mrs. John A. Logan, *Thirty Years in Washington* [1900])

Four

A City of a
Novel Type

In Frances Hodgson Burnett's novel *Through One Administration* (1881), a newcomer to the Washington of the 1870s finds himself growing familiar with the city. In the process, "the public buildings were no longer mere edifices in his eyes, but developed into tremendous communities, regulated by a tremendous system."[1] Twenty years later Mrs. John A. Logan, the wife of a Union general and stalwart Republican senator from Illinois, devoted chapter after chapter of her thick book about Washington to the inner workings of government bureaus. Her goal was to show readers "how marvelously the volume of business of the national government" had grown by describing "the wonders and workings of the elaborate machinery of government in motion, by leading them through the great national buildings and explaining what the army of busy men and women workers do and how they do it." Readers could satisfy themselves about the processing of applications to the Patent Office, the "wonderful instruments, kites, and weather maps" of the Weather Bureau, how Uncle Sam's money was made, and even (in chapter 23) "A day in the Department of Agriculture—The Farmer's Friend and Co-Worker—Free Distribution of Choice and Pure Seeds—How They May Be Had for the Asking."[2]

Mrs. Logan's way of picturing Washington was vastly different from that of antebellum guidebooks. In 1840 or 1860 interest in the federal government primarily meant interest in Congress—its personalities, debates, meeting place. Authors gave page after page to the rules of Congress, the architecture of the Capitol, and the details of its art works. The executive branch got more superficial treatment—the appearance of the White House, the location of the Navy Yard and National Observatory, embellishment of a few other public buildings, and perhaps a glimpse of presidential entertaining.[3]

The new postbellum view reflected the contrast of a rapidly changing world in which the workers of the executive departments were beginning to impact ordinary Americans in ways that ranged from the distribution of land to the awarding of veterans' pensions. The business community, too, was beginning to feel new attention from the federal government through such landmarks of the administrative state as the Interstate Commerce Act of 1887 and the Sherman Anti-Trust Act of 1890. Federal administration did not yet pervade everyday lives and livelihoods, as it would in the later twentieth century, but it certainly had increasing avenues of contact.

Most of these avenues were patrolled and managed from Washington. Along with its other effects, the Civil War tilted the balance of federal employment toward the capital. An increase of four thousand government jobs during the 1860s doubled Washington's share of the national total. The ratio of federal jobs to local employment doubled between 1861 and 1881, when 13,124 federal employees represented 20 percent of all District of Columbia workers (Table 4.1). The number of *new* federal jobs for each decade as a proportion of civilian employment in the District at the start of the decade was higher for the 1860s, 1870s, and 1880s than for any succeeding decades except the 1910s, 1930s, and 1940s (Table 4.2). Not only Mrs. Logan but also other Washington journalists such as Jane Wilson Gemmill (1884), Elizabeth Chapin (1887), and Charles Todd (1889) knew their readers would like to know what those thousands of clerks *did*—where they worked, how much paper they ordered for the Government Printing Office, how many seed packets they mailed out over the course of a year.[4]

The expansion of federal bureaus implied a new understanding of the national city. In the early nineteenth century, Washington was the "national metropolis" in rhetoric but not reality. Talk of a national university and national museum had produced a small Smithsonian Institution and a minor tourist attraction in the form of the Capitol building. The grand commercial ambitions of the founding generation had foundered on the rocks of urban competition, investment shortfalls, geographic disadvantage, and sectional conflict.

After the antebellum disappointments and the partisan feuding of the Reconstruction years, Washington boosters by the turn of the century again found it easy to assert that their city was special. Thomas Presbrey, writing for the Southern Railway, found its only peers in the major capitals of Europe. Newspaper editor Theodore Noyes, in a presidential report to the Board of Trade, claimed that Washington could expect to take its growth automatically from national expansion, for "the greater the current of national

Table 4.1. Washington: Federal Civilian Employment in Relation to Total Employment, 1860–1990

	Total Number of Jobs	Number of Federal Jobs	Federal Jobs as Percentage of Total Employment
1860–61	24,243	2,199	9.1
1870–71	49,041	6,222	12.7
1880–81	66,624	13,124	19.7
1890–91	101,119	20,834	20.6
1900–1901	126,941	28,044	22.1
1910	157,961	38,911	24.6
1920	236,027	94,110	39.9
1930	243,853	73,032	29.9
1940	319,317	139,770	43.8
1950	620,896	223,312	36.0
1960	791,921	239,873	30.3
1970	1,178,990	327,364	27.8
1980	1,530,954	346,000	22.6
1990	2,185,000	377,000	17.3

Sources: Federal employment is from U.S. Department of Commerce, Historical Statistics of the United States (Washington, D.C.: Government Printing Office, 1975), and U.S. Office of Personnel Management, Federal Civilian Workforce Statistics: Annual Report by Geographic Areas (Washington, D.C.: Government Printing Office, 1990).

Notes: For the first five decades, the total employment is taken from the decennial census year and the federal employment from the following year. These base figures through 1940 are for the District of Columbia; for 1950–90, for the Washington Metropolitan Area.

Through 1900–1901, the total employment figures represent the first year and the federal employment figures the second year.

life, the larger and stronger the heart." Real estate developer Arthur Randle agreed optimistically that the seat of government *always* grew into its country's greatest city.[5]

In this same era of revived ambition, Washingtonians not only reaffirmed but also redefined their city's national character. Its function as the *federal* city—the presumably neutral seat of government—was set by Constitution, law, and custom, and its role as an economic center for either the New West or the New South was problematic. Washington might, however, expect to develop as a multifaceted capital that attracted national institutions, private decision makers, public attention, and patriotic pride. Writers increasingly depicted Washington as the *capital* ("metropolis" now being firmly captured by New York and Chicago). As the center of intellectual life and information networks, Washington in this emerging vision could operate the controls on

Table 4.2. Washington: Growth of Federal Civilian Employment in Relation to Total Employment, 1861–1990

	Number of New Federal Jobs	Percentage of New Federal Jobs in Relation to Total Jobs at Start of Decade
1861–71	4,023	16.6
1871–81	6,902	14.1
1881–91	7,710	11.6
1891–1901	7,760	7.7
1901–10	10,867	8.6
1910–20	55,199	34.9
1920–30	–21,738	–8.9
1930–40	66,738	27.4
1940–50	83,542	26.2
1950–60	16,561	2.7
1960–70	87,496	11.0
1970–80	18,631	1.6
1980–90	31,000	2.0

Sources: Federal employment from U.S. Department of Commerce, *Historical Statistics of the United States* (Washington, D.C.: Government Printing Office, 1975), and U.S. Office of Personnel Management, *Federal Civilian Workforce Statistics: Annual Report by Geographic Areas* (Washington, D.C.: Government Printing Office, 1990).

Note: For the first five decades, the beginning total employment is taken from the decennial census year. These base figures through 1940 are for the District of Columbia; for 1950–90, for the Washington Metropolitan Area.

Destroying old greenbacks. In the 1890s, blacks and whites still worked together in federal offices. African Americans in this Treasury Department office had both white-collar and blue-collar jobs. (From Mrs. John A. Logan, *Thirty Years in Washington* [1900])

the engines of industrial prosperity while other cities stoked the furnaces and oiled the gears. Donating his collection to the Library of Congress, Francis Lieber wrote: "I have taken pleasure in inscribing these volumes 'To the National Library.' It is not the official name, but I take the liberty. It is the name you have come to. Library of Congress was good enough for Jeffersonian times; but is not now after the war. . . . I give these books on account of the Nationality in your library, and not of its Congressionality."[6]

The new affirmation of a national city was a rhetorical strategy to bypass the slowly fading conflicts between the agendas of Republicanism and reconciliation. If Washington *was* truly the national capital in fact and in spirit, then regional claims might be secondary. A city that served the nation as a center of institutions and intellect could worry less about regional commercial strategies and rivalries of local elites. Its civic leadership could attend to comprehensively serving the nation as a city of a novel type—what late-twentieth-century economists might label an information city.

Reassertion of national importance also came when Americans were linking local and regional institutions into national organizations. The process has been called the "incorporation of America" and the consolidation of "island communities" into national systems. Industrialists were combining regional manufacturers and locally financed railroads into unified corporations, national trusts, and holding companies whose shares were traded on a truly national stock exchange. Workers countered with efforts to organize national labor federations such as the Knights of Labor (1869) and the American Federation of Labor (1886). A national market for popular culture supported a new generation of mass market magazines and a national system of professional sports as represented by the National League (1876) and American League (1903) of baseball teams. Even academics decided that they were more than local representatives of religious and civil communities and organized themselves as national professions through the American Historical Association (1884), American Economics Association (1885), American Sociological Association (1905), and similar societies that inexorably squeezed out talented amateurs.

The national government played catch-up in this context of organizational development. Slowly in the later nineteenth century and more rapidly during the Roosevelt, Taft, and Wilson administrations it added departments and department heads, bureaus and bureaucrats. Federal civilian employment as a proportion of the American labor force went from 0.5 percent in 1871 to 1.0 percent in 1901 and 1.7 percent in 1921. With an expanding public administration paralleling the growth of corporate management and professional organization, Washington thus became a national city in practice as well as aspiration.

The national city of the early twentieth century, in turn, was the site for a new set of national memorials and museums. The federal government rebuilt the core of Washington in grand cosmopolitan style between 1900 and 1940. Gone was the haphazard development that had dotted the Mall and adjoining areas in the nineteenth century. In its place was a unified monumental core that imitated the imperial capitals of Europe and exemplified the long reach and power of the centralized state. With Capitol, White House, and marble temples to the political giants who had constructed and preserved the federal state, Washington by the mid-twentieth century was not only the home of national decision makers but also the open air cathedral for American patriotism.

The Paris of America

"A National University of Art and Music, fittingly to be located at the National Capital"—that is the pivot for the plot of *Poco A Poco*, a cheerfully satirical novel of Washington life at the turn of the century. William Franklin

Johnson's story gathers an aspiring journalist, a musician from Europe, a senator's daughter, a widow from the West, a business-minded investor, and other young people drawn to Washington by its various opportunities. Members of the group seize on the idea of creating a National University by popular subscription. They prepare a prospectus, secure a congressman as president of the fund-raising syndicate, and gain national publicity. Somewhat to their surprise, the enthusiasts begin to rake in one-dollar subscriptions from around the country, the donations attracted by "patriotism and pride in the greatness of our national Capital City" and the hope that the new university might trigger "a new and glorious Renaissance." The scheme runs afoul of Washington politics and rivalry for the affections of the senator's daughter, but the promoters fight off an indictment for embezzlement and gain the necessary funds from the perfection of a patent for storing electricity. Thereafter the university "takes form with amazing rapidity under the enthusiastic energy of the greatest architects and artists" and soon fulfills its promise to "transform Washington into the first capital city of the world."[7]

Alexander Anderson's 1897 volume on *Greater Washington: The Nation's City Viewed from a Material Standpoint* offers a fuller version of the *Poco A Poco* model of Washington as a city of culture. Anderson, former secretary to the Board of Trade, argued that Washington was destined to be a "paradise for authors" and the "great University City of America" because of access to the Library of Congress and the federal science establishment. It was already headquarters for a number of national organizations interested in "the promotion of great and important public movements" and a focal point for national conventions and travel. In Anderson's view, it could aspire to be the Rome of America in the arts, the Berlin of America in education, and the Paris of America as a city of beauty and pleasure.[8]

Indeed, the rebuilt, prosperous, and intellectually exciting Paris of the Third Republic was a most compatible model for advocates of a new kind of Washington. The capital, said the author of a Washington gazetteer, was "unlike all other American cities. . . . To the stranger she is more like Paris." The *Washington Star* in 1888 enthusiastically proclaimed that "to live at Washington, not to die at Paris, will become the American aspiration." Three years later a visiting professor from France told a local audience what it wanted to hear: that New York was a good place to get rich, but Paris and Washington were better places in which to live.[9]

Washington as a magnet for students, scholars, and literati was a well-rehearsed idea by the 1880s and 1890s. L'Enfant's original plan left a number of sites "unappropriated, and in situations appropriate for Colleges and Academies and of which every Society whose object is national can be accommodated."[10] George Washington had hoped to see the federal government sponsor a national university and had offered his shares in the Potomac Company as a starting endowment. Only James Madison, however, in a message to Congress at the end of his administration, showed much follow-up enthusiasm for "a university within this District on a scale and for objects worthy of the American nation."[11] As the canal company's bankruptcy undercut the value of the first president's offer, the same issues of states rights and rivalries that blocked federal aid to internal improvements also undercut the idea of a federally funded university.

Washington's national museum got off to an equally slow but eventually more fruitful start. The germ was an unexpected bequest by British businessman James Smithson in 1829, bringing the eventual transfer of $550,000 to the federal government in 1838. In an effort to jump-start the project, a number of prominent residents led by Secretary of War Joel Poinsett organized a National Institution for the Promotion of Science in 1840. Looking toward an eventual combination of their own efforts with the Smithson funds, the organizers envisioned a sort of postgraduate science school and sponsor of scientific exploration based on a museum of natural history. Meanwhile, they began to correspond with similar groups and looked for models in London, Dublin, and Paris. As Poinsett argued, the federal government had an essential role in promoting astronomy, geography, hydrology, ethnography, and natural history—what we might now call sciences of national expansion.[12]

In turn, Congress debated whether the Smithson funds should best be used for a national observatory, a museum, a university, a library, or a teachers' college. Lawmakers finally acted in 1846, creating the Regents of the Smithsonian Institution with an open-ended charge that papered over differing expectations. The regents hired Joseph Henry from the College of New Jersey in Princeton to head the new organization and used accumulated interest to open a Gothic building on the south side of the Mall in 1855. Henry focused his work on the direct promotion of science through a National Museum and by publishing scientific papers and reports in the Smithsonian's *Contributions to Knowledge*.[13]

The creation of the Smithsonian Institution was the context for the first comprehensive vision of Washington as an intellectual center in William Q. Force's *Picture of Washington and Its Vicinity for 1848*.[14] Having few distractions of commerce (the hopes of the earlier generation now gone), residents of the District of Columbia could focus on "intellectual culture, the acquisition of knowledge, [and] the improvement of the arts." In turn, "if it become a home for genius, taste, and art . . . thousands will make it their abode." Already the Smithsonian, the Naval Observatory, colleges, and public schools were laying the foundations for an Athens of America.

William Force was more hopeful than realistic, but public institutions of science and letters did grow substantially after the Civil War. New federal agencies with scientific missions or arms included the Department of Agriculture, the Geological Survey, and the Fish Commission. Established agencies included the Smithsonian Institution, Coast Survey, Signal Service, Naval Observatory, and Patent Office. The Smithsonian expanded with a new National Museum in 1881 (now the Arts and Industry Museum) to house exhibits from the 1876 World's Fair in Philadelphia. It followed with the National Zoo in 1890. Lawmakers debated a new building for the Library of Congress for nearly a decade before authorizing construction in 1886. Designed to house more than 3 million volumes and completed in 1897, it was to be the American equivalent of the British Museum or the Bibliothèque Nationale.

Despite these institutions, Washington's scientists were only a handful in the first antebellum decade and its arts a laggard. Once visitors had seen the public buildings, wrote John Ellis in 1869, they would search in vain for other attractions. Fifteen years later, New England social reformer O. B. Frothingham roundly criticized Washington as a disappointment in every way, a city of ill-proportioned buildings and innumerable equestrian statues but no public culture—no decent concert hall, no comprehensive art gallery, little in the way of literary readings or sophisticated theater. It was too small to sustain more than one excitement, he thought, and politics crowded out all other interests.[15]

One source of the circumstances that disturbed the reform-minded Bostonian was the tension between private and public venues for Washington's postwar intellectual life. The organizational problem was how best to connect two sets of newcomers—government scientists on the one hand and men of letters and public affairs on the other. The solution of the 1870s and 1880s was essentially *personal*. Members of the city's small and self-conscious intellectual elite cultivated the private exchange of ideas in contrast to the public social whirl of Gilded Age Washington.

Most famous of these intellectual gardeners was Henry Adams. After moving to Washington in 1877, Adams coalesced an intimate social circle including geologist Clarence King and man of affairs John Hay. Around the "Five of Hearts" (Adams and his wife Marian, King, and Hay and his wife

Clara) revolved a wider circle of interesting politicians and intellectuals such as Henry James (first pleased and then bored by Washington). After Marian's death, Adams reconstructed a breakfast coterie that welcomed those men and women of official Washington who could be amusing.[16]

Encompassing personal social circles was a set of formal organizations that tried to bridge the same gap between science, literature, and public affairs. The Literary Society (1875) heard lectures from eminent scientists, but its heart was genteel poetry and essays. The Philosophical Society (1871) regarded itself as "strictly scientific" but drew membership so broadly that its lectures and publications drifted toward popularization. The Cosmos Club (1878) originated as another effort to bring together Washington's natural scientists, but its members, too, included writers, educators, and men of the learned professions. Both the Philosophical Society and the Cosmos Club allowed the exchange of scientific news reports across disciplines and fields. However, the choice of breadth over depth meant that neither was a forum for critical debate (no more could Henry Adams seriously critique Clarence King's geology than King analyze Adams's use of historical documents). They were valuable institutions for Washington intellectuals, but neither realized the ambition of the Philosophical Society to "have reflex influence upon every part of the United States."[17]

The movers behind these semiscientific organizations in fact had two avenues for national influence. One was to operate like the politicians whom many claimed to scorn. For example, backroom lobbying by Cosmos Club members helped to push through the merger of fragmented geological surveys into the U.S. Geological Survey with headquarters in the capital. In such efforts, social and intellectual exclusiveness helped to turn issues of public policy into quiet dinner table discussions.

The second avenue was to see Washington's scientific community as the center of specialized national networks rather than local social circles. An example was the Anthropological Society of Washington, which brought together the scientists of the National Museum and the Bureau of Ethnology in the Smithsonian. Organized in 1879, the society played an important role in the national professionalization of anthropology, particularly through publishing the *American Anthropologist* (1889) as a national journal. Just as important for the Washington story, however, was the failure to sustain the publication as a local enterprise. Lack of funds forced the transfer of the journal to the Anthropology Section of the American Association for the Advancement of Science, with publication out of New York and London rather than Washington.[18]

The issue with which Washington's intellectuals struggled was the creation of national institutions in a nation where science, high culture, and higher education were still local enterprises. To build churches and park systems, to organize public libraries and orchestras, to endow art museums and universities, to bring men and women of learning together—these were all acts of city building. Whether in Cincinnati, Chicago, or New York, they drew on local fortunes and local entrepreneurship and aimed to create more complete communities. Historians such as Helen Horowitz and Thomas Bender have argued persuasively the importance of local public cultures, not national intellectual networks, as context and motivation for these institution-building efforts.[19]

Washington unfortunately lacked the same city-building inspiration. Its government scientists were migrants to the city who increasingly had the option of alternative positions in the nation's developing universities. Its men of affairs were often sojourners whose financial security was rooted elsewhere. Intellectuals might find Washington enjoyable, but it was only one choice among many competing centers. Its social elites, too, were sojourners who entertained in their homes and had little interest in the charitable endowment of Washington institutions; when they did give money, it was likely to be in the home town where they had gotten rich.

Local promoters of Washington realized the dilemma. Although they did not use the terminology, they clearly hoped that an expanding federal establishment would provide the critical mass that attracted private universities and endowments. Its public libraries and institutions, said Woodbury Wheeler in 1887, rendered Washington "the delight of the educated" and entitled it to be "the center of national culture and civilization." The "presence of many learned and scientific men," according to George Evans in 1892, should make it the capital of the nation's "literary, scientific, and social life." In short, asserted Washingtonian J. H. Crane, the city could look forward to continued growth as the national center of "learning, art, science, and refinement."[20]

Editors and letter writers could proclaim what they wished, of course, but it required private decisions by external philanthropic "investors" to make Washington a comprehensive intellectual center. Although one writer claimed that Washington's equal convenience to North and South assured its future as an educational center, geographic reasoning offered limited insight into a role that required the accretion of private activities that might benefit from proximity to the federal government.[21] Lacking its own complement of capitalists who were endowing new universities from Worcester and Baltimore to St. Louis and Palo Alto, and equally lacking any claim on Morrill Act funding, Washington was a beggar rather than a chooser.

The origins of the Catholic University of America illustrate the possibilities and problems. The idea of a national university for American Catholicism surfaced at the Second Plenary Council of bishops in 1866, gathered interest in the 1870s, and was accepted at the Third Plenary Council in 1884, despite the opposition from the bishops of New York and Rochester. The specific proposal was a "National Catholic School of Philosophy and Theology" under the control of a committee of bishops and aiming to supplement seminary training with advanced research and study. An organizing committee found a site in 1885, incorporated in 1887, and opened the school in 1889.

Washington was both a logical and hotly contested location. Middle western bishops raised philosophical objections to Washington as a corrupting environment and, incidentally, suggested Cincinnati as much more wholesome. More protracted was the regional rivalry with New York. The organizing committee nearly sited the university in northern New Jersey by buying out Seton Hall College. Advocates of South Orange argued that the Northeast was the center of gravity for Roman Catholicism. They feared that a Washington-based institution would undermine a *real* Catholic university in the nation's economic and intellectual center and denigrated the Washington proposal as a "Grand American Catholic University for the Southern States" and "a Southern affair, with a majority of Southerners to control it."[22] In contrast, Bishop John Lancaster Spalding, of Peoria, the leading proponent, described Washington as "neither a Northern nor a Southern nor a Western city, but a common ground upon which we can all meet to establish a national institution."[23]

The final decision for Washington—carried narrowly by Spalding and the chief donor, Mary Caldwell—created serious problems for the high expectations. Despite the new university's national mission and name, fundraising to supplement the Caldwell dollars was largely limited to Washington and Baltimore. Indeed, the archbishop of New York forbade fundraising in his diocese. The result was an institution that opened in 1889 but developed slowly in the following decades in rivalry with other Roman Catholic institutions such as Fordham in New York and Notre Dame in Indiana.

If Roman Catholics came to Washington, Baptists did not. A few Washingtonians angled hopefully for the "Baptist University" that the American Baptist Education Society began to plan in May 1888. The Baptists had their eye on John D. Rockefeller's bank account from the start. They gave serious consideration only to New York and Chicago, although the *Star* editorialized in favor of Washington and a few participants in the decision-making advocated the capital as most appropriate for "our National University."[24] The result of Rockefeller's philanthropy was the University of Chicago, not a university for Washington.

As the Catholic University and University of Chicago stories suggest, ambitions for Washington as a truly national center of education were dreams about public and private benefactions. Opposition from President Charles Eliot of Harvard killed tentative thoughts of reviving George Washington's idea of a true national university in 1872–73. Local leaders were again hopeful in 1888 after a series of articles in the *Forum* by Andrew D. White that presented the case for Washington as the site of an ideal university that could gather "students of the republic in all branches of investigation." In high-minded fashion, White suggested that Washington's libraries, scientific research, and public figures could make it a city of the higher life rather than a place of political scheming or frantic pursuit of wealth. But one might note that White may have been talking about Washington, but he had just put eighteen years into creating Cornell University.[25]

Beyond the realities of Catholic University and Howard University and dreams of a big score, Washington in the 1890s had hopes for several other local institutions.[26] A nascent American University developed with funding and support from local Methodists. The first buildings on a Northwest Washington campus were finished in 1898 but went unused until 1917. Some of the American University founders had hoped to join with the ambitiously named National University and attract federal funds. Instead, National University remained what it had been since its organization in 1869—a collection of small professional schools with part-time instructors and night classes. Columbian University (later George Washington University) was meanwhile evolving gradually from a southern-oriented Baptist college located outside of town into a nationally oriented university in the heart of the city.[27]

Individual institutions fell short of their ambitions, but opportunities for student enrollment were actually impressive. Institutions in the District of Columbia enrolled nearly 10,000 students by 1920 and 18,000 in 1938–39. More important for Washington as a new Paris, the District attracted far more students from other states and nations than it exported to institutions outside its boundaries. The net gain from student migrations was 5,118 for 1920–21, 7,567 for 1930–31, and 8,985 for 1938–39. In the latter year the District even edged past Massachusetts as the nation's largest importer of college students. The results bespoke aggressive recruitment and the attraction of Washington colleges for residents of nearby Maryland and Virginia (24 percent of the outsiders) and of the mid-Atlantic states (35 percent).[28]

What the city still lacked was not colleges and students, but a single flagship university with national influence that spanned religious affiliations and races. James Bryce in 1913 pronounced that Washington's special niche was to develop its museums, galleries, and scientific institutions and added, carefully avoiding the active voice, "there ought to be a great National American University" in the city. The Washington Chamber of Commerce in 1917 continued to explore the possibilities of making Washington the nation's great educational center as one of twenty-five options for developing local business.[29]

Admonitions and boosterism, however, could not overcome the problem of limited local resources. John Bell Larner in 1905 had tried to argue—not very persuasively—that "the advantages of the Capital overbalance . . . the large endowments which are each year being given to the universities of the north and west."[30] Larner actually defined the core of the problem, not its solution. Outside Washington, growing comprehensive private and state universities were overshadowing the federal research establishment and making the capital less central to American scholarship by the 1910s and 1920s than it had been in Henry Adams's golden 1880s. In different form, the situation of higher education replayed the antebellum problem of inadequate commercial capital to outcompete Baltimore and New York.

What Washington had were headquarters of academic and professional organizations for historians, sociologists, architects, and others. The city offered access to decision makers that linked new social sciences to the national state (two presidents, two admirals, and two Adamses would serve as presidents of the American Historical Association by the middle of the twentieth century). The city also compromised sectional differences, making it possible, in one example, for New York and Chicago architects to consolidate separate organizations into an enlarged and genuinely American Institute of Architects.[31] But the real intellectual work, from the creation of skyscraper styles to the definition of approaches to the study of American cities, went on in Boston, New York, Philadelphia, and Chicago. Washington was the intellectual switchboard for information originating elsewhere.

A Magnet for the People

Where one Washington scenario painted the emergence of an Oxford on the Potomac, other Washingtonians were busily envisioning the city as an eastern prelude to twentieth-century Santa Barbara—clear of air, gentle of climate, rich in residential real estate, and untroubled by the hurly-burly of a heterogeneous nation. In other words, the absence of commercial and industrial development could be construed as a virtue that freed Washingtonians of the feverish goads of commercialism.[32] No wharves and factories (or at least factories downwind and out of sight) meant no smoke and soot to stain white buildings or white gloves, no sweat-stained workers on streetcars, and no swearing teamsters to clog the streets with their freight wagons. Their absence also meant no labor organizers, proletarian immigrants, or socialist agitators to bring unease to native-born Americans, disorder to the streets, and the whiff of social revolution to national politics.[33]

This agenda that shunned manufacturing looked to the economic benefits of sojourners of all sorts. Real estate promoters liked the vision of a city of retirement and leisure. Their targets were military retirees and "men of wealth or political prominence" who had established Washington homes without any interest in the city's economic development.[34] Retailers and restaurateurs liked as well the short-term sojourners of conventions and tourism. What Washington had to offer both was amenities and information, ambiance and intellect.[35]

The image of Washington as a second Paris was a direct promotional tool for the convention and tourist trade. E. E. Barton linked the reputation of "our capital city, 'the Paris of America'" and its increasing popularity as the place for the conventions of scientific societies. Theodore Noyes of the Star drew a similar lesson, relating Washington's future as the "leading residence and 'show' city of the continent" to a future recognition as the natural "meeting place of the American people in convention assembled." National institutions, said Ainsworth Spofford, would make it a "perennial attraction to the citizens of the nation."[36]

Convention business built on occasional antebellum events. The year 1846 had brought the First National Fair for the Exhibition of American Manufactures. Held in a quickly erected and roughly finished building of 60 by 500 feet on Judiciary Square, the fair was both a promotion of Washington and a salvo in the debate over the proper tariff on imported manufactured goods. It attracted perhaps sixty thousand visitors in its month of operation. Washingtonian John Silva Meehan noted the "highly respectable strangers, from all parts of the Union" who arrived for the manufacturers' fair and repeatedly marveled at the immense crowds and throngs of visitors.[37]

Expansion from such antebellum beginnings depended on the completion of the American railroad system. Improving service and falling passenger fares facilitated middle-class travel. Railroad companies themselves offered special summer fares to appeal to schoolteachers and families, helped to plan excursions for business groups, and built hotels in scenic places. Better connections made it easy, for example, for some of the millions of visitors to the Centennial Exposition in Philadelphia to take in Washington as well—with a single railroad journey contrasting with an 1850 trip requiring steamer from Philadelphia to Chester, train to Havre de Grace, boat again to Baltimore, and finally a train ride to Washington.[38] Washington tour books and illustrated guides proliferated in the same years to meet the widening market. They increasingly give practical advice on hotels, cabs, and streetcars to help ordinary travelers, rather than describing works of art and the doings of the political elite.

In this new environment of mobility, Washington enjoyed an expanding convention business. Here are some of the meetings of the arbitrarily picked year, 1889: an International Maritime Congress, the Knights Templar Conclave, the Encampment of the Grand Army of the Republic, and sessions of the American Seed Trade Association, American Historical Association, American Surgical Association, Master House Painters and Decorators Association, Mutual Life and Accident Underwriters of America, and Railway Telegraph Superintendents. Over the following years the city continued to draw professional and medical organizations, fraternal societies, business and trade associations, and public interest groups. Despite the setbacks of national depression, the annual count of major gatherings doubled between 1893 and 1903. A few years later, the new Chamber of Commerce defined conventions as "great commercial resources" and, in cooperation with the Board of Trade and the Retail Merchants Association, took the lead in convention recruitment.[39]

Washington's self-image as a national city can be read most clearly as its local leadership argued its advantages and attractions for major expositions and conventions. Washington the national city, they claimed, was the only site that was above sectionalism, the federal capital where people from every state would feel comfortable or inspired. Whereas other cities competed to put on regional fairs and festivals in the years between 1890 and 1914— Louisville's Southern Exposition of 1883–87, Atlanta's Piedmont Exposition of 1887, Denver's annual Festival of Mountain and Plain from 1895 to 1912— Washington could portray itself as a continuing civic festival. Whereas New York and Chicago could argue functional centrality and convenience, only Washington was the nation's symbolic center and the one place that foreigners would expect to visit.

At the end of the 1880s, Washingtonians employed these arguments vigorously in the competition for siting the planned Columbian Exposition, hoping to use newly reclaimed tidal flats west of the Washington Monument.[40] Southern opinion, reported the *Manufacturers' Record*, favored Washington as a location above sectional animosities. An event that truly spoke to the nation as more than a profit-oriented tourist attraction, said the *Star*, could properly be located only in the capital. A survey of mayors and commercial bodies in cities of more than 15,000 population found Washington the first choice of 55 respondents, Chicago of 36, New York of 34, and St. Louis of 8. Most of the New York and Chicago preferences were said to be from home or adjacent states, betraying a parochial rather than a national interest. Washington was also the most common second choice, "the compromise candidate in the sectional contention."[41]

Despite Washington's plans to turn the proposed fairgrounds into a permanent Exposition of the Americas, the capital lacked the size and local economic capacity that made New York and Chicago the obvious leading candidates.[42] Although Congress opted for Chicago in 1890, Washingtonians kept the same arguments polished. In 1910 the Chamber of Commerce proposed to take up President William Howard Taft's idea that there be a celebration on the east coast to mark the opening of the Panama Canal. One was set for San Francisco, but why should the other not be in Washington?[43] Once again in 1939–40, local promoters surfaced a proposal for a world's fair to commemorate the 150th anniversary of laying the cornerstone of the Capitol. Although such an event would balance New York's fair and "welcome the world to Washington," the city was too busy with the coming war to pay much attention.[44]

Notwithstanding the lack of world expositions, individual tourism in the twentieth century gradually took on the dimensions of pilgrimage. In the civil religion of American nationalism, Washington was a "metropolis" in its technical meaning, the home of national temples and cathedrals. If Alexander Shepherd had tried to make Washington decent and functional, local and national interests now attempted to make it noble. A capital worthy of the nation in the 1870s had meant paved streets and decent drainage to better connect the city's scattered parts. By the 1900s and 1910s it meant revitalizing the public spaces of the L'Enfant plan and completing a patriotic program of national sites and monuments.

This new role as a national attractor was explicitly political. Washington was to be a place not only of pleasure and interest, but also of inspiration. It was to be made physically imposing, beautiful, splendid. "To serve its highest purpose," said Wendell Phillips Stafford in 1913, the city "must be a work of art."[45] And the purpose of grand urban artistry was to inspire awe at the history and promise of the nation. A "reverend and august" city that embodied the "majesty and stateliness of the whole nation" was a city doing the political work of state making.

The making of a tourist-centered city was thus part of the larger project of national reconciliation. Mary Ames in 1875 portrayed Washington as the inspiring symbol of the struggle for union. A generation later, it was a symbol not of struggle but of reunification. The physical makeover of this political terrain involved the direct intention of blurring sectional distinctions. The new city was conceived as a monument to freedom and liberty, a symbol of a growing nation that would flourish and inspire as the American people flourished and made their mark on the world. Indeed, it was to be redesigned as a place with as much interest for the citizens of Maine, California, and Florida as for its own residents.[46]

The physical rebuilding of Washington in the early twentieth century is a well-told story.[47] It starts with the challenge of railroad encroachment on the Mall, the physical opportunity of reclaimed tidal flats along the Potomac, and the institutional opportunity of an expanding federal government. The Senate created a Park Commission in 1901 and charged it to consider "the location and grouping of public buildings and monuments to be erected in the District of Columbia and the development and improvement of the entire park system of said District."[48] The Senate Park Commission, often called the McMillan Commission for Senator James McMillan, responded with a decision to reassert the monumental core of the L'Enfant plan with variations to utilize open space along the river. Its emphasis on the Mall and other open spaces south of Pennsylvania Avenue clearly separated the federal city from the everyday city to the north—a sharp contrast to the nineteenth-century tendency to locate federal buildings such as the Patent Office, Pension Office, and Treasury within the emerging downtown. Physical development ideas and plans evolved through the work of the Commission of Fine Arts (1910), the National Capital Park Commission (1924), the National Capital Park and Planning Commission (1926), and the National Capital Regional Planning Commission (1952). For each organization, national goals outweighed concerns with the functioning of the residential city.

Filling in the plan were new public and semipublic buildings. The 1910s brought Union Station, the Lincoln Memorial, the Museum of Natural History, and the cluster of the Pan American Union, American Red Cross, and Constitution Hall of the Daughters of the American Revolution west of the White House. Creation of the National Capital Park and Planning Commission was accompanied by a massive federal building program that turned the south side of Pennsylvania Avenue into the Federal Triangle and added other huge office blocks such as the Interior Department. The 1930s also added the National Archives, National Gallery of Art, and Jefferson Memorial as explicit tourist attractions to embellish what Frederick Gutheim has called the "public city" of federal offices and national institutions.[49]

In twentieth-century guidebooks, these monuments and museums gradually displaced detail on executive departments and buildings.[50] Improved techniques of photograph publication allowed guidebooks to highlight pictorial splendors, displacing dense verbal description of pediments and porticoes with pictures of marble buildings gleaming in the sun or glowing in floodlights.

The buildings themselves and the grand cityscape in which they were placed copied the styles of nineteenth-century Europe. The facades and boulevards were safely cosmopolitan while ignoring the American tradition of naturalized landscape design. The new city also represented the United States as a peer of Europe's old imperial powers and its recently consolidated nations. By sponsoring the new cityscape, moreover, the federal government pointedly asserted its own equivalence to the powerfully centralized governments of France or Germany. It was no accident that the physical reshaping of Washington began with the administrations of Theodore Roosevelt and William Howard Taft, who were simultaneously creating modern, centralized Departments of State and War and drew the support of such centralizers as Elihu Root and Henry Cabot Lodge.[51]

The new monumental core also served the work of national reconciliation. Indirectly, the emphasis on a single people with a single set of national monuments played down the importance of sectional differences. Much more directly, the dedication of the Lincoln Memorial in 1922 expressed the transformation of Abraham Lincoln himself from a northern and Republican hero of emancipation to a national symbol of reunion. The building itself drew on ancient Greece, with no reflection of American regional styles or materials; the texts inscribed on its walls depicted the Great Conciliator rather than a sectional war leader. Completing the ensemble in the 1930s was the Arlington Memorial Bridge that linked Lincoln's memorial to the home of Robert E. Lee and to the Arlington National Cemetery.[52]

The decades after World War II further expanded the objects of pilgrimage. The White House was gradually sanctified as it became more isolated from the public. The eternal flame at the grave of John F. Kennedy, the Iwo Jima Monument, and the Vietnam Veterans Memorial are shrines for newer

Arlington Memorial Bridge under construction. The agenda of reconciliation achieved concrete expression in the Lincoln Memorial and the Memorial Bridge linking Washington to the home of Robert E. Lee. (Still Photographs Department, National Archives)

generations. The expansion of the Smithsonian Institution has created an entire archipelago of national museums that claim to be definitive repositories of American history, art, and industry. The National Air and Space Museum, both by name and exhibits, stakes out a comprehensiveness lacking in more parochial counterparts, whether the Air Force Museum in Ohio or the Cosmodome in Kansas. Its 10 million visitors per year carry a message of American achievement to every corner of the nation.

The resulting public city is awesome. Its buildings are big, its museums are formidable, and its spaces are broad. Visitors to Washington have to hike, not stroll, and many of the hikers are official pilgrims. Especially for the baby boom generation, the high school visit to Washington has been a civic rite of passage. The combination of postwar affluence and improving transportation made it relatively easy for scout troops and high school classes to execute weeklong visits to the ceremonial city, filling the Mall with spring crops of chartered buses and the Metro with surging herds of kids.

But the public city is a civic theater as well as a civic church. As a site for political assertion, it plays a distinct role in fostering national arguments as well as national unity. The open spaces and marble steps invite political statements. The Bonus Marchers of 1932 and the residents of Resurrection City in 1967 came to speak and stay. Most demonstrators have come for a weekend or a day to join the March on Washington for Jobs and Freedom (1963) or the Million Man March (1995), to rally against war in Vietnam, nuclear weapons, or abortion. One hundred thousand like-minded people in Central Park are an impressive set of New York voters. The same number of people in Washington, drawn from across the nation, are an impressive set of voters who are using Washington's political stage to make claims on the conscience of the nation.[53]

Twentieth-century Washington thus became what nineteenth-century Washingtonians could never have anticipated, the symbol rather than the center of national achievement. Monumental Washington is a teacher rather than an entrepreneur, enshrining national values in marble and maintaining them inside display cases. Public disagreement is acceptable in the open air in the form of Pennsylvania Avenue marches and rallies around the Washington Monument. Inside the stone walls, however, that same disagreement sparks unease. Messages of museums and monuments are expected to be simple stories of patriotism and power, not of ambiguity and choice.

The Pencil-Sharpener
Revolution

Edward Rosskam's lavishly illustrated 1939 book, *Washington: Nerve Center*, starts like a standard travel-promoting picture book and ends with a twist. As in the standard guides and picture books of the 1910s and 1920s, Rosskam's early photos show the streets, buildings, and monuments of the tourist city. By the end, however, the reader is paging past pictures of the New Deal at work in the far reaches of the nation in WPA projects and Social Security offices. The explicit message is the positive impact of Washington decisions on all Americans (Eleanor Roosevelt contributed a foreword). As a control point of the expanding federal government, Washington is coordinating a whole country's effort "to keep itself running, to make itself run better." The capital city, says Rosskam, is an information city whose product is more potent than steel or automobiles. It is "the nerve center of a nation determined to work its way and construct its way out of chaos" . . . with the help of 650,000 typewriter ribbons a year.[54]

As Rosskam's adaptation of the Washington picture book suggests, the equilibrium of early-twentieth-century Washington survived the Great War but not the Great Depression. Mobilization in 1917 and 1918 tripled the federal civilian workforce in the District of Columbia and increased the number of northerners in the District by forty thousand between 1910 and 1920, but the new elements faded from the Washington scene nearly as fast as they had appeared. The impact of World War I is invisible in employment and population series that skip from 1916 to 1925.

Permanent expansion of the federal establishment waited until the 1930s. Journalists in the early thirties found new stirrings. John Dos Passos thought that the Bonus Army had awakened Washington to the changes and crises wracking the rest of the nation. *Fortune* in 1934 called the city an "actual capital."[55] The net growth in federal jobs for the 1930s equaled 27.4 percent of the District employment at the start of the decade (see Table 4.2 above). The pencil sharpener revolution of the New Deal, with its proliferation of agencies and programs, made Washington one of the few American cities to experience housing price inflation and rapid suburbanization during the depression decade.

Mobilization in 1940 and 1941 brought more of the same. Like San Diego, Mobile, and Norfolk, Washington was a wartime boomtown where soldiers, sailors, and defense workers crowded available housing, jammed restaurants and theaters, and wandered the streets on hot summer nights.[56] As magazine stories highlighted the young women who flocked to Washington's clerical jobs while boyfriends entered the armed services, federal civilian employment doubled from 1940 to 1942. Even after the government briefly returned to a peacetime footing in 1947–48, civilian employment was half again as high as before the war (see Table 4.1 above). The Washington area population also grew 50 percent during the 1940s.

Recent Washington has alternated decades of slower growth in the 1950s and 1970s with further expansion during the 1960s and 1980s. Federal job growth of 88,000 in the 1960s stands out in the postwar decades. One reason was the need to coordinate an expanding war in Southeast Asia. The other was the proliferation of new civilian bureaucracies under John F. Kennedy, Lyndon B. Johnson, and Richard M. Nixon. Federal programs to improve law enforcement, fight poverty, upgrade transportation, enhance schools, and end pollution often dealt directly with cities and citizens, creating massive and complex flows of grants, reports, and evaluations for civil servants to process.

Activities ancillary to the national government rather than direct employment fueled renewed growth in the 1980s. Examples include tourism, federally funded research and development, expanding sales and engineering staffs for defense contractors, and growing numbers of trade and professional associations.[57] Aggregate metropolitan population, as measured by a geographically expanding metropolitan district (1930–40) or metropolitan area (1950–90), grew from 621,000 in 1930 to 1,464,000 in 1950, 2,861,000 in 1970, 3,924,000 in 1990, and 4,563,000 in 1996.

This exploding metropolis has been increasingly tied into the dense communication network of the northeastern seaboard. Jean Gottman's *Megalopolis* (1961) described the way in which New York and Philadelphia, then Boston and Baltimore, and finally Washington (in the 1930s and 1940s) coalesced into a single urban system that dominated both the eastern seaboard and the nation. Gottman cited data on the density of telephone calls, newspaper circulation, air traffic, and other flows of information to argue the interconnectedness of the new super-metropolitan complex. A decade later Delbert Miller tested the impact of these communication networks by analyzing patterns of interaction among local and national elites in the American Northeast. His data described a New York–Washington axis for the interaction of metropolitan leaders and the circulation of an elite concerned with regional and national decisions, although there was little evidence of a sense of megalopolis as a single regional community.[58]

Black leadership by the 1980s had also begun to tilt northward, with persons born outside the South accounting for 28 percent of metropolitan area entries in the 1985 edition of *Who's Who in Black America*.[59] Washington became home base for northern-national organizations such as the NAACP Legal Defense and Education Fund that took on the role of northernizing southern laws. Howard University also became a more northern than southern institution after the war. In 1934–35, 71 percent of its students came from the Washington area or the South. By 1985–86 that share was down to 43 percent, balanced by 38 percent from the North and 19 percent from abroad.

Aggregate figures on the origins of all students in Washington area colleges and universities have reflected the same connection. Net migration of students into the District of Columbia jumped from 10,000 before World War II to 23,000 by 1951, stabilized in the 1950s, and surged to 37,000 after

1958, making higher education one of Washington's major exports.[60] A simple gravity model of spatial interaction allows the allocation of total migration for a given year on the assumption that the number of students coming to Washington from each state will be directly proportional to its population and inversely proportional to its distance from Washington.[61] Comparison of predicted and actual values consistently shows the overrepresentation of New Yorkers, New Englanders, Floridians, and students from west of the Mississippi at District of Columbia colleges and the underrepresentation of Pennsylvania, the Middle West, and most of the South. The unexpected number of students from the West presumably testifies to the perceived advantages of education in the national capital. The unexpected number of northeasterners, in contrast, suggests that Washington has become part of an educational network that may be an important carrier of northern values.[62]

Taken together, the growing exchange of information and information specialists between Washington and the northeastern states seemed to many observers to have make the capital permanently northern. Donald Bogue and Calvin Beale's inventory of *Economic Areas of the United States* recognized that Washington lies in a cultural and economic transition zone but included it with the "Atlantic Metropolitan Belt" that runs north to Boston. Economic geographer James Watson noted its origins "on the very verge of the South" but described a "mesh of roads, railways, telegraph lines, and urban industrial development" that confirmed Gottman's placement. Emphasizing aspects of consumption rather than production, Wilbur Zelinsky similarly found the northern incorporation of Washington in the distribution of shared tastes. Patterns of magazine readership group Washington with the Northeast and Florida in a discontinuous region sharing "metropolitan" interests.[63]

Changes in political values were also read in terms of national incorporation. John Fenton's study of border state politics posited a unidirectional transition in which the border states were converging on the North in political behavior while the deeper South was moving toward the previous border state pattern. In the Washington area, it is possible to discern a public policy gradient in which the southern style in race relations changed first in the District of Columbia, then in suburban Maryland, and most slowly in suburban Virginia.[64]

One result of the changing approach and rhetoric was to erode the geographic orientation of the "southern" strategy. A new professional development staff helped the Board of Trade redefine its goals as the attraction of national organizations and business headquarters, wholesaling, and regional business offices. The first point recycled the national strategy. The two latter points reworked the historic southern strategy without regional reference. Widely used consulting reports by the Council for Economic and Industrial Research and by Hamer and Associates further changed terms of the discussion by treating demand for manufacturing and wholesaling without direct reference to the rising South as the targeted market.[65]

In accord with the new priorities, the most impressive change in the Washington area economy since 1970 has been the rise of private idea brokers. Elements of this complex were in place in the nineteenth century, but its vast expansion has followed and fed off the growth of the federal government. The metropolis now supports a vast pyramid of information specialists and idea generators. In the broadest layer are tens of thousands of information managers for hire. These are lawyers, business consultants, lobbyists, direct mail specialists, public relations firms, and trade journal editors who work for shifting sets of clients. On this prosperous substrate is an imposing array of trade and professional organizations. On these foundations perch a smaller number of highly influential think tanks, public interest lobbying organizations, and public issue advocacy organizations.

It is difficult to put exact boundaries on the category of information manager or information broker, but a variety of statistics can suggest both its dimensions and growth. One proxy for Washington's growing role as a decision center for the domestic economy is the relative importance of employment in the census category of central administrative offices and auxiliaries for multiestablishment firms in mining, construction, manufacturing, trade, and service industries. These are both headquarters offices and freestanding support groups for marketing, product development, lobbying the federal establishment, and similar activities. Between 1954 and 1972, metropolitan Washington's 320 percent increase in such jobs trailed only that of Boston, Houston, Denver, and Atlanta.[66]

Independent of production-oriented corporations are the sophisticated vendors of producer services. These are the specialized, high-value services that corporations buy as needed—from bond underwriting to advertising copywriting. Whether measured by employment or business volume, contemporary Washington ranks near the top among U.S. metropolitan areas. In 1990, 9 percent of all workers in the Washington Metropolitan Statistical Area were in the category of legal, engineering, and other professional services; the figure was by far the highest among the ten largest metropolitan areas. Overall, metropolitan Washington in 1990 trailed only New York and

Los Angeles in the total receipts for legal services, for business services, and for a catchall category of engineering, accounting, research, management, and related services.[67]

Attorneys who serve businesses and organizations are among the most prominent providers of such services. Between 1950 and 1980 Washington surged from fourteenth place to third place in the number of large and multioffice law firms.[68] The number of outside law firms with Washington offices grew, by one count, from 45 in 1965 to 247 in 1983. Membership in the District of Columbia Bar Association leapt from 17,000 in 1973 to 34,000 in 1981.[69]

With this information infrastructure of idea people and professionals, Washington in the later twentieth century was well positioned as a center for private organizational networks and headquarters—a key element in the Board of Trade development strategy in the 1950s. Despite a proliferation of pressure groups to stand watch around the White House and Capitol during the New Deal, Washington as late as 1959 housed only 15 percent of the organizations listed in the *Encyclopedia of American Associations,* far behind New York (33 percent) and just ahead of Chicago (11 percent).[70] Between the mid-1960s and the mid-1970s, however, Washington's lower rents and accessibility to government decision makers and regulators edged it past New York with a quarter of the country's trade associations. By 1987 the continuing importance of close contact with federal regulators, procurement officers, and congressional committees had pushed the Washington area share of national organizational headquarters above 30 percent, making associations and trade groups the area's third largest industry.[71] The total of such groups is hard to tally, but recent counts of national labor union and association headquarters are around two thousand, with an estimated eighty thousand employees for 1985.[72]

At the top of the postwar information hierarchy are think tanks, another nebulous but important category comprised of not-for-profit organizations that subsist on an omnivorous diet of foundation grants, donations, and government contracts.[73] The first of the breed, and a model for others, was the Brookings Institution, created in 1927 by the merger of two smaller organizations financed by St. Louis businessman Robert Brookings. The Institute for Governmental Research (1916) took the new idea of government efficiency experts, embodied in the New York Bureau of Municipal Research, and applied it to the federal government. The institute gave Washington a source of nonpartisan management advice and helped to spur passage of the Budget and Accounting Act of 1921, which created the Bureau of the

Budget and mandated an executive budget as a management tool. The Institute of Economics and the Brookings Graduate School (1922) were intended to address national and international economic problems in the city where key decisions occurred.[74] As the faculty of a "university without students," the Brookings staff tried out new ideas in the 1930s and 1940s and gained great influence in the 1950s and 1960s by applying managerial economics to formulating and supporting the Fair Deal–Great Society policy synthesis.

A few similar organizations, such as the Center for Strategic and International Studies (CSIS) and the American Enterprise Institute (AEI), paralleled the growth of Brookings in the first postwar decades, but the real take-off for Washington think tanks came with the 1970s. Budgets of existing organizations tripled and quadrupled, and new entries crowded into the idea business. Of the hundred or so think tanks operating in 1989, two-thirds dated to 1970 or later. To mainstream policy shops like Brookings, AEI, and the Urban Institute have been added dozens of groups that advocate from clearly defined positions on the political spectrum—from the left-liberal, such as the Institute for Women's Policy Research and the Friends Committee on National Legislation, to centrist organizations such as Common Cause, to deeply conservative organizations such as the Moral Majority.

From their position on the top of the policy pyramid, think tanks exercise influence out of proportion to their small staffs. Only a handful employ more than a hundred people, and many never reach a staff of a dozen. Yet a *National Journal* survey in 1986 identified 39 people from think tanks and public interest groups among the 150 people who "made a difference" in Washington. As David Ricci writes:

> Today, approximately one hundred think tanks participate in Washington's political conversation. . . . Each year, these institutes conduct thousands of conferences, luncheons, briefings, forums, and seminars, while publishing hundreds of books and innumerable pamphlets, reports, newsletters, backgrounders, and occasional essays. In addition, their members write scores of op-ed articles that appear in dozens of newspapers, and their most articulate fellows perform as commentators on radio and television news programs, often coast-to-coast. In short, a hitherto minor class of talkative entities has grown larger and become more effective on Washington's political stage.[75]

A city of ideas is also a city in which careers are open to talent, and in which women can be intellectual heavy lifters along with men. At both a practical and a symbolic level, women have taken a gradually increasing proportion of the five hundred or so highest-level jobs in the White House and executive departments—from 4 percent under Lyndon Johnson and Richard Nixon and 6 percent under Gerald Ford, to 15 percent under Jimmy Carter and 10 percent with Ronald Reagan, and then jumping to 24 percent with George Bush and 37 percent with Bill Clinton.[76] Under Clinton, the executive branch caught up with the overall Washington economy. Forty percent of working women in the Washington area held professional and managerial jobs in 1990, up from 38 percent in 1980 and the highest proportion among large metropolitan areas. Educational attainment, as measured by the proportion of adult women with a bachelor's degree, also placed Washington at the top of the same group.

Women's wages in the Washington area reflect their educational levels and access to good white-collar jobs. Data prepared by the Institute for Women's Policy Research in 1996 showed that working women in the District of Columbia received an average salary of $24,500, higher than in any of the states. Women in the District earned 88 cents for every dollar paid to men, the highest ratio in the nation.[77] In total, women held 48.5 percent of Washington area jobs, again the highest share among big metropolitan areas.

The cumulative effect of the immense growth of information specialists since 1970 has been to make Washington truly a brain power city. Washington leads the ten largest metropolitan areas in the proportion of residents (age twenty-five or older) with at least a bachelor's degree—39 percent compared to 31 percent for greater Boston and greater San Francisco, 26 percent for New York, and 19 percent for Detroit (Table 4.3). Two-fifths of its workers in 1990 filled managerial and professional positions, the highest proportion among the big ten metropolitan areas and more than ten percentage points above the median for the group. In turn, the Washington area has the highest proportion of engineers and natural scientists (a subcategory of professional jobs). In effect, the Washington of National Institutes of Health biochemists, National Aeronatics and Space Administration engineers, Census Bureau demographers, and U.S. Geological Survey geoscientists is the city dreamed by the promoters of the 1880s and 1890s.

City of Conversation

For most of the twentieth century, Americans strove to build a national city that would belie the strictures of James Bryce and his pointed comment of 1893 that the United States was the only great country without a capital. By a capital, Bryce meant "a city which is not only the seat of political government, but is also by the size, wealth, and character of its population the head

Table 4.3. The Information Economy in the Ten Largest Consolidated Metropolitan Statistical Areas, 1990

	College Graduates [a]	Managerial/ Professional [b]	Engineering/ Legal/Other [c]	Doctoral Degrees [d]
Boston	30.7	34.6	6.1	40,159
Chicago	23.5	28.1	4.6	36,832
Dallas	25.8	28.6	3.7	15,846
Detroit	19.1	26.9	3.6	18,575
Houston	24.2	28.5	4.4	18,202
Los Angeles	22.0	27.7	4.3	72,657
New York	25.8	31.6	5.5	113,353
Philadelphia	22.8	29.4	4.8	29,720
San Francisco	30.9	33.1	4.1	59,479
Washington	38.5	40.2	8.9	59,287

Source: 1990 Census of Population: Social and Economic Characteristics, Metropolitan Areas (CP-2–1B), tables 1, 31, 34–35.

[a] Percentage of population aged twenty-five and older with a bachelor's degree
[b] Percentage of persons in managerial and professional jobs
[c] Percentage of persons providing legal, engineering, and other professional services
[d] Number of persons aged twenty-five and older with doctoral degrees

and center of the country." Neither Washington nor Chicago nor New York could fully claim the combination of "these various elements of power, the conjunction of rank, wealth, knowledge, intellect that naturally make such a city a sort of foundry in which opinion is melted and cast."[78]

In doing battle with Bryce's acerbic comments, Washington's advocates had suggested that the city's special genius in a federated nation was as a "capital of capitals," a center of inspiration for the larger nation.[79] As the ennobling and efficient architecture of the monumental city emerged from the McMillan plan, as bureaucracies expanded, and as conventioneers and tourists grew in numbers, Washington seemed to its advocates to take on the glamour of the larger nation. It was the "most American community," said editor Theodore Noyes in 1915, echoing an earlier comment that it was the "epitome of American life." Indeed, one observer in 1920 argued that Washington was the proper place to understand America in its full variety, the place "to see the American horizon widen till the Mississippi Valley and the Western mountains and the sunset over the Pacific come into view."[80]

Then in the 1980s, the quick popularity of a new term gave a curious twist to Washington's reputation. Washington's governing institutions and bureaucrats, Americans began to comment, did their work "inside the Beltway." The phrase uses isolation behind the physical barrier of a sixty-six-mile circumferential highway, completed in the 1960s, as a metaphor for insulation from popular values. It implies separation and deracination in a cynically negative valuation of Washington's nonregional role. It has a strong partisan dimension, originating as a way for Reagan revolutionaries to attack the administrative and regulatory state constructed from Theodore Roosevelt through Richard Nixon. But its implication of political insiders and inside information also struck a cord with popular writing as Americans adopted a mood of skepticism about federal programs. Appearing first in print around 1983, it surged to a peak of popularity at the end of the decade and remained in common use through the 1990s.[81]

This new characterization of Washington comes laden with several ironies. It burst into popular use just as the arrival of the information economy was making Washington more than ever a center of national life. Between the mid-1960s and the mid-1980s, the National Endowment for the Humanities, National Endowment for the Arts, and National Science Foundation made Washington bureaucrats into the patrons of writers, artists, and scientists nationwide. By 1990 Washington ranked first among U.S. metropolitan areas in the number of convention goers.[82] The city was attracting pilgrims by the millions—not just for the White House and the Lincoln Memorial but for the National Air and Space Museum, the National Museum of American History, the new and improved National Gallery of Art, the Vietnam Veterans Memorial, and a host of smaller museums. Americans continue to visit inside the Beltway even when they claim not to like the people who work there.

The understanding of Washington as a city of insiders recycles old complaints. It echoes negative images from both the Civil War and World War II of a city full of manipulative politicians, draft dodgers, profiteers, and slackers, while real Americans were marching to war or toiling in factories.[83] It draws as well on the complementary criticism of Washington as painfully dull—a city of red-tape merchants and zombie bureaucrats whose pasty faces peer above identical beige trench coats. Writers in search of local color go home frustrated at what seems to be a nonregional city where pervasive influence hides behind orderly blandness. They echo Edmund Wilson's lament that the city "which, after other American cities, seems at first such a relief, so agreeable, turns out, when one has stayed there any length of time, to have little personality of its own and to come to taste rather flat."[84]

In part, the animus against the new Washington extends a century-old complaint about the physical ungainliness and architectural blandness of the bureaucratic city that surrounds and intermingles the museums and monuments. The Pension Building of the 1880s put double rings of clerks around a vast atrium. Now applauded and recycled as the National Building Museum, observers then scorned its ungainliness. It was a "red brick cotton factory," complained Elizabeth Moore Chapin, and the "ugliest building for public purposes ever built in the United States."[85] Fifty years later, the Public Buildings Commission claimed the Federal Triangle between Pennsylvania and Constitution Avenues and filled it with vast tan office buildings in the 1930s for the Commerce Department, Interstate Commerce Commission, and Justice Department. After World War II came a new State Department and then in the 1970s another set of looming office icebergs for Housing and Urban Development, Energy, Transportation, Labor, and the Federal Bureau of Investigation. Washington's private idea people also work not in gleaming towers but in horizontal blocks that turn gray and brown faces to the streets and parks and obey the city's height restrictions with uniform cornice lines.

Ultimately, the inside-the-Beltway criticism is a criticism of the rise of an information economy with fewer people doing "real work." A world of symbolic analysts who form what Alvin Gouldner and Daniel Bell called a "new class" incites many anxieties, especially when they seem to be overpaid for pushing paper.[86] The new class consists of educated professionals who base their claims to authority on rational expertise that can be applied to the good of society as a whole. They contrast with the traditional professions that derived authority from God and mammon as direct servants of churches or property owners. The reliance of the new class on professional standards and portable expertise inspires political critique from both the left and the right. Critics on the left see regulators detached from the real world of factory and field. Those on the right see vapid intellectuals separated from community values. In either case, the criticism implies that ordinary citizens should well be suspicious of a government that requires such a large contingent of code breakers—consultants, communicators, and congressional staff.

The image of an insulated Washington brings a changed meaning to Henry James's characterization of Washington as a "city of conversation" in

Pension Building. Now admired as home for the National Building Museum, the Pension Building in the nineteenth century drew scorn as a factory for routine clerical work. (From Charles Todd, *The Story of Washington* [1890])

The American Scene (1907). For the extraordinarily verbal James, the conversations were those among Henry Adams, literary lions, persons of leisure who could take ideas seriously, and other exemplars of a "Parisian" Washington. Such discourse could go forward among a comfortable intellectual elite untrammeled by the intrusion of a vulgar business community. For novelist Brad Leithauser a century later, however, Washington as a city of conversation meant its participation in the late-twentieth-century economy of information brokering. The morally uncentered protagonist of *Seaward* is a communications lawyer skilled at the ways of the Federal Communications Commission. Terry Seward assumes that every applicant for an FM or a TV license is a "gang of crooks," differentiated only by being "our" clients or "their" clients. But "at some level Terry . . . knew that the presence of 'talk' was the most important thing in the world. For this was his life."[87]

Talk is one of the most important things in Washington, if not necessarily in the world. Information arrives from states, communities, citizens, businesses, and foreign governments. Washingtonians digest and exchange the information, consider needs, make deals, and pass legislation. The new information that results flows out again as responses to grant applications, wire service stories, contracts, orders to the Sixth Fleet, and administrative rules in the thick volumes of the *Federal Register*.

Embedded in this city of public and private decision makers and idea people—in this city of a novel type—is the national shrine. Sentiment as well as specific information converges on Washington. It is not only a national switchboard but also the national city, the place where twentieth-century Americans have recognized and celebrated their civil religion. Washington politics may fall short of ideals, but Washington as a place is the closest the nation has to common ground.

TRANSITIONS

———

Los Angeles on
the Potomac

*I*N 1951 scandalmongering journalists Jack Lait and Lee Mortimer called Washington "Los Angeles without palm trees."[1] Their comparison was a dubious effort to match the high-flying style of the movie industry to fast-and-loose behavior among politicians and power brokers, but the metaphor had broader implications than they realized. Both Washington and Los Angeles *have* grown in parallel in the last half century. They have been idea centers and information cities, they have built new connections beyond the national borders, and their changing neighborhoods and land uses have epitomized many of the metropolitan growth patterns of the later twentieth century. In short, Washington as much as Los Angeles is a Sunbelt city.

Journalists, boosters, and politicians discovered the existence of a Sunbelt in the 1970s. Popularized by Kevin Phillips and then by Kirkpatrick Sale, the term referred to a zone of rapid economic change and metropolitan growth that seemed to stretch across the southern third of the United States. For better (Phillips) or worse (Sale), it was a new economic and political counterweight to the New York–Chicago axis that had dominated the United States for a century.[2]

In drawing the boundaries of this newly identified region, most experts left Washington out. Popular definitions have usually placed the start of the Sunbelt two hundred miles farther south, where the northern borders of North Carolina, Tennessee, Arkansas, Oklahoma, New Mexico, and Arizona form a conveniently straight line. Convenience, however, is a poor criterion for careful analysis. The Sunbelt is not so much a contiguous region sharing a single defining trait, in the style of the Cornbelt, as it is a constellation of dynamic metropolitan centers that have outperformed the rest of the nation. Despite Washington's sometimes choking snowstorms, objective measures of urban growth make the metropolis a close cousin of Atlanta, Austin, and Anaheim.[3]

Most obviously, it is a city built in the later decades of the twentieth century. Despite two hundred years of history, metropolitan Washington has added nearly 80 percent of its population and nearly 90 percent of its developed area since 1940. The national mobilization for World War II, which laid the foundations of the Sunbelt, transformed Washington as much as it changed Norfolk, Dallas, or San Diego. Metropolitan growth rates since 1940 put Washington in the same category with other boom cities of the South and West, not those of the older Northeast.

One result, as the *Washington Post* has pointed out, is an apparent "Los Angelization" of everyday life. Red, Yellow, Orange, and Green Metro lines notwithstanding, present-day Washington has been built around the needs of two-car and then three-car families. It is a prime breeding ground of "edge cities," suburban concentrations of employment and services that function as alternate downtowns for private business (although Bethesda, Silver Spring, and other of Washington's examples remain closely linked to the city center).

Washington has been a great beneficiary of the postindustrial transformation of the national economy. Old factory cities such as Pittsburgh and Cleveland have earned attention for weathering the painful collapse of heavy manufacturing in the past generation and making comebacks as white-collar information and management centers. As a city that never industrialized, Washington was positioned to make the same move without the accompanying costs of disinvestment and structural unemployment.

The Washington economy has also evoked frequent comparisons with Atlanta and Los Angeles. As early as 1958, a Fairfax County, Virginia, economic development official anticipated the rise of the information economy when he claimed that "we are in competition with southern California and Florida, particularly for research type activities." The Federal City Council and the Greater Washington Board of Trade in the 1970s placed Washington among "the dynamic sunbelt cities." Journalists in the 1980s cited Los Angeles, Atlanta, and Dallas as peers and comparators.[4]

As elsewhere in the Sunbelt, defense was the prime Washington growth industry from the 1940s through the 1980s. Washington has far more than its proportionate share of uniformed and civilian Department of Defense workers. The burgeoning offices and establishments of aerospace firms, electronics companies, and other defense contractors fueled its boom in the 1980s. Even when manufacturing facilities are located thousands of miles away, the staggering complexity of modern weapons has required huge technical and engineering staffs along the Beltway for easy liaison with Pentagon procurement officers.[5]

Washington is one of the nation's research and development (R&D) capitals. By 1977 it ranked second behind Los Angeles among all metropolitan areas in the receipt of federal R&D funds. The state of Maryland exceeded the national average for federal R&D funds to universities (calculated on a per capita basis). Data prepared by geographer Edward Malecki show that Washington consistently ranked second in the nation in industrial research laboratories, scientists and engineers in federal jobs, and scientists and engineers in research and development (all standardized by metropolitan population).[6]

A third engine that has fueled rapid growth in the Sunbelt has been permanent and temporary population movements of tourists and retirees. For a historical perspective, it is worth remembering that Washington in the last century served the Northeast as a "winter city"—a sort of Palm Springs with politics. It was also populated, said journalist Julian Street in 1918, by "moderately prosperous retired army and naval officers and their families, living in unostentatious houses and apartments and leading pleasant tepid lives."[7] Although the retired officers are now more likely to be hustling contracts and working on their tennis games than leading tepid lives, Virginia and the District of Columbia still rank with the top ten states for proportion of military retirees in their population.

Sunbelt Washington is a very different creature and concept from southern Washington. The South as a region has been defined by history and culture, military defeat, black-white relations, and the intellectual defense of antimodern values. In contrast, the Sunbelt as a region cannot be defined by the same sorts of political and cultural continuities. People may prosper in the Sunbelt, but they give it no allegiance. There is little common ground between East Carolina farmers and Malibu sophisticates, between Jesse Helms and Tom Bradley.

Unlike the South, the Sunbelt as an identifiable if discontinuous region is essentially new. Its defining character is fast growth on the foundation of new industries and new immigrations. For promoters of a prosperous South, the idea of a Sunbelt has the great advantage that it ignores southern history and ties the region's growth centers to the those of the "forward-looking" West. For the South to be "Sunbelt" is to leap over the century of history that bogged down the efforts of the earlier New South advocates of the nineteenth century.[8]

What links the constellation of boom cities into a Sunbelt? There have been two factors. One is the dominance of information-based industries that have made Sunbelt Washington a networked metropolis, a community where local and regional ties are less important than connections to national and international networks of scientists, journalists, and weapons manufacturers. The second factor is the role of locational and urban amenities and a progrowth environment in attracting footloose activities and new migrants. Washington in the 1990s had plenty of amenities, from big-city culture to Chesapeake Bay and the Blue Ridge only an hour or so away. When combined with a supportive climate for economic growth and land development, especially in northern Virginia, the result has been a Fairfax County that is indistinguishable from North Dallas and a Montgomery County that thinks it is Palo Alto.

GLOBAL CAPITAL

Jack Ryan, the stoic superhero of Tom Clancy's best-selling thrillers of international intrigue and terrorism, is a man of metropolitan Washington. As his career develops through novels such as *Patriot Games* (1987), *Clear and Present Danger* (1989), and *Debt of Honor* (1994), he teaches at the U.S. Naval Academy in Annapolis, climbs to the top in the Central Intelligence Agency (CIA) in Langley, Virginia, and finds himself national security adviser in the White House. As he helps the United States maintain its standing abroad through the Cold War, the drug war, and fierce maneuvering for economic empire, he moves freely among the control centers of the national security apparatus that revolve in a bureaucratic constellation around the North Star of the White House. In the process, the Washington that he sees is a sequence of dark automobiles whisking him from Andrews Air Force Base to top-level meetings in rooms filled with contending decision makers. In these tales of clandestine global networking, the everyday metropolis is a thin backdrop to the "real" action.

Tom Clancy's success suggests a new way of looking at Washington. For more than a century, from Henry Adams's *Democracy* to Allan Drury's *Advise and Consent* and Gore Vidal's *Washington, D.C.*, and then to Joe Klein's *Primary Colors*, novelists have used Washington as the setting to explore the complexities of power and politics. But in the nineteenth century and the first half of the twentieth, the issues around which the fictional action revolved were almost always domestic. How decisions in Washington influence land development and business enterprise in the national hinterland have been compelling subject matter from the old era of railroad barons to the new era of savings and loan scams.

The Cold War years, however, introduced a new subject for Washington novels. For the first time, crisis and corruption could believably revolve around international relations, which were now complex enough and important enough to sustain a plot. The long struggle with the Soviet Union carried far more dramatic weight than the lead-up to the Washington Naval Conference of 1922. The result has been a new genre of Washington-based thrillers whose action pivots on White House and Pentagon decisions. Early examples are Eugene Burdick and Harvey Wheeler's *Fail-Safe* (1962) and Fletcher Knebel and Charles W. Bailey's *Seven Days in May* (1962), followed quickly by Stanley Kubrick's unforgettable depiction of a Washington war room in the 1963 feature film *Dr. Strangelove*. Tom Clancy's politics are far different than Kubrick's, but he has worked the same understanding of Washington as a global capital.

Self-appointed Washington image makers would agree. Boosters in the last two decades have claimed a new identity for the metropolitan area. The *Washington Post* has reported enthusiastically on the emergence of a newly internationalized city. The Greater Washington Board of Trade proclaimed Washington the place to be for firms engaged in international markets.[1] In an advertising campaign a major Washington bank recently called it the most important city in the world. Geographers and regional planners have adapted the same terminology, describing Washington as a "world city" and an "internationalized city" with a "world role" and "international influence."[2] The real estate press prefers the zippier phrase "world class."[3]

At first glance, these claims may seem like the typical output of hot-air vendors in editorial offices and economic development departments. Despite Tom Clancy, it is New York, Los Angeles, and the San Francisco Bay metropolis that scholars have most often identified as the nation's international centers in the late twentieth century.[4] In contrast, Washington's very reason for being is to serve the domestic need of national integration. As a formally neutral *federal city*, it houses the public decision-making apparatus established by the Constitution with the presumed intent of insulating that apparatus from the winds of sectionalism. Since the later nineteenth century, it has also developed into a *national city* with cultural institutions, sources of information, and symbols of national allegiance that have partially fulfilled the challenge of James Bryce that it become "the embodiment of the majesty and stateliness of the whole nation."[5] The range and variety of these national roles is measured by the Smithsonian Institution as a keeper of national cultural values, the U.S. Geological Survey as a source of useful public information, and the Lincoln Memorial as a focus for the emotions of nationalism and national identity.

Although Washington's emerging international image contrasts with much of the city's historic character, the claims merit serious attention. As shaman and spin doctor both know, the act of naming has power in itself, often highlighting certain aspects of a phenomenon while ignoring others. Washington and Washingtonians have appropriated the international label at a time when many U.S. cities have become more directly and fully connected to the world through expanding international trade, investment flows, immigration, and even self-conscious municipal foreign policies.[6] Along with interconnected changes elsewhere around the world, this restructuring of economic activity and social patterns has generated a rich new literature on the character of major cities as centers of transnational organization and control.

Urban internationalization of the sort being experienced by Washington and many other cities can involve any or all of three overlapping processes. One is the development of an economic base that depends heavily on foreign markets for locally produced goods and foreign customers for locally generated services such as transportation, finance, and consulting. This sort of international connection, of course, has long driven the growth of mercantile cities, ports, and European industrial cities. Layered on these older patterns is a second and more recent process: an implosive concentration of the decision-making apparatus of global banks, multinational corporations, and other organizations with international reach. Related to both old and new international economies has been a third process, the development of cosmopolitan communities marked by variety in ethnic and racial groups, languages, and cultural services. Such social and cultural heterogeneity can be seen as the consequence of traditional urban activities as gateways for trade and immigration and as vital social infrastructure for attracting and comforting a very new class of international information workers and transnational capitalists.[7]

The recent literature on the emergence of *world* or *global* cities has been an effort to understand and contextualize the new centralization of world-scale decision-making institutions. Driving much of the work is the desire to frame contemporary urbanization within the broad restructuring of the international division of labor during the 1970s and 1980s. Analysts such as John Friedmann, Michael Peter Smith, Joe Feagin, and Saskia Sassen have tried to identify new forces and outcomes within the long sweep of urban development.[8] They see a reinforcing connection between dispersal of production and centralization of control: the merchants of old international cities traded things; the elite of new global cities coordinate other people's activities. The theoretical work takes off from efforts to understand the changing distribution of responsibilities within individual corporations with geographically proximate headquarters.[9] In Sassen's influential formulation, large complexes of corporate executive and administrative offices call forth concentrations of producer services to supply specialized expertise and informational inputs. Although the logic of dispersal and concentration can apply at any scale from the single metropolitan area upward, world city theorists focus on the global reach of the largest cities and describe a new urban system based on specialization in global finance and business services.

Without challenging the basic idea of a new informational hierarchy capped by global cities, an examination of the internationalization of Washington suggests the need to modify several ancillary premises that are often associated with the model. First, the world city thesis, by its rhetorical strategy and focus on new patterns, tends to ignore older or alternative forms of international connection for cities. Second, this focus on the re-structuring of the global economy downplays the importance of historical endowments and the specifics of past economic and cultural roles for understanding how international roles may have evolved in a particular city. Instead, global cities are seen as detached from their regional and national situations and are treated as nodes in abstract information space.[10] Third, the model emphasizes private economic power, the influence of multinational corporations, and the sovereignty of mobile capital to the substantial exclusion of state-based activities and influence.

Washington fits none of these secondary premises very closely. Like a number of other U.S. cities, it has developed substantial international roles apart from the corporate and financial complex that now drives a global city like New York. In pursuing this point, the following discussion provides historical justification for the findings of Ann Markusen and Vicki Gwiasda about Washington's importance as a node for information production and manipulation distinct from New York.[11] The analysis also supports their argument about the separability of different international functions and the emphasis of related work that finds multiple trajectories toward internationalization.[12] As Markusen and Gwiasda show, cities display different layerings and mixes of international activities. They argue specifically that the locational patterns of trade, government, and education are highly independent of other activities and that finance, research and development, culture, and health and social welfare services are moderately independent. Washington's most important international functions are those with low linkages (government, education) or moderate linkages (culture, research), in contrast to the strongly linked financial services that characterize New York.[13]

In Washington, moreover, what is international is national, based on an elaboration of domestic political and cultural functions. An assessment of Washington against a variety of measures of globalization establishes that the city's international functions are built directly on its historic role as the seat of government. Its international sector has developed and extended its national capital functions such as the federal research establishment, national cultural institutions, administrative agencies, trade associations, and public interest organizations.[14] In these ways, the analysis parallels Richard Child Hill and K. Fujita's description of the global reach of Tokyo as deeply dependent on that city's concentration of state power.[15] Washington's international roles are expansions and elaborations of the same sorts of functions that it performs on the national scene rather than disconnected departures from these functions.

Finally, what is new in Washington is also old. The city's development history supports those global city theorists who refine the broad model by emphasizing the importance of understanding change over time and exploring each city's "rootedness in . . . history, institutions, culture, and politics."[16] The U.S. national metropolis has expanded its international roles by degrees. The decades around 1900, the 1940s, and the 1970s were key periods for the addition or expansion of international functions, followed in each case by a period of absorption involving gradual changes in local culture and tone of life. At every step, control and coordination functions were the leading sectors, followed by new direct services for foreign markets. In turn, these functional changes have led cultural change, with the metropolitan community as a social system responding and adapting to new international roles.

Entering the World

On the brisk morning of October 3, 1889, twenty-seven delegates from the seventeen independent states of Latin America assembled on the Mall to climb aboard a special train provided by the Pennsylvania Railroad for a six-week, six-thousand-mile excursion through the United States. The previous day they had met President Benjamin Harrison and heard Secretary of State James G. Blaine welcome them to the Inter-American Conference—an idea initiated by Blaine in 1881 and seconded by Congress in 1888. On their return, they would join ten U.S. delegates (including Andrew Carnegie) for seventy formal sessions that lasted until April 18, 1890.

The Inter-American Conference marks a milestone in the emergence of a modern, globally connected Washington. Worried about European economic penetration of Latin America and about regional wars that offered openings for European intervention, Blaine hoped to move toward closer commercial ties and a formal system for the arbitration of international disagreements. The results, not surprisingly, fell short of expectations. There was no customs union and no arbitration treaty. But there was a new international organization, the International Union of American Republics, intended to facilitate the collection and distribution of commercial information. Under the aegis of the International Union and the financial sponsorship of the United States was the small Commercial Bureau of the American Republics to gather and publish data on customs regulations, products, and markets as one of the first Washington-based international organizations. Added in 1902 was a Pan American Sanitary Bureau (now the Pan American Health Organization) with its own Washington-based secretariat of seven persons. In turn, the International Union soon evolved into the Pan American Union (1910) and then the Organization of American States (1948).[17]

The Inter-American Conference also reflected the emergence of the first significant era of international conferences and conventions in the late nineteenth and early twentieth centuries. The rapidly increasing speed, safety, and comfort of crossing the Atlantic after 1870 constituted a transportation revolution not too different in effect from that of jet airplanes after 1960. The upper-class tourism that Henry James and Edith Wharton described in their novels was increasingly mirrored by the travels of government officials and scientists to attend Washington meetings, such as the International Medical Congress (1887), International Marine Conference (1889), International Geological Congress (1891), International Woman Suffrage Conference (1902), and International Congress on Hygiene and Demography (1912). Local economic boosters began to claim that "every foreigner turns his face towards Washington," for "here are meetings year by year in increasing variety and numbers, visitors from every corner of the continent, and from every country on the face of the globe, and countless popular assemblies, conventions, and representative congresses of all creeds, professions and nationalities."[18]

Notwithstanding these activities, Washington's international roles remained narrow. International tourism in the nineteenth century was an elite activity rather than a mass phenomenon. Conventions and delegates gathered in Washington because of its scientific establishment or the symbolism of its political role, not the appeal of its cafés, museums, and boulevards.

European visitors sometimes found the city pleasant and sometimes boring, but they never confused it with a major world capital.[19] Only a handful of Washington-based organizations or businesses identified themselves as international in orientation or function in 1900 and fewer than fifty even after the upheavals of World War I (Table 5.1). The strongest focus of such organizations was Latin America, because the early-twentieth-century United States asserted hemispheric rather than global leadership.

With broader diplomatic or military roles still small, the city's cosmopolitanism remained limited. One caustic observer as late as 1920 thought that the main function of the diplomatic corps was to teach Washingtonians the

Table 5.1. Geographically Identified Names of Washington Businesses and Organizations, 1880–1991

	National[a]	Regional[b]	International[c]
1880	36	6	1
1890	40	6	4
1900	108	14	10
1910	150	32	11
1920	342	51	45
1930	441	75	52
1940	528	81	62
1950	995	221	136
1960	1,194	237	189
1970	1,643	193	334
1980	2,108	212	493
1991	4,230	845	1,260

Sources: Washington City Directories, 1880–1940; Telephone white pages for the District of Columbia (1950, 1970, 1980), Washington metropolitan area (1960), and metropolitan Washington (1991). Some 1991 counts have been estimated from column inches.

[a] American, national, or nationwide
[b] Southern, South, Southeast(ern), Dixie, Atlantic, East(ern), east coast, Middle- or Mid-Atlantic, South Atlantic
[c] Global, world, inter-American, Pan-American

art of dining out.[20] European diplomats treated Washington as a minor capital. British representatives used their hill allowance—compensation for
posting on the subtropical Potomac—to join European colleagues in Newport or New York as often as business allowed. The leaders of Washington's
high society confirmed the city's provinciality by going atwitter for nearly a
full year before a brief visit by King George VI of the United Kingdom in
1939.[21]

Hope of the Western World

In January 1943 the U.S. War Department completed the world's largest office building: the Pentagon. Located on the site of an old airport across the
Potomac River from Washington, D.C., the Pentagon supplied office space
for 23,000 workers along 17.5 miles of corridors. Five-sided and only five
stories tall, it had three times the floor space of the Empire State Building.
Three hundred telephone operators directed the calls that came into the single Pentagon number—REpublic 6700—for Secretary of War Henry Stimson, Army Chief of Staff George C. Marshall, and their thousands of military
and civilian subordinates. The building provided the space in which military
planners could coordinate the tasks of raising and equipping the armed
forces that would strike directly at Germany and Japan. The gray sides of the
Pentagon were imposing reminders that Washington in the 1940s was now
balancing the traditional federal concern of promoting domestic tranquility
with a new commitment to project American influence abroad.

World War II cracked open Washington's insularity. In 1942–43 Washington joined and then supplanted London as the decision center for the
global war against the Axis powers. As the command post for the world's
most far-flung military enterprise, it seemed to many observers to have
emerged as the "first city of the world."[22] More than three thousand British
and Commonwealth business people, military officers, and diplomats
staffed organizations such as the British Shipping Mission, Munitions As-
signment Board, and Combined Raw Materials Board in commandeered hotels and apartment buildings. Their Latin American counterparts staffed the
new Inter American Defense Board, one of many wartime organizations that
survived into the Cold War.[23] The number of diplomatic officials assigned to
Washington doubled from 1940 to 1945. The total doubled again from 1945
to 1956 as the internationalization of peacetime foreign policy during the
Truman administration attracted a greatly expanded diplomatic corps.[24] To
quote one overwrought journalist, Washington during the 1940s had become a symbol of freedom in a world of Cold War: "Its decisions have come

to affect men in all parts of the earth. In that sense it is a city of destiny, focusing the world's interest and concern."[25]

Globally engaged Washington certainly had a special attraction and importance for national Jewish organizations. Members of Washington's Jewish community had long taken on political tasks for American Jews as
a whole. As the struggle with Nazi Germany and the creation of Israel became central foreign policy issues, however, organized lobbying became
vital. B'nai B'rith moved its national headquarters to Washington in the late
1930s. The American Jewish Committee, American Jewish Congress, National Council of Jewish Women, and Jewish Labor Committee followed.[26]

Just as important for Washington's emergent role as a venue for international decisions was its campaign for the International Bank for Reconstruction and Development (World Bank) and the closely associated International Monetary Fund (IMF), both of which opened for business in 1946.
The Washington business community, working through the Board of Trade,
helped the Roosevelt and Truman administrations fight the New York banking establishment in a two-stage battle for the new financial institutions
that had been designed at the Bretton Woods conference in 1944. New York
business leaders first opposed the authorizing legislation that created an
alternative focus for world finance. Losing that issue, Wall Street interests
then pushed New York over Washington for the headquarters of the World
Bank and IMF. The arguments for Washington emphasized the intergov-
ernmental character of the new agencies and the need for easy communication through Washington's diplomatic community. The desire of New Deal
Democrats to loosen the grip of New York banks on the nation's international economic policy swayed the decision in favor of Washington.[27]

The tenure of Eugene Meyer, the first World Bank president, summed up
the partial character of Washington's victory. An investment banker who
made a fortune in New York, Meyer became deeply involved in national economic policy with World War I and transferred his base of business activity to
Washington in 1933, when he purchased the *Washington Post*. Under his
chairmanship, the Board of Trade's Postwar Planning Committee in 1945–46
emphasized Washington's potential as a "world capital" with "scores of new
agencies, private, semi-public, governmental, and international."[28] Meyer's
appointment to head the World Bank thus represented a declaration of financial independence by both the city and the federal government. Within the
year, however, it was clear that the World Bank could not function without
supplementing capital assessments on member nations with funds channeled through New York banks. Meyer's replacement by Wall Street lawyer

John McCloy late in 1946 ended Washington's brief victory. The headquarters
and the jobs remained on H Street in a building originally intended for the
State Department, but the power returned to New York.[29]

Postwar Washington faced additional U.S. competition as a world political center. San Francisco and New York continued to house the largest clusters of bankers and lawyers knowledgeable about international trade and
global concerns. Both cities played the key roles in the formation of the
United Nations (UN). Along with Boston, they competed for the permanent
UN headquarters. Its location in Manhattan attracted dozens of related organizations and experts dealing in international affairs to New York rather
than to Washington.

In the same era that European empires were beginning to unravel, racial
segregation in the District of Columbia and adjacent states undercut Washington's attractiveness for multinational organizations. The problems of
segregation derailed Virginia's bid for the UN headquarters, and the reduc-
tion of racial restrictions in the District of Columbia and surrounding suburbs was an important part of the nation's Cold War strategy.[30] Nevertheless, cultural adaptation again lagged behind functional changes. From the
1947–48 reports of the President's Committee on Civil Rights and the National Committee on Segregation in the Nation's Capital to the collapse of
Virginia's program of massive resistance to school integration in 1959, it
took more than a decade to replace the Washington area's southern system
of racial relations with the formally open northern system that was more
welcoming to African and Asian officials.

Although Washington gained another important international institution with the Inter American Development Bank in 1960, there is little published evidence that Washingtonians thought deeply about changes in the
city's international role in the first two decades after World War II. An early
1960s guidebook description of Washington as "the world city of our time"
was an isolated case.[31] The fifteen translation and interpreting services listed
in the 1950 telephone directory grew to only twenty in 1960, scarcely the sign
of a flood of international visitors and business.

The Board of Trade's fruitless campaign to make Washington rather than
New York the site for the 1964 World's Fair displayed the strengths and
weaknesses of postwar Washington as an international center. New Yorkers
confidently argued the merits of their city before President Dwight Eisenhower's site selection commission in 1959. Addressing the President's
Commission on the World's Fair, Mayor Robert Wagner, Senator Jacob Javits, and public works czar Robert Moses variously described their city as the

world capital, the headquarters of the world, a worldwide marketplace, and the world's leading city.[32] Washington's advocates, in contrast, could only counter with "Capital of the Free World" and emphasize the intangible attractions of Washington to U.S. citizens. Their strategists played on Washington's role as the national city and recruited letters of endorsement from mayors, members of Congress, and governors of such landlocked states as Arkansas and North Dakota.[33] New Yorkers touted their city's international functions and claimed the fair, leaving Washingtonians the consolation of their city's national and international symbolism.

Information Capital

In 1965 the Safeway supermarket chain opened a so-called International Safeway grocery store at 1110 F Street N.W. In a decade when Americans were tuning their television sets to learn French cooking from Julia Child and Chinese cooking from Joyce Chen, middle-class Washingtonians responded enthusiastically to the wide array of imported foodstuffs. Thirty years later, the International Safeway was long gone, but specialized groceries and restaurants offering foods from all corners of the map crowded the telephone book.

The change symbolizes another stage in the globalization of Washington. The mid-1970s and 1980s, in contrast to the 1950s, added substance to international claims. The city's international character became a new staple of public discussion. National magazines noted a new "cosmopolitan flavor of a world capital."[34] Business leaders now argued that Washington was growing into a world business city. Civic organizations found it reasonable to assert that Washington was a global political and financial coordinating center with a growing list of foreign businesses. The government of the District of Columbia urged business executives to consider the city's value as a "world center of research and information."[35] Congressman Charles Diggs Jr., the chair of the House Committee on the District of Columbia, opened hearings in 1977 by describing Washington's potential to be "one of the really great cities of the world . . . the Nation's Capital, a federal City, and international city."[36]

The burst of rhetoric reflected an increasing complexity in Washington's engagement with the world economy that coincided with massive corporate and financial restructuring throughout the world. Where the previous stage had depended directly on the growing diplomatic and military presence of the United States in the world, the developments in the seventies and eighties were tied as well to the city's increasing importance and diversity as a national information broker. The overall shift of the U.S. economy toward information and services drove the explosive growth that pushed Washington from eighteenth place among U.S. metropolitan areas in 1930 to eighth place in 1990. In the process, Washington's specialization in national defense and in the prominent information industries of politics, administration, research, education, and cultural tourism allowed boosters such as the Washington-Baltimore Regional Association to claim the title of "information capital of the world."[37]

Most obviously, Washington consolidated its position as a central place for the functions of informal imperialism. It was the center for the coordination of economic policy, diplomatic initiatives, and a vast system of military bases and alliances. If the hundreds of U.S. embassies, consulates, and military bases can be viewed as the dispersed production sites for global influence, the Pentagon and State Department buildings were the federal equivalent of Wall Street office towers. By the early 1970s Washington area employment in international governmental agencies ranged from hundreds of workers with the Arms Control and Disarmament Agency and the Council for International Economic Policy to thousands with the U.S. Information Agency and tens of thousands with the Department of Defense.

In the international as well as the national arena, a vast private and semipublic information industry has grown up around this set of governmental agencies. In this light, it is important to remember that much of the growth of Washington's *domestic* information industry predates the international turn by only a decade or two. Growth in the number of Washington-based international governmental and international nongovernmental organizations has followed the increase of domestic association offices and benefited from the availability of a specialized pool of association staff and executives. Since World War II, such international organizations have spread widely from their European homeland where the rules and forms of diplomacy were created. Their worldwide numbers are now so great that the *Yearbook of International Organizations* divides them among eight different categories. As late as 1962, Washington housed the headquarters or regional office of only 47 international organizations compared with 164 for New York, a ratio of 3.5 to 1 in favor of the economic capital.[38] As of 1985, in contrast, Washington had the principle secretariat of 462 such organizations and a secondary or regional secretariat of 45 more, largely closing the gap on New York, whose total of 701 gave it only a 1.4 to 1 edge. The list of Washington's organizations ranges from specialized academic societies, such as the German Historical Institute, to giants such as the World Bank and the

Organization of American States. Washington-based employment in many of these major multinational organizations grew substantially in the later 1960s and 1970s, in some cases doubling or even tripling.[39] In total number of headquarters, Washington passed such historic centers as Zurich and Geneva to rank sixth among world cities. Its lead over Mexico City doubled. It counted eight times as many secretariats as did Montreal and ten times the number in Toronto.[40]

The proliferation of Washington's international organizations accompanied its increasing importance as a generator of foreign policy ideas. During the early and middle decades of the twentieth century, U.S. foreign policy largely followed the ideas of a New York–based elite that expressed itself through the Council on Foreign Relations and through a series of secretaries of state: Elihu Root, Charles Evans Hughes, Henry Stimson, Dean Acheson, and John Foster Dulles.

Washington's informal foreign policy establishment for two postwar decades was the "Georgetown set." At its core was a generation of young diplomats, spies, and journalists who had enjoyed "good wars" in influencing national policy or running the covert operations of the Office of Strategic Services. After 1945 they gravitated to State Department and CIA jobs and settled among domestic New Dealers in newly fashionable Georgetown. Georgetown's Cold Warriors included members of New York's foreign policy elite, such as Dean Acheson and Averill Harriman, executive branch career men such as Charles Bohlen and Frank Barnes with good connections to Boston and New York, and media figures such as Joseph Alsop, Philip Graham, and Katharine Graham. Over small dinners and late evening drinks, Georgetown's movable salon helped to shape foreign policy until the late 1960s.[41]

Even as members of the Georgetown network began to age, to lose cohesion in the soul-searching of the Vietnam War, and to divide over the Watergate crisis, however, Washington-based institutions began to rival the Council on Foreign Relations as centers of foreign policy expertise. Particularly important were think tanks that had close ties to the defense establishment and to southern and western defense contractors.[42] The new importance of Washington as a source of foreign policy opinion was thus closely associated with the emergence of its intellectual apparatus for articulating a neoconservative domestic agenda, sharing the same ideological bent and similar sources of funding.[43] It can also be read as another stage in the long contest between Europe-firsters and Asia-firsters that underlay midcentury foreign policy debates.

In the 1980s international corporations began to follow governmental and nonprofit organizations. Here, too, the same factors that have made Washington a national information center have also worked on the wider scale of corporate activity.[44] For U.S. firms with international interests, argue the boosters, "greater Washington offers a community of worldwide investment and trade organizations that create an entree to the far corners of the earth. For international firms, Washington offers the U.S. base of operations close to the government regulatory agencies which oversee import/export trade."[45]

The latter point has apparently been convincing, because the local business press reports that more and more European companies have been establishing their main U.S. offices in Washington rather than New York. A prominent business consulting firm ranked Washington fourth among sixty world cities as a desirable location for international headquarters, following Singapore, London, and New York.[46] Behind the boosterism, the particular attraction of Washington for both domestic and foreign firms is the ease of monitoring the rapidly changing U.S. policy environment, lobbying for access to domestic markets, and maintaining contact with state governments, national business and trade associations, and international organizations.[47] In this sphere, Washington's governmental establishment weakly mirrors the attractive power of Tokyo's governmental sector for Japanese and foreign firms, with the difference in intensity reflecting the much more detailed involvement of the Japanese state in economic affairs. Among U.S. corporations, a major move was Mobil's relocation from New York to northern Virginia in search of a higher quality of life and easier international air connections. Between 1979 and 1987 the number of foreign companies with representation in Washington increased from 580 to 950, including three-fourths of the world's reputedly largest corporations.[48] Japan, which accounts for 15 percent of the represented firms, spends an estimated $100 million annually on Washington lobbyists, attorneys, political advisers, and corporate offices.[49]

Education, research, and consulting have also emerged in recent decades as important components of the larger category of producer services.[50] International consulting is most obvious in the activities of the Washington offices of multinational accounting and business management companies. Hundreds of smaller professional firms form a substantial export sector that is invisible in census and trade data on the metropolitan scale. In contrast, it is easy to document the growing number of foreign college and university students in the Washington area, from fewer than 200 in 1938–39 to 1,000 in 1949–50, 3,500 by 1963–64, and 16,000 in the mid-1990s.[51]

Students, of course, can be viewed as a very specialized type of tourist. Long-distance tourism has become mass-market in the last two decades with the help of jumbo jets and First World affluence. Europeans vacation in the Canaries, Japanese take weekends in Singapore and Honolulu, Venezuelans shop in Miami. Washington has been a major destination for the rapidly growing number of foreign visitors to the United States, whose spending in this country first exceeded spending by U.S. tourists abroad in 1989.[52] According to a survey of air travelers administered by the U.S. Travel and Tourism Administration, the city's 1.5 million foreign visitors in 1988 amounted to 10 percent of all such travelers to the United States, placing the city behind only New York, Los Angeles, San Francisco, and Honolulu. The capital city has a special role, of course, as host for officially sponsored junketeers. Another of its special functions is as one of the top dozen world cities for international conventions and meetings. Although data are sporadic and incomplete, Washington and New York appear to have shared a roughly equal and growing number of international meetings in the 1970s and 1980s.[53] This is a function that benefits from the facilities developed for a similar role as a national convention city and continues on a vastly expanded scale Washington's earliest international roles from the nineteenth century.

Beginning in the 1980s, daily life in Washington increasingly supported the international tone of its economy. More than 150 nations were represented by 2,500 diplomatic officers, supported by thousands of technical and clerical staff. Hundreds of other foreign nationals worked for multigovernmental agencies or reported for foreign newspapers and broadcasters. Newspaper stories described foreign real estate investment, multilingualism, and even the number of Washingtonians holding passports (twice the proportion as Detroit or Dallas).[54] The erosion of Washington's cultural insularity made the city more compatible and attractive to foreign business and diplomatic families and global infocrats with strong ideas about suitable cityscapes and societies. Through the 1960s, according to figures maintained by the State Department Office of Protocol, the number of diplomatic family members roughly matched the number of diplomats; in the 1970s the number of family members rapidly doubled the count of diplomats.[55]

A new cosmopolitanism on streets and in neighborhoods now supplemented the sheltered social life of Embassy Row. Fourteen percent of metropolitan area residents were foreign born by 1990, more than tripling the 1960s proportion of 4 percent and placing Washington in the high range of immigrant population for U.S. metropolitan areas.[56] Hispanic and Asian-American populations roughly doubled in the 1980s alone. At the start of the

1990s, 36,000 immigrants per year were listing Washington as their metropolitan area of intended residence. The metropolitan area counted the nation's largest concentration of Ethiopian immigrants, third largest group of Central American immigrants, fourth largest Korean-American community, and sixth largest concentration of newcomers from the former Indochina.[57]

In turn, economic and personal connections appear to have driven improvements in international air connections. Dulles Airport, opened in 1962 to serve as an international hub, remained underutilized until the mid-1980s. In the early 1990s, however, booming growth of international travel through both Dulles and Baltimore-Washington Airports pushed Washington into fifth place among U.S. cities for international air travel.[58]

One summary indicator of Washington's growing global connectivity is the names chosen by its businesses and organizations. Scholars have frequently used such data to measure U.S. regional consciousness and determine, for example, that Topekans feel more middle western than western and Houstonians more southwestern than southern. Washingtonians, such studies suggest, are confused about their place in the U.S. scene, associating themselves strongly with neither the East nor the South.[59] But an examination of Washington as an international city suggests the value of rephrasing the question to carry beyond continental boundaries (see Table 5.1 above).

Dulles Airport terminal. Underutilized when opened in the 1960s, Dulles Airport came into its own as Washington's international connections proliferated in the 1980s and 1990s. (Photograph furnished by Metropolitan Washington Airports Authority)

The 1991 telephone directory for metropolitan Washington contained 1,260 listings that started with terms such as world, worldwide, global, or international. Only 845 listings started with relevant regional terms such as Atlantic, midstates, eastern, or southern. Indeed, Washington joins Miami–Fort Lauderdale and New York as one of three metropolitan areas where "international" listings outnumber those with a regional reference.[60]

City directories and telephone books also confirm the timing of Washington's internationalization. From 1900 to 1940 listings with national, international, and regional terminology grew at essentially the same rate. After 1940, in contrast, international listings began to grow at twice the pace of regional terms and passed them in total number in the mid-1960s. They grew at two and a half times the rate of national terms over the same 1940–90 period. The telephone books—those essential tools of the information age—indicate that late-twentieth-century Washington is situated not only in a particular part of the United States but also within the global networks of the transactional economy.

International Washington
and the Power of History

The evolution of Washington's international roles can be summarized by the character of successive organizations. The Pan American Union, the most important institution of the first stage, began with limited scope and aims in the 1890s and grew slowly. In contrast, the World Bank represents the ways in which Washington's expanding international roles at midcentury were tied to military and diplomatic leadership of the western alliance during World War II and the Cold War. For the most recent stage, the combination and contrast of Mobil Corporation and Georgetown University's Center for Strategic and International Studies suggest the diversification of Washington's role as international decision center.

As the broader comparisons in Table 5.2 indicate, however, it is important to balance the local enthusiasm with a reminder of the wide gaps in Washington's international presence.[61] Its new cosmopolitanism is still limited in comparison to immigrant gateway cities such as Los Angeles, New York, and Miami. It is neither an international port nor a major center for multinational corporate decisions; only one member of *Forbes* magazine's list of "The 100 Largest U.S. Multinationals" is headquartered in the Washington area. Unlike Seattle or Chicago, Washington is not a manufacturing city that sells to world markets. Neither is it a leader in international banking, for its historic lack of manufacturing and foreign commerce limited

Washington banks to real estate loans and left the local responsibility for international finance to nearby Baltimore.[62] This selective specialization supports the theoretical arguments for the separability of international functions and the distinctiveness of globalization trajectories from city to city.

The recent economic history of Washington and its contrasts with other cities support an important analytic distinction between a handful of world cities that structure and dominate a hierarchy of corporate and financial power and a larger number of international cities. A small number of metropolitan regions house the elites of world capitalism—bankers, multinational executives, business consultants, globe-trotting artists. They also retain important roles as manufacturers and traders in world markets. Washington boosters such as congressional delegate Eleanor Holmes Norton may feel no embarrassment in grouping Washington as a peer of world city London or Paris, but it is unlikely that Londoners or Parisians agree.[63] Indeed, Washington seldom appears on scholarly lists of likely global cities, presumably because it lacks the key control institutions for private capital.

At the same time, however, the development of Washington shows the value of examining the wide variety of ways that North American cities meet and have met the world. As is also true in Europe, the roster of substantially internationalized cities is far larger than the short list of global cities. U.S. cities have numerous direct connections to global flows of goods, people, and information that are not channeled through New York or Los Angeles and have promoted and developed these connections in historically distinct ways. Houston is a port and production center that interacts directly with the world of petroleum producers and has gradually substituted sales of expertise for direct sales of petroleum products. Seattle is part of a land bridge between the Pacific and Atlantic economies and now a partner with Vancouver in trying to redefine the Pacific Northwest as an internationalized economic region. The arrival of a Cuban middle class in the 1960s triggered the internationalization of Miami by providing a skilled labor pool for corporate offices and international banks. Atlanta has developed international roles because of its good access to Sunbelt markets and factory sites for foreign corporations, because of active promotion of an international identity, and because of the entrepreneurial accident of the location of the Cable News Network.[64]

In important ways, Washington is an anomaly that requires rethinking several ancillary premises of world city theory and reminds us of the richness of urban experience. Washington is not a global city that directly rivals New York or Los Angeles. Instead, the national metropolis has built its in-

Table 5.2. Metropolitan Area Rankings on International Indicators (among all areas with 1990 populations above 1 million)

Category	Washington	N.Y.	Chicago	Boston	L.A.	S.F.-O.-S.J.[a]	Miami	Atlanta	Houston
Foreign Markets									
Destination for foreign tourists (1988)									
	6	1	7	8	2	3	5	na	na
Manufacturing for export (employment/1,000, 1983)									
	na	21	9	2	15	8	29	25	18
Control Functions									
Diplomatic representation (1992)									
	1	2	4	9	3	5	7	10	5
International organizations (1986)									
	2	1	na	na	3	na	na	na	na
Offices of foreign banks (1988)									
	8	1	3	10	2	5	4	7	6
Headquarters of large multinational corporations (1993)									
	13[b]	1	2	7	11	3	13[b]	13[b]	11
Cosmopolitanism									
Destination for immigrants (1991)									
	9	2	4	10	1	3	6	12	7
Percentage of foreign-born residents (1990)									
	7	4	8	9	2	3	1	27	6
Sister City affiliations (1991)									
	16	5	6	7	1	2	3	15	16

Sources: U.S. Bureau of the Census, *1990 Census of Population: Social and Economic Characteristics, United States,* CP-2-1, pp. 264–68, table 156 [foreign born]; U.S. Bureau of the Census, *Statistical Abstract of the United States, 1991* (Washington, D.C., 1991), 10 [new immigrants]; "Top Numbers Update, 1989," *American Banker* [foreign banks]; "Report on In-Flight Survey of International Air Travelers to USA Destinations," U.S. Department of Commerce, U.S. Travel and Tourism Administration, and *User Friendly Facts: A Resource Book, 1991* (Washington, D.C.: U.S. Travel and Tourism Administration, 1991) [foreign tourists]; *Directory of Sister Cities, Counties, and States by State and County* (Alexandria, Va.: Sister Cities International, 1991); George Mehl, *U.S. Manufactured Exports and Export-Related Employment: Profiles of the 50 States and 33 Selected Metropolitan Areas for 1983* (Washington, D.C.: International Trade Administration, U.S. Department of Commerce, 1987); U.S. Department of State, *Foreign Consular Offices in the United States* (Washington, D.C., 1992); *Forbes Magazine,* July 19, 1993, 182–86 [multinational corporations]; Union of International Associations, *Yearbook of International Organizations, 1985–86* (Munich: K. G. Saur Verlag, 1985).

[a] San Francisco–Oakland–San Jose
[b] Tied with twenty-one other large and small cities with one each

creasingly rich, numerous, and complex international roles and connections on its concentration of public sector rather than private sector activities, on bureaus rather than boardrooms. As a specialized information city, Washington has followed a trajectory perhaps most similar to that of Honolulu, which has deliberately tried to build international activities on a foundation of the government, research, and tourism sectors of its economy. In this light, Washington's growing but still limited international roles are vulnerable less to competition from New York than to a new isolationism and conservative ideology that sees a proud, ambitious Washington as a symbol of oppressive government rather than national achievement.[65]

Washington is also a city that has remained essentially national at the same time that it has taken on international roles. Far from delinking from its roles as a national cultural and administrative center, Washington has directly exploited such roles as a powerful magnet for private sector producer services. It is an international city because it articulates aspects of national character and power and mediates between a large, prosperous nation and a set of constantly changing international relationships that require careful and flexible management. Its international roles are elaborations of its history as a national capital much more than responses to radical economic restructuring.

Although it is a public information capital rather than a corporate control center, the Washington example confirms the basic dynamic of dispersal and centralization. State power and public information are centralized forces that attract a complex of private sector activities in ways similar to the attractions of concentrated financial power. In this light, the federal government can be understood as a producer service that is an important input for domestic and foreign corporations. Government itself, involved as it is with the projection of economic and military power and diplomatic influence, is an activity with internationally dispersed production sites that require central coordination. Washington's role as a command post for Pax Americana thus parallels London's earlier role as an imperial capital.[66] The new international Washington, in short, is the old national city projected on a wider screen.

Six

—

WASHINGTON

AT 2000

Place, Region,
Network

It is sometime in the 1980s. Cassandra Lewis is a black teenager from North-west Washington. With her friends Anita Hughes, Gladys Harper, and Melanie Cartright, she has run an errand to Anacostia and is taking the long way back through an unfamiliar part of Southeast Washington in the vague hope of finding a party. When her car breaks down near East Capitol Street, a young man saunters over from a nearby porch. Cassandra makes an instant judgment: "He was country, stone Bama." A few moments later, after he works some simple magic on the engine, she asks "What do I owe you, Mississippi?"[1]

Cassandra and "Mississippi" are some of the everyday people who populate the stories of black Washington in Edward P. Jones's *Lost in the City*. These are characters who understand the meaning of Washington on several scales. For people like Cassandra Lewis and her friends in "The Night Rhonda Ferguson Was Killed," individual neighborhoods make a difference. Home is a set of blocks not far from Union Station. Anacostia, only five miles away, is foreign territory where they seldom venture: "My grandfather used to say that people in Anacostia still lived with chickens and cows," Anita offers. Regional origins and connections also make a difference. Cassandra types her rescuer as an outsider from the central South, someone without the rich set of family and community ties that link many black Washingtonians to the South Atlantic Tidewater and Piedmont.[2]

In other stories Jones places Washington in its national rather than local context, emphasizing the ways in which the city transcends regional differences. Marie, a woman in her eighties, recalls her mother for an earnest Howard University student doing an oral history project:

My mother had this idea that everything could be done in Washington, that a human bein could take all they troubles to Washington and things would be set right. I think it was all wrapped up with her notion of the govment, the Supreme Court and the president and the like. "Up there," she would say, "things can be made right." "Up there" was her only words for Washington. All them other cities had names, but Washington didn't need a name.[3]

Jones's characters are not descendants of the postbellum black elite. They are twentieth-century Washingtonians, participants and products of the migrations that added complexity to the city's social and cultural mix. By the second half of the twentieth century, Washington had absorbed waves of New Deal bureaucrats, aerospace lobbyists with Cal Tech degrees, and ambitious young women and men hoping to parlay state university diplomas into influential jobs among the thousands of congressional staffers on Capitol Hill. All of the newcomers brought new ideas about the right way to do things and counterbalanced the established families who had previously set the city's social tone. Within the black community, a growing salaried class with steady jobs in the federal service challenged the old elite, while a proletariat of poorly paid service workers and underemployed laborers tended to push both groups into the background. Regional affiliation since the war has therefore involved the overlapping claims of multiple Washingtons—old and new white, old and new black.

This final chapter revisits Washington after midcentury on three different scales. It looks again at ways that Washingtonians have understood and interacted with their Potomac landscape. It considers the sorts of regional connections that old and new residents have forged and tended. And it examines the contrasting manner in which the city has developed and functioned within the very large-scale frameworks of modernism.

Washington and Its River

In the 1920s and 1930s, members of the Washington Board of Trade looked forward to their annual spring shad bake. As the fish swarmed up Chesapeake inlets and rivers to spawn, Washington business leaders descended on a Chesapeake resort—Quantico on the lower Potomac; Chesapeake Beach in Calvert County, Maryland; or Sherwood Forest and Bay Ridge near Annapolis. The purpose was to gorge on local seafood with boiled potatoes and coleslaw on the side. "With the aid of those toothsome products of Chesapeake Bay, the famous planked shad, the old-fashioned clam chowder and other delicacies," said the 1922 program, "your Committee will sustain the reputation for hospitality for which the salt-washed shores of tide-water Maryland have long been famous."[4]

World War II interrupted the tradition and eroded the excursion's regional roots. Wartime gasoline and tire rationing substituted dinner at the Shoreham Hotel for a drive to the Chesapeake Bay. The "Shad Bake" became a generic "Spring Outing" in 1947. There were a few more visits to the shore, but the popular new site was the Indian Spring Country Club at Silver Spring, Maryland. The event itself became a generic businessmen's outing whose golf, beer, and hot dogs could have been the order of the day in Detroit, Rochester, or Kansas City as easily as Washington.[5]

The changing habits of the Board of Trade tell half the story of Washington's changing relationship to its site and landscape since the 1880s. The sequence started with the transformation of the early Tidewater town into a city whose center of gravity and focus of attention moved uphill and upstream for three generations after the Civil War. By the 1950s middle-class Washington was a Piedmont city that had largely lost contact with and awareness of its Tidewater roots. In contrast, growing national environmental consciousness and renewed attention to Washington's Tidewater setting in recent decades have helped to rebalance the upland city of mid-century as a Chesapeake metropolis.

As late as the 1880s, nearly all Washingtonians lived in the original city between the Potomac and the surrounding hills or in Georgetown. Old Washington families held on to houses near Lafayette Park and the White House. Successful postwar businessmen and newcomers with money to spare erected mansions a bit to the north toward Dupont, Thomas, and Scott Circles. This increasingly fashionable West End also boasted the city's first luxury apartment buildings in the 1880s. Modest town houses slowly filled the districts closer to the Capitol for small business owners and bureaucrats. The surrounding hills themselves were a rural patchwork of woods, fields, and country houses. Dotted with an occasional crossroads community such as Tenleytown and crowned with earthworks and forts still fresh from the war, they remained an escape from the bustle and heat of the city.

Change began slowly when land developers pushed the first subdivisions beyond the original city boundaries, buying up farms to the north of the central business core and cutting streets across their slopes. Visitors to the first suburbs took the Fourteenth Street horsecar line two miles beyond Boundary Street (now Florida Avenue) to Mt. Pleasant (1866) and Columbia Heights or the Seventh Street horsecars to LeDroit Park (1870s). By the

1880s Brookland and Takoma Park had appeared along the Metropolitan Branch of the Baltimore and Ohio Railroad, while developers looked forward to marketing Petworth and Brightwood Park with the help of the new electrified trolleys.[6]

The mechanically powered transit revolution between 1890 and 1930 pulled the middle class away from the row houses of Northeast and Southeast Washington. Streetcars in the 1890s, automobiles after 1910, and new bridges on Connecticut and Massachusetts Avenues allowed real estate developers to leap northwestward across Rock Creek with an eye on Montgomery County, Maryland. Francis Newlands led the way by acquiring 1,700 acres along Connecticut Avenue from Rock Creek into Maryland, building a streetcar line to serve his Chevy Chase Land Company, and fostering smaller developments such as Cleveland Park along the route.[7] Just as horsecar and streetcar lines served Northwest Washington more intensively than eastern and southeastern neighborhoods, longer-distance suburban and interurban railroads spread more thickly to the north than the south. Draw a line from the eastern corner to the western corner of the original District—from Seat Pleasant, Maryland, to Falls Church, Virginia. By 1915 northward commuters could reach Rosslyn and McLean in Virginia, Bethesda, Chevy Chase, Forest Glen, Silver Spring, Hyattsville, College Park, and Kenilworth in Maryland. To the south, their few choices were Arlington Junction, Alexandria, and Congress Heights. Important new institutions chose the same uphill locations—American University, Walter Reed Army Hospital, the National Institutes of Health.[8]

The Piedmont environment of the twentieth-century middle and upper classes had a few local touches, such as cascades of spring dogwood, to remind southerners of Richmond and Greensboro. But most neighborhoods could just as easily be tucked into the hill-and-ravine outskirts of Philadelphia or the suburban uplands of northern New Jersey. Bethesda, Takoma Park, McLean, and Chevy Chase have been generically northeastern in housing styles and tone. Their golf courses—recall the Board of Trade entertainment—could just as well encircle Hartford or New York.

Artists and mapmakers reflected the uphill orientation in the late nineteenth and twentieth centuries. The first inklings of change actually came in perspective drawings in the 1850s and 1860s. Casimir Bohn and Edward Sachse's midcentury views of the city westward from the Capitol reduce the Potomac and the Virginia hills to distant elements that blend with the horizon rather than using them as prominent parts of the composition.[9] In the same period, publishers replaced maps that aligned the Potomac and East-

ern Branch as dominant horizontal and vertical elements with newer depictions that placed north and south strictly at the top and bottom of the page
or sheet. In the new cartography, rivers dropped toward the bottom as framing elements.[10]

Washington maps continued to change in the later decades of the nineteenth century. By the 1880s and 1890s cartographers no longer placed the
Capitol, the formal seat of government, at the center of their maps. Instead,
the site of the Capitol drifted slowly toward the lower right corner of many
maps, allowing greater attention to the western and especially the northern
sections of the city at the expense of the Tidewater side of the District. Maps
of 1890 and 1891, for example, allocated two to three times more space to
the northern quadrants of Washington than to the southern quadrants, a
sharp contrast with maps of 1876 and 1881 that were tilted just slightly off
center to the south.[11]

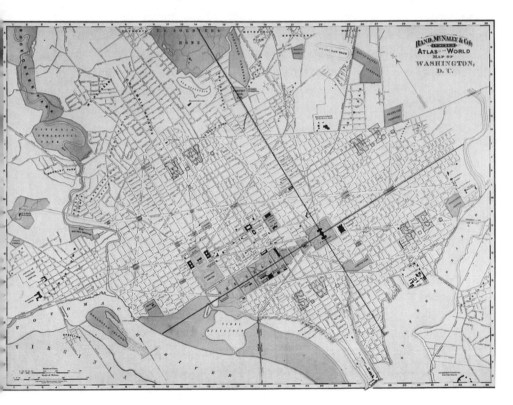

Washington in 1893, Rand McNally and Co. By the end of the nineteenth century,
mapmakers scarcely noticed Washington's rivers when they depicted the capital.
(Geography and Map Division, Library of Congress)

Recentered maps further deemphasized the two rivers. The lower Potomac and Alexandria vanished completely. The river and its Virginia shore were easy to obliterate under indexes and "ready reference" guides, as were the upper reaches of the Anacostia.[12] Some cartographers managed to squeeze in Fort McNair and a sketchy indication that the main stem and the Eastern Branch actually joined. Others cut off the junction entirely, leaving the Potomac and Anacostia Rivers as little more than decorative blue borders with little connection to the city and no visible connection to each other.[13]

The artists and photographers who produced perspective views in the late nineteenth and early twentieth centuries made similar compositional decisions. The more developed Washington's constructed environment of buildings, streets, and monuments, the less attention its rivers seemed to need. When Theodore Davis drew the city for the readers of Harper's in 1869, he offered a bird's-eye view from the White House to the Capitol with the Anacostia River squeezed to a narrow band on the edge of the picture, scarcely distinguishable from a bank of clouds. Thirteen years later, he drew the city in a south-to-north orientation with no water at all to break the vista of brick and stone.[14] Photographs up and down Pennsylvania Avenue became a staple of pictorial guides. Twentieth-century bird's-eye views and early aerial photos from the 1920s emphasize the built city, ignore the Eastern Branch, and reduce the Potomac at best to a visual entryway.[15]

When Washington officials did become concerned with the Potomac in the mid-twentieth century, their upstream emphasis reflected both the orientation of the city and changing ways of thinking about rivers. National river basin regionalism of the 1930s and 1940s tended to emphasize headwater areas over downstream reaches and estuaries. The interest was to dam and harness rivers and their basins for hydropower, flood control, erosion control, navigation, and irrigation. Attention centered on how best to use river basin planning to help the landside economy of farms and factories, with fisheries and natural systems largely ignored.

In this context, development proposals for the Potomac River focused on tributary dams and the economic development needs of the Appalachian headwaters. The Interstate Commission on the Potomac River Basin (ICPRB), instituted in 1940 by compact between four states and Congress, focused on water quality problems created by mining, siltation, and sewage disposal. The 1950 report of the President's Water Resources Policy Commission, *Ten Rivers in America's Future*, looked at water quality, economic development, and governmental options. The Corps of Engineers, meanwhile, published studies of flood control and urban water supply needs in 1934, 1946, and 1950. These documents were preludes to a massive congressionally mandated Potomac River Basin Report, begun in 1957 and issued in 1963. As in earlier studies, the Corps looked forward to controlling floods, expanding urban water supply, and serving recreation through dam building. The report recommended the construction of 418 headwater reservoirs and 16 major reservoirs, including one on the main river that would have created a lake from Seneca Creek to Harper's Ferry.[16]

The Corps proposals were a decade too late for implementation. Taxpayers protested the costs, local communities feared the destruction of rural landscapes, and the National Parks Association led an opposition coalition of national conservation organizations. The coalition argued that the proposals would destroy much of the now-historic Chesapeake and Ohio Canal and that alternative technologies would allow pollution abatement and adequate water supply with lower costs and fewer environmental impacts. In March 1965 Lyndon Johnson proposed the Potomac as a "model river" for enhancement of scenic and recreational values. The initiative kicked into gear a new set of committees, task forces, and reports, especially The Nation's River (1968), which emphasized preservation of the Potomac shoreline from Washington upstream to Cumberland, Maryland.[17] Through various permutations, the new effort led to National Park Service studies for a 191-mile-long "Potomac National River" and designation of the Chesapeake and Ohio National Historic Park of 20,000 acres on the Maryland side of the river above Washington.

An early correction to the upstream emphasis was Frederick Gutheim's talk on "The Lower Potomac River" at a public meeting of the ICPRB. He reminded listeners that the Potomac did not stop at the Fourteenth Street Bridge. It flowed another one hundred miles, opening out to eleven miles wide by the time it fully merges into the Chesapeake Bay. The upper river may have been cleaned up, but the lower river was still polluted. The upper river may have been in demand for middle-class recreation, but the lower river flowed through economically depressed counties with the potential for new investment. "The lower estuary is an integral part of the Potomac," Gutheim argued. "I believe that after three centuries of slumbering, this great region, heretofore relatively isolated and undeveloped, is about to awaken and to play its part in the future growth of the Potomac Basin and the Washington metropolitan region."[18]

The contrast between the perspectives of the Corps of Engineers in 1963 and Gutheim in 1965 encapsulated a deep change in American thinking about rivers from the 1950s to the 1970s. Gutheim's talk was part of a change of consciousness that included a new awareness of the value of wetlands as "million dollar marshes" and passage of the Coastal Zone Management Act in 1972. Potomac River studies and conferences began to pay attention to downstream reaches and to link environmental problems of the river to those of the bay.[19] Chesapeake Bay states simultaneously worked toward cooperative efforts to protect the waters of the bay, leading to a Chesapeake Bay Commission in 1980 and to Chesapeake Bay Agreements in 1983 and 1987 among Pennsylvania, Maryland, Virginia, the District of Columbia, and the U.S. Environmental Protection Agency to be implemented by state land use regulations.[20]

On a more local scale, Washington planners since the 1970s have rediscovered the long-neglected Anacostia River. The National Capital Planning Commission in 1972 reported on *The Urban River* and opportunities for open space, recreational access, and vistas along both the Potomac and the Anacostia. In a way not often seen since the nineteenth century, the report's text and maps present the waterways and their junction as the defining feature of Washington's site and the creators of the city's most expansive public spaces.

Anacostia redevelopment continued to figure prominently in planning proposals in the ensuing quarter century.[21] Most recently, the National Capital Planning Commission's *Extending the Legacy* (1997) called for a makeover of the space within the original Washington City—the monumental core and close-in neighborhoods. The central suggestion is to recenter Washington on the Capitol with strong axes to the north, south, and east to balance the Mall to the west. Redevelopment of South Capitol and East Capitol Streets would help with "integrating the Potomac and Anacostia rivers into the city's public life." New uses for both sides of the Anacostia, particularly in the area between Greenleaf's Point and the Navy Yard, could restore the "historic awareness of Washington as a vital river city."[22]

Particularly since the 1960s, recreational choices have brought contemporary Washingtonians into contact with the same areas. One might speculate that the renewed interest is tied to the postwar democratization of sailing as middle-class recreation (perhaps balancing the interest of the 1930s and 1940s in creating the Blue Ridge Parkway, Appalachian Trail, and Shenandoah National Park).[23] Census data on "homes held for occasional use," first available for 1980, identify concentrations of recreational activity in the mountain counties of the upper Potomac drainage, on the Tidewater Virginia peninsulas, the eastern shore of Chesapeake Bay, and the Atlantic coasts of Delaware, Maryland, and North Carolina. Speaking for characters

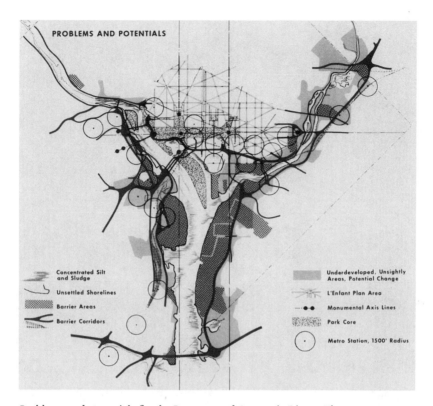

Problems and potentials for the Potomac and Anacostia Rivers. The 1972 report on *The Urban River* helped Washingtonians rediscover the Potomac and Anacostia shores as locations for recreational space, public facilities, and investment. Its maps recalled earlier depictions of Washington at the head of the Potomac estuary. (From National Capital Planning Commission, *The Urban River: A Staff Proposal for Waterfront Development in the District of Columbia* [1972])

with jobs in Washington and Baltimore, novelist John Barth wrote in 1987 that "the purpose of Maryland's mainland, where one lives and works, is to yearn toward its Eastern Shore, where one plays and dreams." The yearning seems to include the Sunday edition of the *Washington Post*, which has 5 percent sales penetration as far to the southeast as Nags Head on the Outer Banks of North Carolina.[24]

Midlantic Metropolis

To introduce "Washington: The City of Leisure" to readers of the *Atlantic Monthly* as the twentieth century opened, Maurice Low used the capital's summer climate: "Looking up from my desk at the close of a day almost

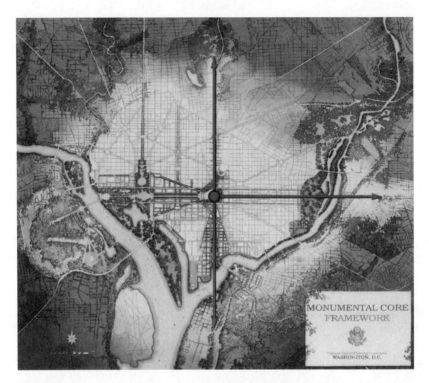

The monumental core and Washington's rivers. The National Capital Planning Commission in 1997 suggested ways to recapture the importance that the Anacostia River had held in Pierre L'Enfant's original plan for Washington. (From National Capital Planning Commission, *Extending the Legacy: Planning America's Capital for the Twenty-first Century* [1997])

tropical in its sensuous languorousness, with a sky so brilliant blue that it seems to take on the color of the flowers beneath rather than to reflect them, with the air laden with the perfume of magnolias and other heavy odors of our Southern flowers . . ."[25]

Throughout the twentieth century, even if society has seemed to northernize, Washington's "air" has been southern. Winter storms follow the route of Robert E. Lee and Stonewall Jackson, driving clouds of snow like gray-clad armies up the Piedmont between the Appalachians and the sea. Warm air weighted down with moisture seeps more slowly but just as inexorably northward along the summer coast—the "humid Southern sun-blurred breeze" of Gary Snyder. August tourists can feel their own experience in Karl Shapiro's lines: "From summer and the wheel-shaped city / That sweats like a swamp and wrangles on / Its melting streets . . ."[26] As the warm night falls, the visitor might also think of Jean Toomer's southward view from the grounds of the Soldier's Home on a hilltop due north of the Capitol: "The ground is high. Washington lies below. Its light spreads like a blush against the darkened sky. Against the soft dusk sky of Washington. And when the wind is from the South, soil of my homeland falls like a fertile shower upon the lean streets of the city."[27]

Southern climate is a metaphor for southern culture, as Toomer's novel about black Americans in the 1920s makes clear. Incorporation of northern values and connections within Washington's public institutions of government, education, and commercial promotion have been balanced by the per-

Chesapeake Bay Bridge. Opened in 1952 and augmented with a second span in 1973, the Chesapeake Bay Bridge offered Washingtonians easy access to the Eastern Shore of Maryland for recreation. By 1980, several Eastern Shore counties were part of Washington's vacation home hinterland. (Photograph furnished by Maryland Transportation Authority)

sistence of southern characteristics and connections in private values and behavior. Even in recent versions of the "big change," Washington commentators of both races have agreed that southern styles of social behavior lasted at least into the 1970s before yielding to Manhattanization.[28] More people in the Washington area read *Southern Living* than *New York*. In complementary fashion, residents of the South Atlantic states (and the West) are more likely to keep up on local developments by subscribing to the *Washingtonian* than are northeasterners and middle westerners.[29]

Washington sports teams in the mid-twentieth century approached racial integration with southern caution. After he moved the Redskins of the National Football League from Boston to Washington in 1937, owner George Preston Marshall consciously marketed the team as an all-white standard bearer through the 1940s and 1950s. With competing teams to the north, Marshall's natural market for radio broadcasts and ticket sales lay in the South. In the off-season, the racially distinct Redskins cultivated the market with exhibition tours through southern cities. The marketing strategy presumably benefited from the fame of Texan Sammy Baugh, the 'Skins first star quarterback. The Washington Senators of the American League were also slow to add black American players to their roster (although management deemed Cuban players acceptable).[30]

Washington's role in the propagation of indigenous South Atlantic musical traditions offers a specific illustration of the intensification of southern cultural ties. The migrations of the 1930s and 1940s brought the evolving bluegrass music of the eastern Appalachians to Washington. As the most accessible and "southern" of the major eastern markets, Greater Washington has supported specialized clubs and radio stations since the 1950s, summer festivals and publications since the 1960s.[31]

A number of practitioners of the Piedmont blues style that emerged in Virginia and the Carolinas in the early twentieth century similarly moved to Washington as the first stop "up the road" to the North. Early centers and markets for Piedmont blues were smaller cities such as Spartanburg, Durham, and Richmond, but Washington has had the advantage of a larger musical market and opportunities to support a family with nonmusical jobs. Blues artists in the Washington area often keep family ties to the rural South and fold its places into their lyrics—John Cephas calls his guitar style the "Williamsburg Lope" and worked a Richmond setting into "West Carey Street Blues." Archie Edwards in "My Old Schoolmates" talks about a visit to Franklin County, Virginia, and ends with the 250-mile drive back to Washington.[32]

Professional and amateur musicians are one specialized subgroup within a much larger migration stream that has continued to reinforce Washington's southern character. In the 1960s and 1970s Washington counted twice as many residents born in the Carolinas as in New York and Pennsylvania.[33] Aggregate migration data for 1935–40, 1955–60, and 1975–80 show a consistent overrepresentation from the South Atlantic states, Southwest, and Far West compared with the numbers predicted by a simple gravity model. Delaware, Pennsylvania, New Jersey, the Ohio Valley, and the Great Lakes states have been underrepresented. In the aggregate, the South exclusive of Maryland, Delaware, and Virginia accounted for 32 percent of migrants to the District of Columbia in the later 1930s, 34 percent of migrants to the larger metropolitan area in the later 1950s, and 30 percent in the later 1970s.[34]

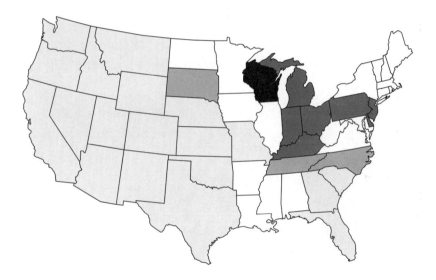

☐ Migration ≥ 120% of predicted values, all periods*

▨ Migration ≥ 120% of predicted values, two of three periods

▨ Migration ≤ 80% of predicted values, all periods

■ Migration ≤ 80% of predicted values, two of three periods

*1935–40; 1955–60; 1975–80

Migration to Washington. In the middle decades of the twentieth century, metropolitan Washington drew new residents disproportionately from the West and the South. (Map by the author)

Table 6.1. Percentage of All Regional Terms in Names of
Washington Businesses and Organizations, 1912–1997

	North [a]	East [b]	Middle/ Atlantic [c]	South [d]
1912	7	14	14	65
1930	2	10	23	65
1943	2	17	24	57
1948	2	28	25	45
1960	2	28	25	45
1970[*]	2	30	36	32
1970[**]	6	25	31	38
1988	4	28	45	23
1997	6	30	47	17

[a] North(ern), North Atlantic, Northeast(ern), North Star, Northland
[b] East(ern), East Coast, East Atlantic
[c] Middle Atlantic, Mid-Atlantic, Mid-States, Mid-East
[d] South(ern), South Atlantic, Southeast(ern), Southland, Dixie

[*] 1912–70: District of Columbia, from R. L. Polk Co. city directories
[**] 1970–97: D.C., suburban Maryland, and northern Virginia, from
telephone directory white pages

Migrants with paychecks from the Department of Defense are especially
likely to have had southern connections, for the growth of military administration in Washington has meant the expansion of an institution historically dominated by southerners. Despite declines after both world wars, the
postwar American officer corps continued to draw disproportionately from
persons of southern birth and premilitary education. As late as 1980, the
South supplied more than its per capita share of all enlistees.[35] Even military
men and women with northern backgrounds are likely to have had the experience of southern living through service at southern bases, which accounted for 48 percent of all military postings in 1980.[36] Since the early years
of the century, many military personnel have tended to stay in or return to
the Washington area after retirement. More than one out of every one hundred residents of the District of Columbia and Virginia are military retirees

(the Virginia figures, of course, reflect concentrations in both the Washington and Hampton Roads areas).[37]

A substantially larger portion of Washington's new southerners have been blacks from the Carolinas and Georgia who have maintained both folk culture and family connections. Anthropologist Brett Williams has documented surviving southern folkways dealing with food, fishing, gardening, and healing. If the Metroliner and air shuttle to New York are the armatures that support a Washington-Northeast communications network, Interstate 95 from Washington to Savannah provides the basis for an equally active Washington-Southeast social network. Black colleges in the Carolinas have alumni groups in Washington. Gospel ensembles in Washington keep open an active creative exchange by hosting choirs and quartets from the Carolinas and Georgia and making their own annual visits to particular South Atlantic churches. Black churches are likely to hold "Carolina Days," and social clubs for migrants from specific South Atlantic communities have survived for decades. Family members visit between Washington and the Carolinas, attend annual reunions, and shift residence back and forth between South and city. Many Washington families regularly send their children or grandchildren south for the summer, keeping alive a sense that the South is home as much as the city up the road.[38]

Travel patterns facilitated by postwar highway building have also reintensified Washington's connections with nearby rural districts where historic southern culture survived into the later twentieth century in relative isolation from the industrial growth of the New South. Chesapeake Bay and its tidal rivers have long been a local migration field and an economic resource for watermen operating out of the lower Potomac. The northern counties of Virginia and the upper Potomac Basin similarly looked to Washington as a communication and retail center.[39] Annapolis, Fredericksburg, and Culpeper were all incorporated into the Washington exurbs during the 1970s.

Local opinion leaders have searched in recent years for the right phrase to capture the sense of an emerging subregion. The 1970s brought interest in identifying Washington with the Sunbelt to emphasize its independence from the aging Northeast core. The decade also generated promotional excitement about the more localized idea that Washington and Baltimore function as a single supermetropolis. Business leaders in both cities promoted the idea of a Baltimore-Washington Common Market in the mid-1970s and organized the Baltimore-Washington Regional Association in 1978. Advocates such as Baltimore civic leader James Rouse stressed the attractions of a single market and the complementarity of Baltimore's port and Washington information industries. Support for the Regional Association came from the Greater Baltimore Association, Federal City Council, and Greater Washington Board of Trade.[40]

Indeed, the 1980s brought substantial integration of local markets for many service businesses. Washington law firms opened Baltimore branches, and Baltimore firms expanded their presence in Virginia. Maryland banks dominated Washington's northern suburbs, Washington retailers anchored Baltimore shopping malls, and commercial real estate brokers and large construction companies operated from Fredericksburg to Baltimore. The Baltimore Orioles, who had long sold a quarter of their tickets to Washingtonians, deliberately located their new Camden Yards ball park on the southern edge of downtown Baltimore, a site even more convenient and enticing to Washingtonians than their old stadium.[41]

The culmination of the supercity campaign came in 1992, when the Bureau of the Census defined Washington-Baltimore as a new Consolidated Metropolitan Statistical Area (CMSA). To the delight of boosters interested in making certain that the Chesapeake metropolis attracts due attention from outside investors, the new CMSA ranks fourth in population (at 6.7 million in 1990 and an estimated 7.2 million in 1996) and second in the size of its office market.[42] In the words of one corporate location consultant, "it absolutely makes a difference when you're trying to sell this region to companies, particularly those overseas."[43] Such boosters were especially pleased that the Census Bureau bowed to strong pressure and violated its guidelines by placing the smaller central city before the larger in the hyphenated name. Not only was "Washington" more recognizable than "Baltimore" to businesses in Bangkok and Barcelona, but the choice also avoided overtaxing northern Virginians with a new identity.[44]

Metropolitan area definitions recognize economic integration and commuting patterns, not cultural and social identity. Washington-Baltimore may well have the economic standing to sell itself as "midway between the Northeast and the Sunbelt, midway between the West Coast and London."[45] But as the debate over the CMSA name suggests, there is still a sense of difference. The two cities are seen as white collar and blue collar, teleport and seaport, paper pusher and steelmaker. One is the natural home of yuppies, the other of long-rooted ethnic neighborhoods. An emblematic Washington movie is All the President's Men, but Baltimore is better captured in Barry's Levinson's Diner and Tinmen. Nevertheless, advocates of a single metropolis argue that the differences between the two cities were more reputation than reality by the 1990s, especially as Baltimore manufacturing jobs declined from 180,000 in 1972 to 119,000 in 1992, as Baltimore's new waterfront brings the city into the tourist age, and as Baltimore and Washington suburbs melt together.[46]

Even more inclusive is the idea of a Chesapeake "Crescent" arcing from Norfolk to Baltimore with Washington as its organizing core.[47] Heavy telephone traffic between Washington, Baltimore, Richmond, and Norfolk foreshadowed the crescent as early as the 1950s.[48] The area is linked by the strong presence of the federal government from Aberdeen Proving Grounds north of Baltimore to the NASA and Navy complexes in Norfolk–Newport News. Other connections are consolidation of Virginia banking and the growth of Chesapeake Bay recreation.[49] A recent advertisement by Commonwealth Land Exchange, Inc., showed the I-95/I-64 route from Baltimore and Washington and announced that its Stafford, Virginia, offices were "Located at the Heart of the Golden Crescent." The advertisement would make sense to Maryland novelist Tom Clancy, whose *Debt of Honor* (1994) makes the Golden Crescent into a day-to-day world stretching from Johns Hopkins University to the Maryland coast, to work places in Washington and North Virginia, to flights in and out of Andrews Air Force Base, and to meetings at Camp Peary near Yorktown, Virginia.

We can also trace the changing regional consciousness in the choice of regional terminology for the names of businesses and organizations.[50] City directories for the District of Columbia for 1912 through 1970 and combined city and suburban telephone directories for 1970, 1986, and 1997 have been examined for the use of three sets of regional terms as the initial word in business or organizational names. As Table 6.1 above indicates, "North" and its variations have been also-rans from the start. More interesting are a complex of "middle" terms. "East" may imply connection to the northeastern seaboard. It may also group with "Atlantic" and "Middle" as a set of neutral names that avoid identification with either North or South. Taken in aggregate, these three regional identifiers passed southern terms in popularity soon after World War II and surged further ahead after 1970.[51]

The idea of a distinct Chesapeake region is part of the reseparation of the historic South into subregions with distinct characteristics and trajectories. The traditional triad of North/South/West may be fragmenting in the face of new patterns of world trade and immigration, new arrangements for marketing natural resources and manufactured goods, and the mobility of people and information. Joel Garreau's "nine nations of North America" cross several international borders, split the West into four parts, and divide the South into a core and four edges. Geographer Wilbur Zelinsky uses popular culture to parcel the South among distinct subareas that put Floridians with New Yorkers and Texans with Nevadans. Economic and population trends are pulling an "outer South" of Virginia, Florida, and Texas away from a "middle South" of Georgia and the Carolinas and an "inner South" of Alabama, Mississippi, and Arkansas.[52]

In a sense, Washington is constructing a new "Midlantic" identity by selective borrowing from both models of its regional character. Washington is defined as a key location for control functions in the national and international economies, but one that is separate rather than subordinate to New York and the Northeast.[53] At the same time, it retains strong connections to the multiple Souths of Tidewater towns, Carolina farms, and Texas military bases. The articulation of a contemporary consumption region around this emergent control center incorporates direct links to the traditional South but filters them through the needs of an information-era metropolis. Indeed, the idea of Midlantic Washington as the center of national information networks is a curious and unanticipated realization of George Washington's early dream of a middle empire ruled from the Potomac.

Finally, the idea of a revitalized and redefined southernness is a powerful reminder that regions are not simply residual categories that preserve fragments of a simpler society in the maelstrom of modernization. Instead, they are active cultural products that are constantly reinterpreted and reformed by residents and newcomers as internal and external circumstances change. There are substantial parallels to our understanding of city neighborhoods and ethnic groups as social categories that are repeatedly readapted within changing environments. Urbanization, bureaucratization, and globalization are most certainly powerful and transformative, but they have not eliminated the desire to define ourselves in terms of smaller communities and distinct places.

A City of the Twentieth Century

"Postmodern" is a slippery term. It may have been the big idea in the academic world of the 1990s, but it seems to take on new meanings with every critical and scholarly explanation. It implies everything from a specific aesthetic taste for architectural pastiche to a fundamentally skeptical philosophy of knowledge.

In one version postmodernism explicitly rejects nineteenth- and early-twentieth-century efforts to develop comprehensive theories and models of social change. The founding fathers and grandfathers of social science were systematizers. Working in the shadow of the Enlightenment, they looked

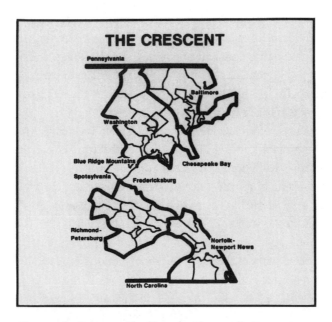

Chesapeake Crescent. The idea of a Chesapeake Crescent emphasizes the urbanization of the western margins of the Chesapeake Bay. (From George Grier and Eunice Grier, *Greater Washington at
Mid Decade* [1985]; used by permission of George Grier)

for the big patterns that could integrate the variety of social and economic
life and make sense of the big changes sweeping across the Atlantic economy and then the world. Karl Marx, Herbert Spencer, Max Weber, Thorstein
Veblen—these giants of social thought emphasized widely differing sets of
causes, but they all wanted to understand the transformation of Euro-Amer-
ican society in the age of urbanization. The same can be said for the twentieth-century theorists who have tried to understand the dynamics of change
on the global scale, whether the model is Robert Redfield's theory of the
modern transformation of folk society, Lenin's linkage of imperialism and
capitalism, Immanuel Wallerstein's model of world systems, or William
McNeill's description of the opening and closing of the Eurasian ecumene.

Postmodernism rejects such efforts as not simply wrong but wrong-
headed. Social systems, say the postmodernists, are too fragmented, multiple, and uncentered for any model to encompass. All encompassing "meta-
narratives" and comprehensive models inevitably privilege the powerful and
ignore alternative voices. They are dangerous and deluded, for the roots of
totalitarianism lie in the ambitious "project of the Enlightenment" and the

idea that rational thought is adequate to reorder human behavior. As a result, postmodernism rejects universalism as a false front that conceals the intent of one group to dominate another. With good reason, the secular universalism of communism is seen as a front for Russian imperialism, market ideologies as fronts for Coca-Cola imperialism, and the religious universalism of Christianity as a front for cultural imperialism.

Comprehensive models are also seen as bound to failure. Because societies are inevitably messier than the theories that try to comprehend them, grand schemes will obscure more than they illuminate, for they are always based on assumptions and selectivity among data. Big theories thus ask more of the intellect than is possible. Because all knowledge is "local" or based in particular situations, say postmodernists, what is left is the stance of the ethnographer or the artist. The former can try to understand fragments in detail without feeling guilty about working on a small scale. The latter can represent and reflect glimpses of the world that audiences can do with as they will. In each case, the goal is to elicit and articulate place stories, personal stories, and group stories that form a collage of understanding.

Cities in this postmodern view are constantly rotating kaleidoscopes. Grand planning theories in the Enlightenment tradition are judged to do more harm than good by trying to freeze urban variety. Georges Haussmann, Le Corbusier, and Robert Moses all refused to see their schemes as both self-serving and impossible to fully implement because the parts of cities do not fit together in a stable mosaic (a comforting metaphor that finds pattern in multiplicity). Neither social nor philosophical glue now holds the fragments together. At best those pieces of understanding are chips of glass in constant motion, catching light in ever-changing ways. All we can really know is particular experiences and the changing ways that we give them meanings. Only the artist can know the city, certainly not the social ecologist.

A second version of postmodernism combines aesthetic and political criticism. The contemporary city, say the critics, is artificial. It is a place of mass-produced and unauthentic environments, a land of parts that are as interchangeable as the plastic decorations that can turn the Kon-Tiki Room into Ye Olde English Pub overnight. It is also an environment of appetites in which a culture of consumption has substituted for an authentic connection to the production of real value (do we hear Marx and Veblen here?). Metaphors for the postmodern city are the New York–New York hotel and casino in Las Vegas and Universal Studio's Citywalk in Burbank, California, deliberately constructed environments in which the shopping mall is packaged as a "real" urban experience.

The alternative to the artificially homogenized city, say these postmodern critics, is to reauthenticize everyday experience as part of a political effort that counters capitalist hegemony by reaching out to workers, ethnic groups, women, and others on the margins and undersides of power. What matters most is to identify a multiplicity of groups that stand in opposition to the overarching claims of the state, or transnational capitalism. In this effort, place and region are viewed as possible points of cultural and political resistance. This interpretation has been proposed by sociologists and regional planners such as Manuel Castells, particularly on the basis of national separatist movements in Europe. Pierre Clavel's study of "opposition planning" in Appalachia applies it to the United States. Clavel finds that regional identity itself becomes a tool of sociopolitical resistance against economic and political exploitation, asserting that "cultural differentiation also can reinforce local capacity. Resistance to external control, whether the resistance is organized by the local bourgeoisie or by some other group (such as the antigrowth coalition), requires a positive motivation and a set of symbols around which to develop a program."[54]

Both of these postmodernisms, with their converging emphasis on the local over the comprehensive, have their points. They have certainly informed this essay, with its effort to understand a particular place and its peoples in history and context. But neither analytic nor political postmodernism fully comprehends Washington. In the face of the postmodern critique, it has been and remains intensely *modern*. It is a city that has shaped and been shaped by the twentieth century. The sense of place and region in Washington has functioned *within* comprehensive systems and patterns and has been fueled by the city's growth as a capital.

Washington is deeply centered, conceptually and physically. Both the American nation and its federal government, after all, are epitomes of the Enlightenment. They are consciously created, comprehensive institutions, and they are embodied in the national city. Indeed, a basic purpose of the federal government is to make universal claims and inspire universal obligations. Despite government downsizing, Washington institutions and workers operate on vast scales and at high levels of generality. Their charge and tasks are rooted in the nineteenth-century creation and defense of the nation-state and in the twentieth-century articulation and expansion of state functions.

Washington is also far from the fragmented landscape that is said to characterize the postmodern metropolis. It has an instantly identifiable core of great size and inertia. Visitors may not know where to find the center of

Orange County, California, but the functional and symbolic heart of Washington is never in doubt. Thanks to James McMillan, Daniel Burnham, and many others, the cityscape revolves around a clearly ordered set of public spaces and places. Since the City Beautiful era, it has been a laboratory for comprehensive planning for transportation, parks, and core redevelopment.

In turn, Washington's public core is encompassed by an intensive employment district that spans both sides of the Potomac and serves the single dominant industry of government and its friends. Business as well as federal employment has gradually lost its local roots. The leaders of the Board of Trade since 1950 have included fewer southerners and more northerners, along with a core of second- or third-generation Washingtonians. Many of the northerners have been professional managers with national careers and cosmopolitan allegiances.[55] They have provided a receptive audience for the restatement of the southern commercial strategy in nonregional terms, shifting local economic discussion from the language of geographic imperialism to the spatially neutral industrial categories of modern economic analysis.[56] Serving this functional and symbolic heart is a thriving system of radial commuter rail and subway lines—the standard twentieth-century solution to integrate cities as different as New York and Singapore.

Surrounding the ceremonial and functional core are four distinct "realms." Like the classic modern city, these parts have distinct identities, but they are understood in relation to the whole—they are parts of a single social and economic machine like Cleveland's east and west sides or Chicago's north, south, and west sides. Their key economic institutions are all tied functionally to central institutions and decision makers. They are parts of an easily assembled puzzle, not chips in a kaleidoscope.[57]

Close-in is a diamond-shaped set of gentrified neighborhoods that has emerged in the half century since World War II.[58] This realm is anchored by Foggy Bottom, Adams-Morgan, Capitol Hill, and Southwest. In many of these areas, white households have replaced blacks through their clout in the real estate market and the power of conscious redevelopment. This is the city of apartments and row houses, chic restaurants and sojourning lobbyists, singles and childless couples, sexual energy, and raw careerism—the counterpart of neighborhoods in Manhattan, San Francisco, and the North Side of Chicago.

Northwest Washington beyond Rock Creek Park, Montgomery County, and the fringe of Prince Georges County housing the University of Maryland constitute the homeland of Washington's liberal establishment. This quadrant has continued the northwestward expansion of the nineteenth century's West End and Francis Newlands's turn-of-the-century developments. It is the location of fashionable institutions and schools and the medical research complex of the National Institutes of Health. Montgomery County has accommodated much of the Jewish population of the metropolitan area. The county's residents tend to maintain close ties to the northeastern states; as consumers they are the area's most New York–focused and fashion-conscious suburbanites.[59]

The Virginia suburbs, especially Faixfax County and its westward extensions, are far more southern. They retained residual traces of segregationist values such as a racially closed housing market until the 1970s. The presence of the Pentagon and the Central Intelligence Agency has tended to attract migrants (including military retirees) with previous experience of Sunbelt military bases and defense contractors. If Montgomery County reproduces the suburbs of Philadelphia and New York, Fairfax County reproduces the up-to-date urban South of northside Atlanta and North Dallas with an emphasis on the pleasures of unregulated entrepreneurship.

The southeastern half of the metropolitan area—Northeast and Southeast Washington and Prince Georges County, Maryland—contrasts with both Fairfax and Montgomery Counties. Here is the minority metropolis, with low-income black city neighborhoods blending into middle-class black neighborhoods across the District line. In contrast to Montgomery and Fairfax Counties, Prince Georges County has followed a path in which the rural South has adapted to the economic and political empowerment of blacks. Historically part of the corn and tobacco farming Tidewater, the county saw the most entrenched opposition to racial desegregation. The arrival of middle-class blacks seeking a suburban alternative to the District of Columbia, however, has made it a mixed society in which both races share political power.[60]

Nor—to conclude a brief canvass—is Washington a city of postmodern politics. The central political issue since the 1940s has been the modern *American* problem of finding political voice and economic opportunity for black citizens. Organized pressure for changes in the city's strict codes of racial segregation appeared in 1947–48 with an executive order barring racial discrimination in federal employment, reports from a President's Committee on Civil Rights, and findings by a National Committee on Segregation in the Nation's Capital. Catholic schools desegregated in 1950, most private restaurants and theaters in the District between 1951 and 1953, and public schools and parks in 1954. Suburban Maryland counties implemented freedom-of-choice plans for their public schools in 1955, and northern Virginia school systems integrated after the collapse of Massive Resistance in 1959. Resisting the changes were southern members of the House Committee on the District of Columbia, who attacked integration of District parks, public housing, employment, and schools from the 1940s until as late as 1962.[61]

As elsewhere around the country, blacks followed the reaffirmation of basic rights with a drive for self-determination. The first step in Washington was limited home rule in the District of Columbia in 1974.[62] The initial direction of the new government came from a liberal black-white coalition, but the disparity of populations (70 percent black) led, in turn, to black control of local politics in the later 1980s and 1990s under the erratic direction of Mayor Marion Barry (1979–90, 1995–98).

These efforts at political change have operated within the paradigm of nineteenth-century politics. The periodic interventions of Congress, from the abolition of territorial government in 1874 to the imposition of a financial control board in 1995, are the local version of the state legislative intervention that long plagued U.S. cities. Political groupings and leadership since home rule have functioned within the paradigm of entrenched machines and occasional bursts of reform. Marion Barry's use of city government jobs and contracts to build a base of political support is classic machine politics. So was his ability to maintain working-class support despite criminal conviction and to secure a new term in 1994. The one-term mayoral interregnum of Sharon Pratt Kelly is another story of reformers as fading morning glories.[63]

Metropolitan Washington thus remains a national and international city, understandable as a phenomenon of the modern age. The national roles developed over two centuries and the international roles over one century, driving economic growth and social change. Washington is a Tidewater city, river city, and southern city, but it is also networked, centered, and large scale—and dealing politically with the legacy of the nineteenth century.

Place and Politics

This study began as an effort to link my long-standing interest in cities and their national influence with a renewed scholarly concern with cultural regions. Numerous scholars in the last decade have reinvigorated the study of regions as cultural and political categories and as policy tools. At one extreme, such attention can blur into a romantic cultural conservatism that may help to validate submerged nationalisms. At the other extreme is the attempt to use scholarship to identify points of resistance to global capitalism. In between is the more modest and realistic goal of studying and understanding region as one of the middle institutions that mediate between individuals and global systems. Institutions in the middle may also be nonprofit organizations, churches, or city-states, and each type has its own growing literature. Analysis of regions as mediators draws substantially on social science models of economic and social behavior, but it is thoroughly historical in its focus on the changing character and affiliations of particular places over time.

In addressing Washington, I have tried to study this mediating dynamic in both horizontal and vertical dimensions. Washington is linked to its site and its adjoining regions, and it functions within transregional networks. From the interaction of lateral ties and networks arises much of Washington's complexity. It is central *and* liminal, national core *and* economic periphery, focus and articulator of national political culture *and* border zone among regional cultures. It is place, community, and political terrain.

The metropolis has grown as part of the multigenerational effort to construct and define a national state, to shape its character, and to project its influence abroad. If there is a "project of the Enlightenment," the American nation and its capital are front and center. Its founding generation viewed the capital both as a national symbol and as a practical tool for overcoming centrifugal regionalism.

The city, moreover, has been involved from the start in regional struggles for economic, social, and political influence. Regions have hierarchies of dominance and subordination, contact zones of growth and shrinkage. As a border community, Washington has been a site of contestation and uncertainty where new social patterns have struggled to emerge. Nowhere has this been more clear than in the history of black freedom and empowerment, for Washington's particular location has also made it a practical as well as a symbolic site for identifying and "discussing" the position of black Americans. For white Americans, this has meant the series of controversies over the antebellum slave trade, voting rights after the Civil War, segregation in the federal service in the early twentieth century, and integration of public facilities in the later twentieth century. For blacks it has also meant debates about the ability to sustain a centralized elite and the value of such an elite.

The character of regional contests has changed over the city's two centuries. In the nineteenth century contestation was explicitly economic and political. The city was engaged in rivalries for commercial control of the West, debates and war over slavery and its expansion, battles over the political and economic reconstruction of the South. In the twentieth century the regional encounter has been much more an implicit contest of cultures. Outside the realm of civil rights, region has been social rather than political. It is a facet of everyday life, a continuing category that is repeatedly reconstructed and reformed at the level of individual, family, and neighborhood.

The specific findings for Washington question the common theoretical assumption of regional hegemony and unidirectional change in which an economically dominant and culturally aggressive core region absorbs peripheral areas and supplants their traditional cultures. Regional change in Washington has not operated in parallel in the public spheres of business and politics and the private realms of personal behavior and allegiance. Washington at the end of the twentieth century experienced substantial and almost certainly permanent accommodation to the public values of the North and was integrated into the communication networks of the Northeast core. At the same time, improvements in transportation and communication enhanced its role as a metropolitan focus for southern culture. Its border location worked as much to concentrate and reconfirm southern connections as to facilitate northern incorporation. Such southern ties were not "relict cultural slopes" but rather an updating of connections as a southern destination point and staging ground for return contact.[64]

The endurance of Washington's southern character despite strong cosmopolitan influences supports the larger argument for an enduring South that can modernize without northernizing. "New" has meant northern and megalopolitan, but it has also meant southern and Chesapeake. In Washington the evidence thus suggests that regional orientation is now a reserved rather than an oppositional realm. Regional identity and connections provide many black Washingtonians with a separate sphere that supplements big-city life. For middle- and upper-status residents of both races, they offer alternative arenas of consumption within the reach of an affluent metropolis. Rather than to the ideas of Manuel Castells and Pierre Clavel, I find a greater similarity to the work of John Shelton Reed, who has argued that the members of the new middle class in southern cities make self-conscious choices to incorporate traditional "southern" values and behaviors into their nontraditional lives. Whether raised inside or outside the region, such inhabitants of the new urban South construct behavioral patterns that define distinctiveness within a larger modernizing society.[65] In the same way, the regional rootedness of blacks and the voluntary regionalism of whites are means of self-definition within a mobile society. Southernness in Washington survived the changes of the second half of the nineteenth century largely intact and adapted to the further changes of the middle twentieth century. The city is substantially more northern now than it was in 1865, more national, more international, but also southern in new as well as old ways.

We can conclude by returning to the fiction of Edward Jones. The stories in *Lost in the City* are reminders of the multiple ways that contemporary Washington as a city structures the lives of these residents. Place survives as an important influence on daily life (in Jones's fiction, in the form of neighborhood identities), but it is a variable that is continually redefined and reinterpreted. Over two centuries, for example, the Potomac River has steadily lost importance as part of a national production system and gained as a place and item of recreational consumption. Region—repeatedly reinforced by generations of newcomers to the metropolitan area—remains an important identifier and social tag. As a border city between East and West and then between South and North, Washington has encapsulated and mediated some of the essential divisions among Americans. As the story of Marie's mother reminds us, Washington has always had a special meaning as the national metropolis. Its institutions have created national and international connections and networks that frame and alter regional patterns.

In the process, Washington has been the backdrop on which different groups of Americans have drawn their ideas about the nation's identity and destiny. Was the United States to be a coastal or continental nation? The location of Washington was an emphatic statement of the importance of the western territories. Were the southern states to set the standards for the nation, with New England an isolated appendage like Canada's maritime provinces? Or was the commercial and industrial North to direct national growth? The character of Washington reflected the ebb and flow of regional economic power and cultural influence. Would the United States evolve from a federation into a centralized state? Was the growing nation to become a major actor in international politics? Here, too, the changing mix of Washington's monuments and organizations demonstrated and facilitated the expanding reach of national government.

Politics is about social claims as well as economic goals—claims for legal rights, social standing, and cultural validation. Washington's institutions and cityscape have represented and embodied values that speak to general rather than parochial interests. The capital has thus been an intensely political setting where the claims of regions or groups can take on the aura of nationality rather than specificity. Virginia land speculators asserted that they had the good of the republic at heart; educational and scientific entrepreneurs describe their work as filling national needs; blacks, radical Republicans, and southerners have contested which system of race relations best serves the needs of the nation.

For two hundred years we have used Washington to anticipate and visualize our national future. Where Washington has fallen short, as in racial equality and economic opportunity, so has the United States. But also on the political terrain of Washington we have sketched the images of ideal Americas—a benevolent nation, a unified nation, an educated nation, a prosperous nation, a just nation.

NOTES

CHAPTER 1

1. Theoretical understanding of the ways that images are constructed and function is still limited. See Anselm Strauss, *Images of the American City* (New York: Free Press, 1961); Rob Shields, *Places on the Margin: Alternative Geographies of Modernity* (London: Routledge, 1991); and Lloyd Rodwin and Rob Hollister, *Cities of the Mind: Images and Themes of the City in the Social Sciences* (New York: Plenum, 1984).

2. Kennedy quoted in Arthur M. Schlesinger Jr., *A Thousand Days* (Boston: Houghton Mifflin, 1965), 673.

3. Willie Morris, *The Last of the Southern Girls* (New York: Knopf, 1973), 62.

4. Citations of different turning points include Atlee Shidler, quoted in Barbara Palmer, "Myths of Washington," *Washingtonian*, January 1980, 90 [Civil War and Reconstruction]; Fletcher Knebel, "Washington: America's Home Town," *Look*, April 26, 1960, 36–41 [World War I]; Federal Writers' Project, *Washington, D.C.: A Guide to the Nation's Capital* (New York: Hastings House, 1942), 3 [New Deal]; Ben Bagdakian, "The Five Different Washingtons," in Bill Adler, ed., *Washington: A Reader* (New York: Meredith Press, 1967), 262–65 [New Deal]; David Brinkley, *Washington Goes to War* (New York: Knopf, 1988) [World War II]; Michael Frome, *Washington: A Modern Guide to the Nation's Capital* (Garden City, N.Y.: Doubleday, 1960), 9 [1950s]; Joseph Rauh, quoted in *Washingtonian*, October 1985, 248 [1950s]; Haynes Johnson, "The Capital of Success," *Washington Post Magazine*, February 2, 1986 [1960s]; Sam Smith, *Captive Capital: Colonial Life in Modern Washington* (Bloomington: Indiana University Press, 1974), 17 [1960s and 1970s]; Julius Hobson Jr., quoted in David Ruffin, "Washington, D.C.: A Thriving Center of Power and Culture," *Black Enterprise* 17 (May 1987): 78 [1970s]; *Guest Informant: 1994 Washington, D.C., Area Edition* (Woodland Hills, Calif.: LIN Cellular Communication Group, 1994) [1970s]. The publishers of the standard national and regional *Who's Who* series shifted the District of Columbia out of the South/Southwest volume in 1976–77.

5. Gore Vidal, *Washington, D.C.* (Boston: Little, Brown, 1967), 251.

6. Stennis quoted in Howard Means, "The Northernization of Washington," *Washingtonian*, August 1978, 83.

7. Residual southernness remained a commonly invoked explanation of local behavior and politics into the 1990s. See Lee May, "Socially, Color Line Is Still Drawn in Nation's Capital," *Los Angeles Times*, January 17, 1989; "Once Again Snowstorm Halts U.S. Government," *New York Times*, January 27, 1987; "Washington, D.C.: A Second Revolution," *Economist* 303 (April 16, 1988): special section 1–18.

8. Eisenhower, from news conference, May 11, 1955, quoted in James Clapp, *The City: A Dictionary of Quotable Thoughts on Cities and Urban Life* (New Brunswick, N.J.: Center for Urban Policy Research, 1984), 75; Nixon quoted in Frank DeFord, "Home without Homeowners: Washington, D.C.," *Sports Illustrated*, July 2, 1979, 68.

9. Larry McMurtry, *Cadillac Jack* (New York: Simon and Schuster, 1982), 235. Joel Garreau, in *The Nine Nations of North America* (Boston: Houghton Mifflin, 1981), 104, describes Washington as an aberration and also quotes Jimmy Carter on Washington as an island.

10. See Paul Knox, "The Restless Urban Landscape: Economic and Sociocultural Change and the Transformation of Washington, D.C.," *Annals of the Association of American Geographers* 81 (June 1991): 181–209.

11. Karl Shapiro, *Collected Poems, 1940–1978* (New York: Random House, 1978), 136.

12. Classic examples of the delineation of hinterland zones include Mildred Hartsough, *The Twin Cities as a Metropolitan Market*, Studies in Social Sciences, no. 18 (Minneapolis: University of Minnesota, 1925); Chauncy Harris, *Salt Lake City: A Regional Capital* (Chicago: University of Chicago Department of Geography, 1940); Edward Ullman, *Mobile: Industrial Seaport and Trade Center* (Chicago: University of Chicago Department of Geography, 1943); and Howard Green, "Hinterland Boundaries of New York City and Boston in Southern New England," *Economic Geography* 31 (October 1955): 283–300.

13. Donald W. Meinig, *The Shaping of America: A Geographical Perspective on 500 Years of History*, vol. 1: *Atlantic America, 1492–1800* (New Haven, Conn.: Yale University Press, 1986); Robert D. Mitchell, "The Formation of Early American Cultural Regions," in James Gibson, ed., *European Settlement and Development in North America* (Toronto: University of Toronto Press, 1978), 75.

14. The trans-Appalachian expansion of cultural regions is discussed in Mitchell, "Early American Cultural Regions"; Henry Glassie, *Patterns in the Material Folk Culture of the Eastern United States* (Philadelphia: University of Pennsylvania Press, 1968); and Terry G. Jordan and Lester Rowntree, *The Human Mosaic* (New York: Harper and Row, 1986), 10. Examples of detailed analysis include Richard L. Power, *Planting Corn Belt*

Culture: The Impress of the Upland Southerner and Yankee in the Old Northwest (Indianapolis: Indiana Historical Society, 1953); Terry G. Jordan, "The Imprint of the Upper South on Mid-Nineteenth Century Texas," *Annals of the Association of American Geographers* 57 (December 1967): 667–90; and Donald Meinig, *Imperial Texas* (Austin: University of Texas Press, 1969).

15. The growth and interaction of cultural regions in the American West is treated by Donald Meinig in "The Mormon Culture Region," *Annals of the Association of American Geographers* 55 (June 1965): 191–220, *Southwest: Three Peoples in Geographical Change* (New York: Oxford University Press, 1971), and "American Wests: Preface to a Geographical Introduction," *Annals of the Association of American Geographers* 62 (June 1972): 159–84.

16. See Glassie, *Material Folk Culture*; Conrad Arensberg, "American Communities," *American Anthropologist* 57 (December 1955): 1143–62; Hans Kurath and Raven I. McDavid Jr., *The Pronunciation of English in the Atlantic States* (Ann Arbor: University of Michigan Press, 1962); Fred Kniffen, "Folk Housing: Key to Diffusion," *Annals of the Association of American Geographers* 55 (December 1965): 549–77; Peirce F. Lewis, "Common Houses, Cultural Spoor," *Landscape* 19 (January 1975): 1–22; Terry G. Jordan, *Texas Log Buildings* (Austin: University of Texas Press, 1978); Wilbur Zelinsky, "An Approach to the Religious Geography of the United States: Patterns of Church Membership in 1952," *Annals of the Association of American Geographers* 51 (June 1961): 139–93; James Shortridge, "Patterns of Religion in the United States," *Geographical Review* 66 (October 1976): 420–34; Edward T. Price, "The Central Courthouse Square in the American County Seat," *Geographical Review* 58 (January 1968): 29–60; Daniel Elazar, *American Federalism: The View from the States* (New York: Crowell, 1972).

17. Raymond Gastil, *Cultural Regions of the United States* (Seattle: University of Washington Press, 1975), 26–33 (quotations, p. 26), 180, 190, 196; Wilbur Zelinsky, *The Cultural Geography of the United States* (Englewood Cliffs, N.J.: Prentice-Hall, 1973), 77–82; Bruce Bigelow, "Roots and Regions: A Summary Definition of the Cultural Geography of America," *Journal of Geography* 79 (November 1980): 218–29.

18. John F. Rooney Jr., Wilbur Zelinsky, and Dean R. Louder, eds., *This Remarkable Continent: An Atlas of United States and Canadian Society and Cultures* (College Station: Texas A&M University Press, 1982).

19. Ary J. Lamme III, "From Boston in One Hundred Years: Christian Science, 1970," *Professional Geographer* 23 (October 1971): 229–32; Wilbur Zelinsky, "The Roving Palate: North America's Ethnic Restaurant Cuisine," *Geoforum* 16 (1985): 51–72; John Rooney, "The Pigskin Cult and Other Sunbelt Sports," *American Demographics* 8 (September 1986): 38–43; Rooney, Zelinsky, and Louder, *Remarkable Continent*, 215, 244, 272–74. Popular acceptance of "Sunbelt" as a new regional term is another example of regional patterning that spans traditional boundaries. See Richard Bernard and Bradley Rice, eds., *Sunbelt Cities: Politics and Growth since World War II* (Austin: Univer-

sity of Texas Press, 1983), 1–30, and Carl Abbott, "New West, New South, New Region: The Discovery of the Sunbelt," in Raymond Mohl, ed., *Searching for the Sunbelt* (Knoxville: University of Tennessee Press, 1990).

20. Robert Dorman, *The Revolt of the Provinces: The Regionalist Movement in America, 1920–1945* (Chapel Hill: University of North Carolina Press, 1993); Michael O'Brien, *The Idea of the American South, 1920–1941* (Baltimore: Johns Hopkins University Press, 1979); William G. Robbins, "The 'Plundered Province' Thesis and the Historiography of the American West," *Pacific Historical Review* 55 (November 1986): 577–98; Gene Gressley, "Regionalism and the Twentieth-Century West," in Jerome O. Steffen, ed., *The American West: New Perspectives, New Dimensions* (Norman: University of Oklahoma Press, 1979), 197–234.

21. Jacob M. Price, "Economic Function and the Growth of American Port Towns in the Eighteenth Century," *Perspectives in American History* 8 (1974): 121–86; James E. Vance, *The Merchant's World: The Geography of Wholesaling* (Englewood Cliffs, N.J.: Prentice-Hall, 1970), 68–79; Robert G. Albion, *The Rise of New York Port, 1815–1860* (New York: Scribner's, 1939); David Gilchrist, ed., *The Growth of the Seaport Cities, 1790–1825* (Charlottesville: University of Virginia Press, 1967); James Livingood, *The Philadelphia-Baltimore Trade Rivalry, 1790–1840* (Harrisburg: Pennsylvania Historical and Museum Commission, 1947); Allan Pred, *Urban Growth and the Circulation of Information: The United States System of Cities, 1790–1840* (Cambridge: Harvard University Press, 1973) and *Urban Growth and City Systems in the United States, 1840–1860* (Cambridge: Harvard University Press, 1980); A. L. Kohlmeier, *The Old Northwest as the Keystone in the Arch of American Federal Union* (Bloomington, Ind.: Principia Press, 1938); John M. Clark, *The Grain Trade in the Old Northwest* (Urbana: University of Illinois Press, 1966); David Ward, *Cities and Immigrants* (New York: Oxford University Press, 1971), 11–49; David R. Meyer, "Emergence of the American Manufacturing Belt: An Interpretation," *Journal of Historical Geography* 9 (April 1983): 145–74.

22. Edward Ullman, "Regional Development and the Geography of Concentration," *Papers and Proceedings of the Regional Science Association* 4 (1958): 179–98.

23. Jean Gottman, *Megalopolis: The Urbanized Northeastern Seaboard of the United States* (New York: Twentieth-Century Fund, 1961).

24. J. M. S. Careless, "Frontierism, Metropolitanism, and Canadian History," *Canadian Historical Review* 35 (March 1954): 1–21; Donald Kerr, "Metropolitan Dominance in Canada," in John Warkentin, ed., *Canada: A Geographical Interpretation* (Toronto: Methuen, 1968), 531–55; Donald F. Davis, "The Metropolitan Theme and the Writing of Canadian Urban History," *Urban History Review* 14 (October 1985): 95–114.

25. For a variety of ways to frame world development in core-periphery terms, see William H. McNeill, *The Rise of the West: A History of the Human Community* (Chicago: University of Chicago Press, 1963) and *The Great Frontier: Freedom and Hierarchy in Mod-*

ern Times (Princeton, N.J.: Princeton University Press, 1983); Andre Gunder Frank, *Capitalism and Underdevelopment in Latin America* (New York: Monthly Review Press, 1969); Immanuel Wallerstein, *The Modern World System: Capitalist Agriculture and the European Economy in the Sixteenth Century* (New York: Academic Press, 1974), *The Capitalist World Economy* (New York: Cambridge University Press, 1979), and *The Modern World-System II: Mercantilism and the Consolidation of the European World Economy* (Orlando, Fla.: Academic Press, 1980); Alejandro Portes, "On the Sociology of National Development: Theories and Issues," *American Journal of Sociology* 82 (July 1976): 55–85; Bernard Bailyn, "The Challenge of Modern Historiography," *American Historical Review* 87 (February 1982): 1–24, and *The Peopling of British North America: An Introduction* (New York: Knopf, 1986); and Peter J. Hugill, "Structural Change in the Core Region of the World-economy, 1830–1945," *Journal of Historical Geography* 14 (April 1988): 111–27.

26. Charles O. Paullin, *Atlas of the Historical Geography of the United States* (Washington, D.C.: Carnegie Institution, 1932); Richard Bensel, *Sectionalism and American Political Development, 1880–1980* (Madison: University of Wisconsin Press, 1984).

27. *Manchester Guardian*, November 17, 1832, quoted in Asa Briggs, *Victorian Cities* (New York: Harper and Row, 1965), 52.

28. Two classic studies that have framed our understanding of these changes are H. Stuart Hughes, *Consciousness and Society: The Reorientation of European Social Thought* (New York: Knopf, 1958), and Henry May, *The End of American Innocence* (New York: Knopf, 1959).

29. Kenneth Boulding, *The Organizational Revolution* (New York: Harper and Row, 1953).

30. Louis Galambos, "The Emerging Organizational Synthesis in American History," *Business History Review* 44 (Autumn 1970): 279–90; Robert Berkhofer Jr., "The Organizational Interpretation of American History: A New Synthesis," *Prospects* 4 (1979): 611–29; John Kenneth Galbraith, *American Capitalism* (Boston: Houghton Mifflin, 1952); Robert Wiebe, *The Search for Order, 1877–1920* (New York: Hill and Wang, 1967) and *The Segmented Society: An Introduction to the Meaning of America* (New York: Oxford University Press, 1975).

31. Michael Sorkin, ed., *Variations on a Theme Park: The New American City and the End of Public Space* (New York: Hill and Wang, 1992); Sharon Zukin, *Landscapes of Power* (Berkeley: University of California Press, 1991).

32. John Shelton Reed, *My Tears Spoiled My Aim and Other Reflections on Southern Culture* (Columbia: University of Missouri Press, 1993), 104–5.

33. Walter Nugent, "Where Is the American West? Report on a Survey," *Montana* 42 (Summer 1992): 2–23 (quotation, p. 13); Carl Abbott, "United States Regional History as an Instructional Field: The Practice of College and University History Departments," *Western Historical Quarterly* 21 (May 1990): 197–217.

34. William Sharpe and Leonard Wallock, "Reading the Modern City," in Sharpe and Wallock, eds., *Visions of the Modern City: Essays in History, Art, and Literature* (Baltimore: Johns Hopkins University Press, 1987), 26–27.

35. In my hall closet are caps with Cincinnati Reds and Cleveland Browns logos—affirmations of urban loyalties from my Ohio upbringing in the days when Wally Post roamed the outfield at Crosley Field and Otto Graham handed off the ball at Municipal Stadium.

36. James Sterling Young, *The Washington Community, 1800–1828* (New York: Columbia University Press, 1966).

37. Gary Snyder, *Turtle Island* (New York: New Directions Publishing, 1974), 44.

CHAPTER 2

1. The tentative name for the new city is from the Georgetown newspaper *The Times, and the Potowmack Packet*, October 20, 1790, reporting on Washington's upriver trip, quoted in Nelson R. Burr, "The Federal City Depicted, 1612–1801," in Walter W. Ristow, ed., *A La Carte: Selected Papers on Maps and Atlases* (Washington, D.C.: Library of Congress, 1972), 126–43.

2. Milton C. Cummings Jr. and Matthew C. Price, "The Creation of Washington, D.C.: Political Symbolism and Practical Problem Solving in the Establishment of a Capital City for the United States of America, 1787–1850," in John Taylor, Jean G. Lengelle, and Caroline Andrew, eds., *Capital Cities: International Perspectives* (Ottawa: Carleton University Press, 1993), 220–22.

3. Bruce A. Ragsdale, "George Washington, the British Tobacco Trade, and Economic Opportunity in Prerevolutionary Virginia," *Virginia Magazine of History and Biography* 97 (April 1989): 133–62.

4. George Washington to Charles Carter, ca. August 1754, quoted in Marc Egnal, *A Mighty Empire: The Origins of the American Revolution* (Ithaca, N.Y.: Cornell University Press, 1988), 87; Washington to Thomas Johnson, July 20, 1770, quoted in John Lauritz Larson, "'Bind the Union Together': The National Union and the Struggle for Internal Improvements," *Journal of American History* 74 (September 1987): 366.

5. Washington's choice of a southeasterly center point for the federal district required Congress to amend the Residence Act to allow the inclusion of territory not authorized in the original legislation (the lands south of the Eastern Branch in Maryland and the territory on the Virginia side).

6. George Washington to Thomas Jefferson, March 31, 1791, quoted in Cummings and Price, "Creation of Washington," 223.

7. Plans and preparations are described in Stephen E. Ambrose, *Undaunted Courage:*

Meriwether Lewis, Thomas Jefferson, and the Opening of the American West (New York: Simon and Schuster, 1996), 69–107.

8. See Jefferson's reference to a "nation of Virginia" in 1799 in Peter Onuf, *The Origins of the Federal Republic: Jurisdictional Controversies in the United States, 1775–1787* (Philadelphia: University of Pennsylvania Press, 1983), 27.

9. The territorial dispute was resolved in 1780, when the two states agreed to an extension of the Mason-Dixon line beyond Maryland as Pennsylvania's southern border.

10. Egnal, *Mighty Empire*.

11. From Beverly Letter Book, 1761–93, quoted in T. H. Breen, *Tobacco Culture: The Mentality of the Great Tidewater Planters on the Eve of Revolution* (Princeton, N.J.: Princeton University Press, 1985), 184.

12. Drew McCoy, "James Madison and Visions of American Nationality in the Confederation Period: A Regional Perspective," in Richard Beeman, Stephen Botein, and Edward C. Carter II, eds., *Beyond Confederation: Origins of the Constitution and American National Identity* (Chapel Hill: University of North Carolina Press, 1987), 228–34.

13. Arthur Pierce Middleton, *Tobacco Coast: A Maritime History of Chesapeake Bay in the Colonial Era* (Newport News, Va.: The Mariners' Museum, 1953), 40–42; Allan Kulikoff, *Tobacco and Slaves: The Development of Southern Cultures in the Chesapeake, 1680–1800* (Chapel Hill: University of North Carolina Press, 1986), 226–28.

14. *Virginia Journal*, November 25, 1784, quoted in Peter S. Onuf, "Maryland," in Michael Allen Gillespie and Michael Lienesch, eds., *Ratifying the Constitution* (Lawrence: University Press of Kansas, 1989), 188.

15. Thomas Jefferson to James Madison, December 8, 1784, in Julian Boyd, ed., *Papers of Thomas Jefferson* (Princeton, N.J.: Princeton University Press, 1953), 7:558; Joseph Harman Jr., "Sic et Non: Thomas Jefferson and Internal Improvements," *Journal of the Early Republic* 7 (Winter 1987): 335–50.

16. The map is reproduced in Burr, "The Federal City Depicted."

17. *Virginia Journal*, August 17, 1786, in Onuf, "Maryland," 189. Also see Larson, "'Bind the Union Together,'" 366.

18. Charles Royster, *Light-Horse Harry Lee and the Legacy of the American Revolution* (New York: Knopf, 1981), 70–77.

19. Breen (*Tobacco Culture*) considers the political consequences of the switch to grain through the lens of cultural change and the self-image of Virginia agriculturalists. Joyce Appleby, in a series of essays, considers the political consequences from the perspective of changing clusters of economic interest. See "The 'Agrarian Myth' in the Early Republic" and "What Is Still American in Jefferson's Political Philosophy"

in Joyce Appleby, *Liberalism and Republicanism in the Historical Imagination* (Cambridge: Harvard University Press, 1992).

20. Thomas M. Doerflinger, *A Vigorous Spirit of Enterprise: Merchants and Economic Development in Revolutionary Philadelphia* (Chapel Hill: University of North Carolina Press, 1986), 74, 92–93, 107–15, 288–89, 337.

21. Calvin Jillson and Rick K. Wilson, *Congressional Dynamics: Structure, Coordination, and Choice in the First American Congress, 1774–1789* (Stanford, Calif.: Stanford University Press, 1994), 285–86; H. James Henderson, *Party Politics in the Continental Congress* (New York: McGraw-Hill, 1974), 318–21, 432–35.

22. McCoy, "James Madison and Visions of American Nationality," 239–43; Lance Banning, "Virginia," in Gillespie and Lienesch, *Ratifying the Constitution,* 266.

23. Jack P. Greene, "The Constitution of 1787 and the Question of Southern Distinctiveness," in Greene, *Imperatives, Behaviors, and Identities: Essays in Early American Cultural History* (Charlottesville: University Press of Virginia, 1992), 338, 340.

24. Kenneth Bowling, *The Creation of Washington, D.C.: The Idea and Location of the American Capital* (Fairfax, Va.: George Mason University Press, 1991), 3; McCoy, "James Madison and Visions of American Nationality," 237; Greene, "The Constitution of 1787," 332, 336.

25. Adrienne Koch, ed., *Notes of Debates in the Federal Convention of 1787, Reported by James Madison* (Columbus: Ohio State University Press, 1966), 124, 429.

26. Greene, "The Constitution of 1787," 334, 341; Calvin Jillson and Cecil Eubanks, "The Political Structure of Constitution Making: The Federal Constitution of 1787," *American Journal of Political Science* 28 (August 1984): 435–58.

27. For the influence of the new agriculture on urban growth in the Chesapeake, see Carville Earle and Ronald Hoffman, "Staple Crops and Urban Development in the Eighteenth-Century South," *Perspectives in American History* 10 (1976): 5–78, and Jacob M. Price, "Economic Function and the Growth of American Port Towns in the Eighteenth Century," *Perspectives in American History* 8 (1974): 121–86.

28. Bowling, *Creation of Washington,* 8.

29. Henderson, *Party Politics,* 342.

30. Madison in the Constitutional Convention, August 11, 1787, quoted in McCoy, "James Madison and Visions of American Nationality," 251.

31. Anonymous essay attributed to Stephen Hallet, L'Enfant's draftsman in 1791, quoted in Howard Gillette Jr., *Between Justice and Beauty: Race, Planning, and the Failure of Urban Policy in Washington, D.C.* (Baltimore: Johns Hopkins University Press, 1995), 7, and in Pamela Scott, "L'Enfant's Washington Described: The City in the Public Press, 1791–1795," *Washington History* 3 (Spring–Summer 1991): 110.

32. Cummings and Price, "Creation of Washington," 216.

33. Bowling, *Creation of Washington*, 10; McCoy, "James Madison and Visions of American Nationality," 226–28, 251. The same point was made in an anonymous essay by Georgetown merchant George Walker in the *Maryland Journal and Baltimore Advertiser*, January 23, 1789, reproduced in Kenneth R. Bowling, "The Other G. W.: George Walker and the Creation of the American Capital," *Washington History* 3 (Fall–Winter 1991–92): 4–21.

34. The map is reproduced and analyzed in Lester J. Cappon, ed., *Atlas of Early American History: The Revolutionary Era, 1760–1790* (Princeton, N.J.: Princeton University Press, 1976), 58. The map underestimated the westward trend of the coast from Virginia southward.

35. Joseph Martin, *A Comprehensive Description of Virginia and the District of Columbia: Containing a Copious Collection of Geographical, Statistical, Political, Commercial, Religious, Moral, and Miscellaneous Information, Chiefly from Original Sources* (Richmond, Va.: J. W. Randolph, ca. 1834), 497.

36. Larson, "'Bind the Union Together.'"

37. Donald W. Meinig, *The Shaping of America: A Geographical Perspective on 500 Years of History*, vol. 2: *Continental America, 1800–1867* (New Haven, Conn.: Yale University Press, 1993), 339–42.

38. Gillette, *Between Justice and Beauty*, 18–20.

39. George Watterston, *Picture of Washington* (Washington, D.C.: William M. Morrison, 1840), 76.

40. Tobias Lear, *Observations on the River Potomack, the Country Adjacent, and the City of Washington* (New York: Samuel Loudon and Son, 1793), 12; William Q. Force, *Picture of Washington and Its Vicinity for 1848* (Washington, D.C.: W. Q. Force, 1848), 28–31; R. S. Fisher, *Gazetteer of the State of Maryland . . . to Which Is Added a General Account of the District of Columbia* (Baltimore: James S. Waters, 1852), 106; *Bohn's Hand-Book of Washington* (Washington, D.C.: Casimir Bohn, 1856), 80; David Baillie Warden, *A Chorographical and Statistical Description of the District of Columbia, the Seat of the General Government of the United States* (Paris, 1816), 23–25; Jonathan Elliot, *Historical Sketches of the Ten Miles Square, Forming the District of Columbia, with a Picture of Washington, Describing Objects of General Interest or Curiosity, at the Metropolis of the Union; also, A Description of the River Potomac—Its Fish and Wild Fowl* (Washington, D.C.: J. Elliot Jr., 1830), 419–47. Joseph Martin (*Comprehensive Description of Virginia*, 480–91) estimated in 1834 that the Potomac fisheries employed more than 1,000 workers and took 22.5 million shad and 750 million herring, packed into 995,000 barrels.

41. Undated and untitled map drawn by Thomas Jefferson, Manuscripts Department, Library of Congress.

42. Bowling, *Creation of Washington*, 221–24. Perhaps the analogy of New York's East River harbor off the fast-flowing Hudson was in the back of some minds.

43. Lear, *Observations on the River Potomack*, 13. Also see Martin, *Comprehensive Description of Virginia*, 497: "one of the safest and most commodious harbors in America, and is sufficiently deep for the largest Ships, for about 4 ms. above its mouth."

44. Francis Baily, in *Journal of a Tour in Unsettled Parts of North America in 1796 & 1797*, ed. Jack D. L. Holmes (Carbondale: Southern Illinois University Press, 1969), described the "hilly and romantic country" around about Washington. David Baillie Warden (*Chorographical and Statistical Description*, 61) rambled on about the "sublime scenery of a majestic river, beautified by the luxuriant hangings of woods, rocks, and meadows."

45. See Views 14 and 217 in the Machen Collection, Historical Society of Washington, D.C., or the views by George Isham Parkyns (1795) and George Beck (1801) in John W. Reps, *Washington on View: The Nation's Capital since 1790* (Chapel Hill: University of North Carolina Press, 1991), 47, 64.

46. Warden, *Chorographical and Statistical Description*; William Elliot, *The Washington Guide* (Washington City: Franck Taylor, 1837).

47. Jonathan Elliot, *Historical Sketches of the Ten Miles Square*, 92; Watterston, *Picture of Washington*, 5; Force, *Picture of Washington*, 17; John Davis, *Travels of Four Years and a Half in the United States of North America*; Duke de la Rochefoucault-Liancourt, *Travels through the United States of America* (London, 1799); George Walker, "A Description of the Situation and Plan of the City of Washington, Now Building for the Metropolis of America," broadside published in London, March 12, 1793, in Geography and Map Division, Library of Congress; John Hayward, *A Gazetteer of the United States of America* (Hartford: Case, Tiffany and Co., 1853), 611.

48. Andrew Ellicott, *Plan of the City of Washington in the Territory of Columbia* (Philadelphia: Thackara and Vallance, 1792), in Geography and Map Division, Library of Congress.

49. S. S. Moore and T. W. Jones, *The Traveller's Directory . . . of the Main Road from Philadelphia to Washington* (Philadelphia: Matthew Carey, 1802); "Map of Washington City," from *Harper's Magazine*, 1852, in Geography and Map Division, Library of Congress.

50. Ellicott, *Plan of the City*, 1794; Warden, *Chorographical and Statistical Description*; William Elliot, *Washington Guide*; "Geographical, Statistical, and Historical Map of the District of Columbia," from *A Complete Historical, Chronological and Geographical American Atlas* (Philadelphia: H. C. Carey and Isaac Lea, 1822), in Reps, *Washington on View*, 69; D. McClelland, *Map of the City of Washington: Established as the Permanent Seat of the Government of the United States of America* (Washington, D.C., 1846), insert of federal district; *District of Columbia* (New York: J. Higginson, 1850); *Map of the District of Colum-*

bia including the *Cities of Washington, Georgetown, and Alexandria* (1873), Geography and Map Division, Library of Congress.

51. From the Geography and Map Division, Library of Congress, see J. Melish, *Description of the United States* (N.p., 1820–30); T. G. Bradford, *Comprehensive Atlas* (Boston, 1835); and *District of Columbia and Adjacent Country, 1874, Compiled Expressly for Keim's Handbook to Washington and Its Environs* (N.p., 1874).

52. T. Packer, "General View of Washington," hand-colored lithograph, ca. 1840, View 302, Machen Collection, Historical Society of Washington, D.C.

53. Peder Anderson, *View of the City of Washington: The Metropolis of the United States of America: Taken from Arlington House[,] the Residence of George Washington P. Custis Esq.* (Boston: T. Moore, 1838), in Reps, *Washington on View*, 83.

54. Reps, *Washington on View*, 81; Force, *Picture of Washington*, opposite p. 18. A cruder version of the same perspective is a "View from the Lunatic Asylum," ca. 1861, in Reps, *Washington on View*, 166, and ca. 1872 in View 72, Machen Collection, Historical Society of Washington, D.C. Rivers also dominated bird's-eye views of Washington and vicinity during the Civil War, looking south over the city to Virginia and the widening Potomac. See Reps, *Washington on View*, 157, 159.

55. Diary of Manasseh Cutler, quoted in Charles Todd, *The Story of Washington* (New York: Putnam, 1889), 370–74; Jane Wilson Gemmill, *Notes on Washington, or Six Years at the Nation's Capital* (Philadelphia: E. Claxton and Co., 1884), 271. The track may have been that described by Christian Hines as located between F, K, Twenty-first, and Twenty-third Streets in Christian Hines, *Early Recollections of Washington City* (Washington, D.C.: Chronicle Book and Job Print, 1866), 42.

56. Kathryn Allamong Jacob, *Capital Elites: High Society in Washington D.C., after the Civil War* (Washington, D.C.: Smithsonian Institution Press, 1995), 9, 38.

57. Frederick Gutheim, *The Potomac* (New York: Rinehart, 1949), 248; Constance McLaughlin Green, *Washington: Village and Capital, 1800–1878* (Princeton, N.J.: Princeton University Press, 1962), 109, 231; Hines, *Early Recollections*, 43.

58. Augustus Foster, quoted in Todd, *Story of Washington*, 363.

59. Bladensburg at the time of the Revolution had thirty-five households, including seven merchants. Kulikoff, *Tobacco and Slaves*, 228.

60. Bernard L. Herman, "Southern City, National Ambition: Washington's Early Town Houses," in Howard Gillette Jr., ed., *Southern City, National Ambition: The Growth of Early Washington, D.C., 1800–1860* (Washington, D.C.: Center for Washington Area Studies, George Washington University, 1955), 35.

61. Herman, "Washington's Early Town Houses," 21–46; Richard C. Wade, *Slavery in the Cities: The South, 1820–1860* (New York: Oxford University Press, 1964).

62. The following paragraphs draw on Mary Beth Corrigan, "Ties That Bind: The Pursuit of Community and Freedom among Slaves and Free Blacks in the District of Columbia, 1800–1860," in Gillette, *Southern City, National Ambition*, 69–90; Gillette, *Between Justice and Beauty*, 27–43; Letitia Woods Brown, *Free Negroes in the District of Columbia, 1790–1846* (New York: Oxford University Press, 1972); Leonard Curry, *The Free Black in Urban America, 1800–1850: The Shadow of the Dream* (Chicago: University of Chicago Press, 1981); and Green, *Village and Capital*.

63. George Watterston, *The L——— Family at Washington, or A Winter in the Metropolis* (Washington, D.C.: N.p., 1822); Margaret Bayard Smith, *A Winter in Washington, or Memoirs of the Seymour Family* (New York: E. Bliss and E. White, 1824). For one interpretation of the books, see Fredrika J. Teute, "'A Wild, Desolate Place': Life on the Margins in Early Washington," in Gillette, *Southern City, National Ambition*, 47–68.

64. Martin, *Comprehensive Description of Virginia*, 509–12; E. A. Cohen and Co., *A Full Directory for Washington City, Georgetown, and Alexandria* (Washington, D.C.: William Green, 1834); William Elliot, *Washington Guide*; Anthony Reintzel, *The Washington Directory, and Governmental Register, for 1843* (Washington, D.C.: Jno. T. Towers, 1843); *The Washington Directory, and National Register, for 1846; In Two Parts, Compiled and Published Annually by Gaither and Addison* (Washington, D.C.: John T. Towers, 1846); Edward Waite, *The Washington Directory, and Congressional and Executive Register, for 1850* (Washington, D.C.: Columbus Alexander, 1850).

65. Caleb Atwater, *Mysteries of Washington City, during Several Months of the Session of the 28th Congress, by a Citizen of Ohio* (Washington, D.C.: G. A. Sage, 1844), 177–86; Force, *Picture of Washington*, 133. Alexandrians themselves would have disagreed strenuously with this image of rustication. The purpose of retrocession to Virginia in 1846 was to allow Alexandria to push a railroad toward the Shenandoah Valley in the hope of fending off Baltimore merchants. See Harold W. Hurst, "The Merchants of Pre–Civil War Alexandria: A Dynamic Elite in a Progressive City," in J. Kirkpatrick Flack, ed., *Records of the Columbia Historical Society* (Charlottesville: University of Virginia Press, 1989), 52:327–43; David R. Goldfield, *Urban Growth in the Age of Sectionalism: Virginia, 1847–1861* (Baton Rouge: Louisiana State University Press, 1976).

66. Margaret Hall, Letter 14, December 8, 1827, Margaret Hall Papers, Library of Congress.

From Town to Metropolis

1. Margaret Hall, Letter 16, January 2–7, 1828, and Letter 17, January 28, 1828, Margaret Hall Papers, Library of Congress.

2. Caleb Atwater, *Mysteries of Washington City, during Several Months of the Session of the 28th Congress, by a Citizen of Ohio* (Washington, D.C.: G. A. Sage, 1844).

3. Judah Delano, *The Washington Directory* (Washington, D.C.: William Duncan, 1822);

The Washington Directory (Washington, D.C.: S. A. Elliot, 1827 and 1830); E. A. Cohen and Co., A Full Directory for Washington City, Georgetown, and Alexandria (Washington, D.C.: William Green, 1834).

4. George Watterston, Picture of Washington (Washington, D.C.: William M. Morrison, 1840), 7.

5. For example, Alexander McIntire to Jonathan Elliot, January 18, 1823, Jonathan Elliot Papers, in vol. 8-D, reel 38, Peter Force Papers, Library of Congress; George Watterston, Wanderer in Washington (Washington, D.C.: Washington Press, 1829); E. A. Cohen and Co., A Full Directory; Jonathan Elliot, Historical Sketches of the Ten Miles Square, Forming the District of Columbia, with a Picture of Washington, Describing Objects of General Interest or Curiosity, at the Metropolis of the Union; also, A Description of the River Potomac—Its Fish and Wild Fowl (Washington, D.C.: J. Elliot Jr., 1830).

6. R. S. Fisher, Gazetteer of the State of Maryland . . . to Which Is Added a General Account of the District of Columbia (Baltimore: James S. Waters, 1852), 109; Joseph Martin, A Comprehensive Description of Virginia and the District of Columbia: Containing a Copious Collection of Geographical, Statistical, Political, Commercial, Religious, Moral, and Miscellaneous Information, Chiefly from Original Sources (Richmond, Va.: J. W. Randolph, ca. 1834), 471.

7. Bohn's Hand-Book of Washington (Washington, D.C.: Casimir Bohn, 1856).

8. Alexander Mackay, The Western World (Philadelphia: Lea and Blanchard, 1849), 2:108; George Sala, My Diary in America in the Midst of War (London: Tinsley Brothers, 1865), 2:68–70.

9. "Washington in 1859," Harper's New Monthly Magazine, December 1859, 1; "Washington City," Atlantic Monthly, January 1861, 1–8.

10. John Silva Meehan, Journal for 1845–46, entries for December 27, 1845, May 26, July 2, 1846, J. S. Meehan Papers, Library of Congress; John Davis, Travels of Four Years and a Half in the United States of North America: During 1798, 1799, 1801 and 1802 (London, 1803).

CHAPTER 3

1. Frederick Douglass, A Lecture on Our National Capital (Washington, D.C.: Smithsonian Institution Press, 1978), 12.

2. Douglass, Lecture on Our National Capital, 21–22, 26.

3. Fishback to Douglass, May 12, 1877, reel 3, Frederick Douglass Papers, Library of Congress. The apologia, published in the National Republican, May 13, 1877, was an unconvincing effort to plane away the sharp edges of his criticism. See John Blassingame and John McKivigan, eds., The Frederick Douglass Papers, Series One: Speeches, Debates, and Interviews, vol. 4: 1864–1880 (New Haven: Yale University Press, 1991), 443, 475, 618–20.

4. Rupert Vance, *Human Geography of the South* (Chapel Hill: University of North Carolina Press, 1932); William H. Nicholls, *Southern Tradition and Regional Progress* (Chapel Hill; University of North Carolina Press, 1960); Selz C. Mayo, "Social Change, Social Movements, and the Disappearing Sectional South," *Social Forces* 43 (October 1964): 1–10; John C. McKinney and Edgar Thompson, *The South in Continuity and Change* (Durham, N.C.: Duke University Press, 1965); John C. McKinney and Linda Bourque, "The Changing South: National Incorporation of a Region," *American Sociological Review* 36 (June 1971): 399–412; Numan Bartley and Hugh Davis Graham, *The South and the Second Reconstruction* (Baltimore: Johns Hopkins University Press, 1975); Jack Bass and Walter DeVries, *The Transformation of Southern Politics* (New York: Basic Books, 1976).

5. John Shelton Reed, *The Enduring South* (Lexington, Mass.: Lexington Books, 1972); "Fifteen Southerners," *Why the South Will Survive* (Athens: University of Georgia Press, 1981); Louis D. Rubin, ed., *The Lasting South* (Chicago: H. Regnery and Co., 1957); Carl Degler, *Place over Time: The Continuity of Southern Distinctiveness* (Baton Rouge: Louisiana State University Press, 1977). Also see U. B. Phillips, "The Central Theme of Southern History," *American Historical Review* 34 (October 1928): 30–43; John Shelton Reed, *Southerners: The Social Psychology of Sectionalism* (Chapel Hill: University of North Carolina Press, 1983); David R. Goldfield, *Cottonfields and Skyscrapers: Southern City and Region, 1607–1980* (Baton Rouge: Louisiana State University Press, 1982); Charles Roland, "The Ever-Vanishing South," *Journal of Southern History* 48 (February 1982): 3–20; and Carl Degler, "Thesis, Antithesis, Synthesis: The South, the North, and the Nation," *Journal of Southern History* 53 (February 1987): 12–13. Wilbur Zelinsky's classic article, "Where the South Begins: The Northern Limit of the Cis-Appalachian South in Terms of Settlement Landscape," *Social Forces* 30 (December 1951): 172–78, adduces historical data to answer a question posed in the present tense.

6. Jack Temple Kirby, *Media-Made Dixie: The South in the American Imagination* (Baton Rouge: Louisiana State University Press, 1978).

7. Vivien Green Fryd, *Art and Empire: The Politics of Ethnicity in the United States Capitol, 1815–1860* (New Haven, Conn.: Yale University Press, 1992).

8. The two other rotunda paintings completed between 1840 and 1855 were *The Landing of Columbus at the Island Guanahani, West Indies*, and *Discovery of the Mississippi by DeSoto*, both topics that were safely continental rather than sectional.

9. *Seventh Census, 1850: Report of the Superintendent of the Census for December 1, 1852* (Washington, D.C.: Robert Armstrong, Printer, 1853), 16–19.

10. When Washington natives relocated outside the Chesapeake, their leading choices were Pennsylvania, Ohio, New York, Missouri, Indiana, and Illinois.

11. Letitia Woods Brown, *Free Negroes in the District of Columbia, 1790–1846* (New York:

Oxford University Press, 1972); James Oliver Horton, "The Genesis of Washington's African American Community," in Francine Curro Cary, ed., *Urban Odyssey: A Multicultural History of Washington, D.C.* (Washington, D.C.: Smithsonian Institution Press, 1996), 20–41; Emily Edson Briggs, *The Olivia Letters* (New York: Neale Publishing Co., 1906), 24.

12. Howard Gillette Jr., *Between Justice and Beauty: Race, Planning, and the Failure of Urban Policy in Washington, D.C.* (Baltimore: Johns Hopkins University Press, 1995), 31–32.

13. J. Valerie Fifer, "Washington, D.C.: The Political Geography of a Federal Capital," *Journal of American Studies* 15, no. 1 (1981): 5–26.

14. The presidents of the 1840s were Virginia-born William Henry Harrison followed by southerners John Tyler, James Knox Polk, and Zachary Taylor. The chief justice from 1836 to 1864 was Roger Taney of Maryland.

15. Albert Bunn, *Old England and New England, in a Series of Views Taken on the Spot* (London: Richard Bentley, 1853), 1:242–49.

16. Lawrence A. Gobright, *Recollections of Men and Things at Washington during the Third of a Century* (Philadelphia: Claxton, Remsen and Haffelfinger, 1869).

17. Briggs, *Olivia Letters*, 181; Kathryn Allamong Jacob, *Capital Elites: High Society in Washington, D.C., after the Civil War* (Washington, D.C.: Smithsonian Institution Press, 1995), 38–39; John B. Ellis, *The Sights and Secrets of the National Capital* (New York: U.S. Publishing Co., 1869), 418–20.

18. Virginia Clay Clopton, *A Belle of the Fifties: Memoirs of Mrs. Clay, of Alabama, Covering Social and Political Life in Washington and the South, 1853–66* (New York: Doubleday, Page and Co., 1904), 143; Donn Piatt, quoted in Ellis, *Sights and Secrets*, 417.

19. J. B. Jones, *The Rival Belles, or Life in Washington* (Philadelphia: T. B. Peterson and Brother, 1878).

20. Mary Jane Windle [McLane], *Life in Washington, and Life Here and There* (Philadelphia: Lippincott, 1859); Albert Gallatin Riddle, *Alice Brand: A Romance of the Capital* (Cleveland: Cobb, Andrews and Co., 1875), 268; Mrs. N. P. Lasselle, *Annie Grayson, or Life in Washington* (Philadelphia: Henry B. Ashmead, 1853), 254.

21. Henry Adams, *The Education of Henry Adams* (New York: Modern Library, 1931), 44.

22. Windle, *Life in Washington*, 136–38.

23. Allen Tate, *The Fathers* (Denver: Alan Swallow, 1960).

24. Lindsay Lomax Wood, ed., *Leaves from an Old Washington Diary, 1854–1863* (New York: Dutton, 1943); Briggs, *Olivia Letters*, 339.

25. Mary Clemmer Ames, *Ten Years in Washington: Life and Scenes in the National Capital, As a Woman Sees Them* (Hartford, Conn.: Worthington, 1875), 70–71.

26. Samuel Douglas Wyeth, *The Federal City, or Ins and Abouts of Washington* (Washington, D.C.: Gibson Brothers, 1868), unpaginated introduction; Ainsworth R. Spofford, *The Founding of Washington City* (Baltimore: Maryland Historical Society, 1881), 61–62.

27. Virginia Jeans Laas, ed., *Wartime Washington: The Civil War Diaries of Elizabeth Blair Lee* (Urbana: University of Illinois Press, 1991), 53, 64. Mrs. Lee cited Calvert, St. Marys, and Charles Counties.

28. Ibid., 65.

29. The most accessible source on life in wartime Washington remains Margaret Leech, *Reveille in Washington, 1860–1865* (New York: Harper and Brothers, 1941).

30. *Washington Chronicle*, June 3, 1864, quoted in Gillette, *Between Justice and Beauty*, 49.

31. Elizabeth Lee diary entry for September 30, 1863, quoted in Laas, *Wartime Washington*, 309. For the succession of visitors, see the diaries of William Q. Force for 1864–65, ser. 2, William Q. Force Papers, Library of Congress.

32. Allan Johnston, *Surviving Freedom: The Black Community of Washington, D.C., 1860–1880* (New York: Garland Publishing, 1993), 11, 111, 123–25. As a result, the 1880 census found that 90 percent of older black Washingtonians (aged 50 or over) and 80 percent of younger adults (aged 20–49) had been born in Maryland or Virginia. Also see Gillette, *Between Justice and Beauty*, 40–41; Green, *Village and Capital*, 263, 293; Frederick Gutheim, *The Potomac* (New York: Rinehart, 1949), 275; and "Census of the District of Columbia [1867]," in U.S. Office of Education, *Special Report on the Condition and Improvement of Public Schools in the District of Columbia* (Washington, D.C., 1871), 28–38.

33. Wilson quoted in Alan Lessoff, "Progress and Civic Identity in Reconstruction Washington, D.C.," paper delivered at the annual meeting of Organization of American Historians, 1995.

34. Gillette, *Between Justice and Beauty*, 50–52.

35. Lois Horton, "The Days of Jubilee: Black Migration during Civil War and Reconstruction," in Cary, *Urban Odyssey*, 72–73; Johnston, *Surviving Freedom*, 195; Gillette, *Between Justice and Beauty*, 54–59.

36. On the origins and work of the territorial government, see William M. Maury, *Alexander "Boss" Shepherd and the Board of Public Works*, George Washington Studies, no. 3 (Washington, D.C.: Center for Washington Area Studies, George Washington University, 1975); Alan Lessoff, *The Nation and Its City: Politics, "Corruption," and Progress in Washington, D.C., 1861–1902* (Baltimore: Johns Hopkins University Press, 1994); and Gillette, *Between Justice and Beauty*, 59–68.

37. Elizabeth Miller, "The Washington Business Community in the Nineteenth Century: Dreams and Disappointments," paper delivered at the D.C. Historical Studies

Conference, 1980, in library of Historical Society of Washington, D.C.; Harvey W. Crew, ed., *Centennial History of Washington, D.C.* (Dayton, Ohio: United Brethren Publishing House, 1892), 413; *Report of the Joint Committee on Manufactures of the Legislative Assembly of the District of Columbia* (Washington, D.C., 1872), 22.

38. George A. Townsend, *New Washington, or The Renovated Capital City* (Washington, D.C.: N.p., 1874), 7; Ainsworth R. Spofford, *The Founding of Washington City* (Baltimore: Maryland Historical Society, 1881), 51, 61; *Morrison's Stranger's Guide to Washington City* (Washington, D.C.: W. H. and O. H. Morrison, 1868), 8; *Gazetteer of the District of Columbia for 1871–72* (Washington, D.C.: Morris and Drysdale, 1871), 31.

39. Maury, *Alexander "Boss" Shepherd*, 50.

40. *Industrial and Commercial Resources of Washington, D.C., Alexandria, Virginia, and the States of Maryland and Delaware* (New York: Historical Publishing Co., 1887).

41. Briggs, *Olivia Letters*, 315; "How Shall We Govern the National Capital?," *Nation*, June 11, 1874, 376; John Addison Porter, *New Standard Guide to the City of Washington and Environs* (Washington, D.C.: Arlington Publishing Co., 1886), 15.

42. Jacob (*Capital Elites*) develops the temporal and social distinctions within Washington society with great finesse.

43. George Lathrop, *Harper's New Monthly Magazine*, March 1881, 542; *Cleveland Leader*, September 30, 1883, quoted in Jacob, *Capital Elites*, 169; Woodbury Wheeler, *The Sights of Washington and Its Vicinity and How to See Them* (New York: New York Cheap Publishing Co., 1887), 8; E. E. Barton, *Historical and Commercial Sketches of Washington and Environs* (Washington, D.C.: E. E. Barton, 1884), 37. Also see Julian Ralph, *Dixie, or Southern Scenes and Sketches* (New York: Harper and Brothers, 1896), 372.

44. Paul Laurence Dunbar, "Negro Society in Washington," *Saturday Evening Post*, December 14, 1901, 9. Also see Archibald Grimke's assertion in 1906 that Washington drew blacks from all over the country, cited in Willard Gatewood, *Aristocrats of Color: The Black Elite, 1880–1920* (Bloomington: Indiana University Press, 1990), 63. Gatewood's book is the most thorough and detailed examination of the origins and institutions of the black elite.

45. Johnston, *Surviving Freedom*, 13, 57.

46. Constance McLaughlin Green, *The Secret City: A History of Race Relations in the Nation's Capital* (Princeton, N.J.: Princeton University Press, 1967), 133, 162–63; Haynes Johnson, *Dusk at the Mountain: The Negro, the Nation, and the Capital* (Garden City, N.Y.: Doubleday, 1963), 217–18.

47. Paul Laurence Dunbar, "Negro Life in Washington," *Harper's Weekly*, January 13, 1900, 8; Desmond King, *Separate and Unequal: Black Americans and the U.S. Federal Government* (Oxford, England: Clarendon Press, 1995), 45–46, 221. The estimate of 250 officials and clerks comes from Andrew F. Hilyer, "A Compilation of Commendable

Things of the Negro Race in the District of Columbia," cited in Steven Mintz, "A Historical Ethnography of Black Washington, D.C.," *Records of the Columbia Historical Society* (Charlottesville: University of Virginia Press, 1989), 52:245.

48. Kelly Miller, "Howard: The National Negro University," in Alain Locke, ed., *The New Negro: An Interpretation* (New York: Albert and Charles Boni, 1925), 312–22; Rayford W. Logan, *Howard University: The First Hundred Years, 1867–1967* (New York: New York University Press, 1969).

49. Based on data furnished by the Howard University registrar.

50. Logan, *Howard University*; Carroll D. Wright, "The Economic Development of Washington," *Proceedings of the Washington Academy of Sciences* 1 (1899): 183; Green, *Secret City*, 207–10; Willard B. Gatewood Jr., "Aristocrats of Color: South and North, the Black Elite, 1880–1920," *Journal of Southern History* 54 (February 1988): 3–20.

51. Ronald M. Johnson, "Those Who Stayed: Washington's Black Writers of the 1920s," *Records of the Columbia Historical Society* 50 (1980): 484–99; Letitia W. Brown and Elsie M. Lewis, *Washington in the New Era, 1870–1970* (Washington, D.C.: Government Printing Office, 1972), 23–28; Logan, *Howard University*.

52. Gatewood, *Aristocrats of Color*, 260–61; Johnston, *Surviving Freedom*, 58–60.

53. Mintz, "Historical Ethnography," 245–47.

54. Frank Lincoln Mather, ed., *Who's Who of the Colored Race: General Biographical Dictionary of Men and Women of African Descent* (Chicago: N.p., 1915); Thomas Yesner, *Who's Who in Colored America, 1928–29* (Brooklyn: N.p., 1928); James G. Fleming and Christian E. Burckel, *Who's Who in Colored America, 1950* (Yonkers-on-Hudson, N.Y.: Christian Burckel and Associates, 1950).

55. Gatewood, *Aristocrats of Color*.

56. Ibid., 259; James O. Horton and Lois E. Horton, in "Race, Occupation, and Literacy in Reconstruction Washington, D.C.," in James O. Horton, *Free People of Color: Inside the African American Community* (Washington, D.C.: Smithsonian Institution Press, 1993), 185–97, offer a careful analysis of the extent and effects of public education for blacks.

57. Mary Church Terrell, "Society among the Colored People of Washington," *Voice of the Negro* 1 (March 1904): 150–56; Kelly Miller, "Where Is the Negro's Heaven?," *Opportunity* 4 (December 1926): 371.

58. "Prosperous Washington," *Washington Post*, June 11, 1912, 55; Washington Board of Trade, Sixteenth Annual Report, November 1906, 58; J. Clinton Ransom, "Washington and Its Industries," *Southern Commercial*, October 1, 1906, 5.

59. Washington Board of Trade, Twenty-seventh Annual Report, 1917–18, 12–13; Washington Chamber of Commerce, First Annual Report, January 14, 1908, 3; Con-

stance M. Green, *Washington: Capital City, 1879–1950* (Princeton, N.J.: Princeton University Press, 1963), 30–31; *The Book of Washington, Sponsored by the Washington Board of Trade* (Washington, D.C.: Washington Board of Trade, 1930), 3, 7, 250.

60. U.S. National Capital Planning Commission and Frederick Gutheim, *Worthy of the Nation: The History of Planning for the National Capital* (Washington, D.C.: National Capital Planning Commission, 1977), 166–67; Harold A. Stone, Don K. Price, and Kathryn H. Stone, *City Manager Government in Nine Cities* (Chicago: Public Administration Service, 1940); Carl Abbott, *The New Urban America: Growth and Politics in Sunbelt Cities*, rev. ed. (Chapel Hill: University of North Carolina Press, 1987); Jessica Ivy Elfenbein, *Civics, Commerce, and Community: The History of the Greater Washington Board of Trade, 1889–1989* (Dubuque, Iowa: Kendall-Hunt Publishing Co., 1990).

61. Washington Board of Trade, Fifteenth Annual Report, November 1905, 50, Nineteenth Annual Report, November 1909, 59; *Washington Enterprise*, August 8, 1906; "Prosperous Washington," *Washington Post*, June 11, 1912, 53; Washington Chamber of Commerce, First Annual Report, January 14, 1908, 5; *Southern Commercial*, October 15, 1906, 5.

62. Washington Board of Trade, Tenth Annual Report, November 1900, 57–58, Eleventh Annual Report, 1901, 55 (quotation), Twenty-fifth Annual Report, 1915–16, 7–8; Louis P. Shoemaker, *Manufacturing in the District of Columbia and Its Influence on the United States, Copied from the Evening Star and Reprinted by the Business Men's Association* (Washington, D.C.: N.p., 1905); George H. Gall, *Washington: Industrial, Commercial, and Civic Features* (Washington, D.C.: Washington Chamber of Commerce, 1908); *Washington Condensed: Five Thousand Facts for Ready Reference* (Washington, D.C.: Bert S. Elliott, 1909), 10; *Jobbers and Shippers Trade Journal*, August 8, September 15, 1906. Trade and manufacturing would presumably support an expanded financial role. According to J. Selwyn Tait, president of the Washington and Southern Bank, the city "should rapidly become to the South the banking center which New York is now to the country at large." Quoted in George Gall, *The New Washington and the South* (Washington: Southern Commercial Congress, 1915), 43.

63. John F. Stover, *The Railroads of the South, 1865–1900: A Study in Finance and Control* (Chapel Hill: University of North Carolina Press, 1955), 233–53, 263–73; Burke Davis, *The Southern Railway: Road of the Innovators* (Chapel Hill: University of North Carolina Press, 1985), 38, 66; Howard D. Dozier, *A History of the Atlantic Coast Line Railroad* (Boston: Houghton Mifflin, 1920); *Washington Condensed: Five Thousand Facts for Ready Reference* (Washington, D.C.: Bert S. Elliott, 1909), 3–4.

64. Southern Railway Co., Seventeenth Annual Report, 1910–11, 8 (first quotation); Fairfax Harrison, *The South and the Southern Railway: The Statement of a Record and of an Ambition: An Address before the Virginia Bankers Association* (Washington, D.C., 1916), 15; *Southern Field* 9 (May 1904): 6, (September 1904): 8; Frank Presbrey, *The Southland* (Washington, D.C.: Southern Railway Co., 1898), n.p. (second quotation).

65. *Washington Enterprise*, September 8, 1906; *Southern Commercial*, October 1, 1906, 18 (quotation); Washington Board of Trade, Fifteenth Annual Report, November 1905, 50.

66. *Washington Star*, August 15, 1911, February 20, 1912.

67. Map inserted in *Greater Washington*, May 1929; Joint Industrial Council, Industrial Survey of the Washington Metropolitan Area, Washington, D.C., 1928.

68. Washington Board of Trade, *It's a Capital Idea* (1st–5th editions, 1955–59); *Headquarters USA . . . the Story of Profit and Prestige on the Potomac: An Area Survey by Industrial Development and Manufacturers Record*, reprinted from *Industrial Development*, February 1959, 18–39.

69. For early and later citations of comparators, see Washington Board of Trade, Twelfth Annual Report, 1902, 10; *Southern Commercial*, October 1, 1906, 9, 16; William B. Wrench, Executive Director, Fairfax County Economic and Industrial Development Committee, in *Washington Metropolitan Area Economic Development: Hearings before the Joint Committee on Washington Metropolitan Problems*, July 8–10, 1958, 85th Cong., 2d sess., 64; "Marketing Concept for the Baltimore/Washington Common Market," June 1976, in Washington Board of Trade Papers, Gelman Library, George Washington University.

70. Adams, *Education*, 100.

71. Federal Writers' Project, *Washington, D.C.: A Guide to the Nation's Capital* (New York: Hastings House, 1942), 167; E. Merton Coulter, "What Has the South Done about Its History?," in George B. Tindall, ed., *The Pursuit of Southern History: Presidential Addresses of the Southern Historical Association, 1935–63* (Baton Rouge: Louisiana State University Press, 1964), 20–21; Wilhelmus Bogart Bryan, *Bibliography of the District of Columbia* (Washington, D.C.: Government Printing Office, 1898).

72. Washington Board of Trade, Twenty-seventh Annual Report, 1917–18, 12–13; Washington Chamber of Commerce, First Annual Report, January 14, 1908, 3; *The Book of Washington, Sponsored by the Washington Board of Trade* (Washington, D.C.: Washington Board of Trade, 1930), 3, 7, 250; Green, *Capital City*, 30, 437; Johnson, *Dusk at the Mountain*, 211–12.

73. Information on the origins of the leaders of the Washington Board of Trade and Washington Chamber of Commerce to 1940 was drawn from the obituary and biography files, Washingtoniana Collection, Martin Luther King Jr. Memorial Library, Washington, D.C., and from the following biographical sources: John P. Coffin, *Washington: Historical Sketches of the Capital City of Our Country* (Washington, D.C.: N.p., 1877); *Leading Merchants and Manufacturers of the City of Washington: A Resume of Trade, Enterprise, and Development* (New York: International Publishing Co., 1887); *Eminent and Representative Men of Virginia and the District of Columbia of the Nineteenth Century*

(Madison, Wis.: Brant and Fuller, 1893); A. K. Parris and W. A. Means, eds., *Investor's Handbook of Washington Securities* (Washington, D.C.: N.p., 1900); Allan B. Slauson, ed., *History of the City of Washington: Its Men and Institutions* (Washington, D.C.: Washington Post Co., 1903); *District of Columbia: Concise Biographies of Its Prominent and Representative Contemporary Citizens and Valuable Statistical Data* (Washington, D.C.: Potomac Press, 1908); Albert D. Miller, *Distinguished Residents of Washington, D.C.: Science-Art-Industry* (Washington, D.C.: National Capital Press, 1916); *Prominent Personages of the Nation's Capital* (Washington, D.C.: N.p., 1924); John Clagett Proctor, ed., *Washington Past and Present: A History* (New York: Lewis Historical Publishing Co., 1930); *Who's Who in the Nation's Capital, 1921–22* (Washington, D.C.: Consolidated Publishing Co., 1921), *1923–24* (Washington, D.C.: W. W. Publishing Co., 1924), *1926–27* (Washington, D.C.: Ransdell, 1926), *1929–30* (Washington, D.C.: Ransdell, 1930), *1934–35* (Washington, D.C.: Ransdell, 1934), and *1938–39* (Washington, D.C.: Ransdell, 1938).

74. Mintz, "Historical Ethnography," 237.

75. Edward P. Jones, *Lost in the City* (New York: Morrow, 1992), 220.

76. Langston Hughes, *The Big Sea* (New York: Hill and Wang, 1963), 208–9.

77. Marita Golden, *Long Distance Life* (New York: Doubleday, 1989), 38. Also see Spencer Crew, "Melding the Old and New: The Modern African American Community, 1930–1960," in Cary, *Urban Odyssey*, 216–17.

78. Elizabeth Moore Chapin, *American Court Gossip, or Life at the National Capitol* (Marshalltown, Iowa: Chapin and Hartwell, 1887), 177, 184.

79. King, *Separate and Unequal*, 7, 47; Mintz, "Historical Ethnography," 247; Gatewood, *Aristocrats of Color*.

80. King, *Separate and Unequal*, 10.

81. Kelly Miller to William Dudley Foulke, Civil Service Reform Association, September 18, 1923, in King, *Separate and Unequal*, 48–49. Aggregate data on blacks as a proportion of total federal employees are fragmentary. One study found that the percentage of federal jobs held by blacks declined from 6 percent in 1910 to 4.9 percent in 1918. A different data series shows a decline from 10 percent in 1923 to 9 percent in 1930. See King, *Separate and Unequal*, 49, 228–29.

82. King, *Separate and Unequal*, 3, 5, 9, 13 (quotation), 14, 20, 28–29.

83. Dixon to Wilson, July 27, 1913, in Arthur S. Link, ed., *Papers of Woodrow Wilson* (Princeton, N.J.: Princeton University Press, 1978), 27:88–89.

84. August Meier and Elliott Rudwick, "The Rise of Segregation in the Federal Bureaucracy, 1900–1930," *Phylon* 28 (Summer 1967): 178–84; King, *Separate and Unequal*, 23, 30–31.

85. "Washington, D.C.," *Fortune*, December 1934, 130.

86. Green, *Secret City*, 214; Hughes, *Big Sea*, 206.

87. John Dos Passos, *In All Countries* (New York: Harcourt, Brace, 1934), 268.

88. Mary Church Terrell, *A Colored Woman in a White World* (Washington, D.C.: Ransdell, 1940), 383, 385.

89. W. Y. Barnet, "Washington Entertains Bankers," *Banking and Mercantile World* 7 (November–December 1905): 206; Lyman P. Powell, *Historic Towns of the Southern States* (New York: Putnam, 1900); Ralph, *Dixie*, 341–46; Harrison Rhodes, *American Towns and People* (New York: Robert M. McBride and Co., 1920), 127.

90. King, *Separate and Unequal*, 251.

91. Anonymous essay on the "History" of the Washington Literary Society, Literary Society Papers, Library of Congress, quoted in Jacob, *Capital Elites*, 230.

92. Henry James, *The American Scene* (London: Chapman and Hall, 1907), 303.

93. John Borchert, "America's Changing Metropolitan Regions," *Annals of the Association of American Geographers* 62 (June 1972): 352–73; Allan Pred, *City-Systems in Advanced Economies* (New York: Wiley, 1977).

94. *Washington Star*, June 10, 1912, November 19, 1916.

WOMEN, WORK, AND REGION

1. H. S. Sutton, *Rhoda Roland: A Woman from the West in Washington* (New York: Abbey Press, 1902).

2. Margery W. Davies, *Woman's Place Is at the Typewriter: Office Work and Office Workers, 1870–1930* (Philadelphia: Temple University Press, 1982), 51; Cindy Aron, "To Barter Their Souls for Gold: Female Clerks in Federal Government Offices, 1862–1890," *Journal of American History* 67 (March 1981): 835; John B. Ellis, *The Sights and Secrets of the National Capital* (New York: U.S. Publishing Co., 1889), 387; Frances Hodgson Burnett, *Through One Administration* (New York: Scribner's, 1881), 66–67; Jane Wilson Gemmill, *Notes on Washington, or Six Years at the National Capital* (Philadelphia: E. Claxton and Co., 1884), 34, 172–73.

3. Davies, *Woman's Place*; Stuart Blumin, *The Emergence of the Middle Class: Social Experience and the American City, 1760–1900* (New York: Cambridge University Press, 1989).

4. U.S. Department of Commerce, *Historical Statistics of the United States* (Washington, D.C.: Government Printing Office, 1960).

5. Davies, *Woman's Place*, 51–78; Alice Kessler-Harris, *Out to Work: A History of Wage-Earning Women in the United States* (New York: Oxford University Press, 1982), 147–48.

6. Davies, *Woman's Place*, 178–79.

7. Mrs. John S. Logan, *Thirty Years in Washington, or Life and Scenes in Our National Capital* (Hartford: Worthington, 1901), photographs facing p. 250.

8. For available data on employment, see Aron, "To Barter Their Souls for Gold."

9. For example, George Watterston, L——— *Family at Washington, or A Winter in the Metropolis* (Washington, D.C.: N.p., 1822); Mrs. N. P. Lasselle, *Annie Grayson, or Life in Washington* (Philadelphia: Henry B. Ashmead, 1853; J. B. Jones, *The Rival Belles, or Life in Washington* (Philadelphia: T. B. Peterson and Brother, 1878).

10. James Edwards, *The Court Circle: A Tale of Washington Life* (Washington, D.C.: N.p., 1895).

11. Logan, *Thirty Years in Washington*, 520; William Franklin Johnson, *Poco A Poco: A Novel* (Akron, Ohio: Saalfield Publishing Co., 1902), 35.

12. Elizabeth Clark-Lewis, *Living In, Living Out: African-American Domestics in Washington, D.C., 1910–1940* (Washington, D.C.: Smithsonian Institution Press, 1994), 122.

13. Adam Badeau, *Conspiracy: A Cuban Romance* (New York: Worthington, 1885), 63.

14. Burnett, *Through One Administration*, 20.

CHAPTER 4

1. Frances Hodgson Burnett, *Through One Administration* (New York: Scribner's, 1881), 66.

2. Mrs. John A. Logan, *Thirty Years in Washington, or Life and Scenes in Our National Capital* (Hartford: Worthington, 1901), i, iii. In a similar vein, although less fully detailed, is Ernest Ingersoll, *Rand McNally and Company's Handy Guide to the City of Washington* (Chicago: Rand McNally, 1899).

3. Federal buildings such as the National Printing Office are intermingled with private organizations (American Colonization Society) and local government services (Columbian Institution for the Deaf, Dumb, and Blind) in the short list of places to see in William D. Haley, *Philp's Washington Described: A Complete View of the American Capital and the District of Columbia* (London: Sampson Low, Son and Co., 1861). The Capitol appears in enormous detail in Samuel Douglas Wyeth, *The Federal City, or Ins and Abouts of Washington* (Washington, D.C.: Gibson Brothers, 1868).

4. Jane Wilson Gemmill, *Notes on Washington, or Six Years at the National Capital* (Philadelphia: E. Claxton and Co., 1884); Elizabeth Moore Chapin, *American Court Gossip, or Life at the National Capitol* (Marshalltown, Iowa: Chapin and Hartwell, 1887); Charles Todd, *The Story of Washington* (New York: Putnam, 1889).

5. Frank Presbrey, *The Southland* (Washington, D.C.: Southern Railway Co., 1898); Theodore W. Noyes, in Washington Board of Trade, Eighth Annual Report, November 1898, 27–28; Arthur E. Randle, "The Future of Washington [1899]," in Ulmo

S. Randle, *Reminiscences* (Washington, D.C.: N.p., 1924). These assertions of Washington's national role followed closely on the publication of James Bryce's *The American Commonwealth* (1893), which argued that the United States had no true capital and dismissed Washington in two paragraphs.

6. Francis Lieber to Ainsworth Spofford, May 20, 1870, Lieber Papers, Library of Congress, quoted in James Kirkpatrick Flack, *Desideratum in Washington: The Intellectual Community in the Capital City, 1870–1900* (Cambridge, Mass.: Schenkman, 1975), 20.

7. William Franklin Johnson, *Poco A Poco: A Novel* (Akron, Ohio: Saalfield Publishing Co., 1902), 9–11, 307.

8. Alexander Anderson, *Greater Washington: The Nation's City Viewed from a Material Standpoint* (Washington, D.C.: Hartman and Chadwick, Printers, 1897).

9. *Gazetteer of the District of Columbia for 1871–72* (Washington, D.C.: Morris and Drysdale, 1871), 57; "The Good Times Coming," *Washington Star*, March 17, 1888, in Theodore W. Noyes, *Newspaper Libels, the National Capital, and Notes of Travel* (Washington, D.C.: Byron S. Adams, 1894), 52; *Washington Star*, March 27, 1891. Also see *Washington, D.C., with Its Points of Interest Illustrated* (New York: Mercantile Illustrating Co., 1894), 50.

10. References and explanatory observations by Pierre L'Enfant, first published in 1792, are in John W. Reps, *Washington on View: The Nation's Capital since 1790* (Chapel Hill: University of North Carolina Press, 1991), 22.

11. Constance M. Green, *American Cities in the Growth of the Nation* (New York: Harper and Row, 1965), 232; James Madison, Eighth Message to Congress, December 3, 1816, in Fred L. Israel, ed., *The State of the Union Messages of the Presidents, 1790–1966*, vol. 1: 1790–1866 (New York: Chelsea House–Robert Hector Publisher, 1966), 142.

12. Joel R. Poinsett, *Discourse on the Objects and Importance of the National Institution for the Promotion of Science, Established at Washington, 1840, Delivered at the First Anniversary* (Washington, D.C.: Peter Force, 1841); A. Hunter Dupree, *Science in the Federal Government: A History of Policies and Activities to 1940* (New York: Harper and Row, 1964), 70–76; Constance McLaughlin Green, *Washington: Village and Capital, 1800–1878* (Princeton, N.J.: Princeton University Press, 1962), 139–40, 166–67. Congress in 1842 entrusted the National Institution with scientific specimens from the Wilkes Expedition, but the institution's amateur curator botched their care. The National Institution convened a national congress of scientific men in 1844 but then faded as the Smithsonian finally got started.

13. Dupree, *Science in the Federal Government*, 76–90.

14. William Q. Force, *Picture of Washington and Its Vicinity for 1848* (Washington, D.C.: W. Q. Force, 1848), 2–16.

15. John B. Ellis, *The Sights and Secrets of the National Capital* (New York: U.S. Publishing

Co., 1889), 55; O. B. Frothingham, "Washington as It Should Be," *Atlantic Monthly,* June 1884, 841–48.

16. Patricia O'Toole, *The Five of Hearts: An Intimate Portrait of Henry Adams and His Friends, 1880–1918* (New York: Clarkson Potter, 1990).

17. Asaph Hall, presidential address for 1885, quoted in Flack, *Desideratum in Washington,* 61. The problem of breadth over specialization was briefly recognized in 1883, when an Applied Mathematics section was formed within the Philosophical Society.

18. Flack, *Desideratum in Washington.*

19. Helen Horowitz, *Culture and the City: Cultural Philanthropy in Chicago from the 1880s to 1917* (Lexington: University Press of Kentucky, 1976); Thomas Bender, *New York Intellect: A History of Intellectual Life in New York City, from 1750 to the Beginning of Our Time* (New York: Knopf, 1987).

20. Woodbury Wheeler, *The Sights of Washington and Its Vicinity and How to See Them* (New York: New York Cheap Publishing Co., 1887), 5, 8; George Evans, *Visitors' Companion at Our Nation's Capital: A Complete Guide for Washington and Its Environs* (Philadelphia: George C. Evans, 1892), 62; J. H. Crane, letter to the editor, *Washington Star,* February 18, 1891.

21. "Prosperous Washington," *Washington Post,* June 11, 1912, 21.

22. Bishop Bernard McQuaid, Rochester, quoted in C. Joseph Nuesse, *The Catholic University of America: A Centennial History* (Washington, D.C.: Catholic University of America Press, 1990), 39.

23. John Tracy Ellis, *The Formative Years of the Catholic University of America* (Washington, D.C.: American Catholic Historical Association, 1946), 127.

24. Richard J. Storr, *Harper's University: The Beginnings* (Chicago: University of Chicago Press, 1966), 3–34, esp. quoting George Boardman to Frederick T. Gates, July 17, 1889, 33; *Washington Star,* May 27, 1888, November 20–21, 1889.

25. *Washington Star,* September 22, December 29, 31, 1888, January 26, February 2, 1889. The *Star* (May 14, 16, December 5, 7, 1889) was also briefly excited by a bill on establishing a national university introduced by Senator George Edmunds.

26. Georgetown College and Gallaudet College were highly specialized and were not seen as the seeds for national research universities.

27. Columbian College became Columbian University in 1873 with the help of an $85,000 gift from W. W. Corcoran. Constance McLaughlin Green, *Village and Capital,* 102, 378, and *Washington: Capital City, 1879–1950* (Princeton, N.J.: Princeton University Press, 1963), 59.

28. George F. Zook, *The Residence of Students in Universities and Colleges,* U.S. Bureau of

Education Bulletin, 1922, no. 18 (Washington, D.C.: Government Printing Office, 1922); Frederick J. Kelly and Betty A. Patterson, *Residence and Migration of College Students* (Washington, D.C.: Government Printing Office, 1934); Frederick J. Kelly and Ruth E. Eckert, *Residence and Migration of College Students, 1938–39* (Washington, D.C.: Government Printing Office, 1945).

29. James Bryce, *The Nation's Capital* (Washington, D.C.: Byron S. Adams, 1913), 43; "Greater Capital Plans to be Outlined Tonight," *Washington Evening Star*, June 1, 1917.

30. John Bell Larner, "Washington as an Educational Center," reprinted from the Souvenir Volume prepared by the Bankers Association of the District of Columbia for the American Bankers Association (Washington, D.C., 1905).

31. The New York–based American Institute of Architects merged with the Chicago-based Western Association of Architects in 1889 and moved its offices to Washington in 1898. See William A. Tobin, "In the Shadow of the Capitol: The Transformation of Washington, D.C., and the Elaboration of the Modern United States Nation-State" (Ph.D. diss., Stanford University, 1994), 24–25, 31–35.

32. In a variation, the Board of Trade periodically argued that the proper choice of manufacturing categories and site could ensure industrial growth without detrimental effects. Washington Board of Trade, Eighth Annual Report, 1898, 46–47, Tenth Annual Report, 1900, 58–59. Also see Green, *Capital City*, 174.

33. A. Maurice Low, "Washington: The City of Leisure," *Atlantic Monthly*, December 1900, 768–69; Isaac F. Marcossin, "The New Washington," *Munsey's Magazine*, December 1911, 328; E. E. Barton, *Historical and Commercial Sketches of Washington and Environs* (Washington, D.C.: E. E. Barton, 1884), 37.

34. Louis P. Shoemaker, *Manufacturing in the District of Columbia and Its Influence on the United States, Copied from the Evening Star and Reprinted by the Business Men's Association* (Washington, D.C.: N.p., 1905); Carroll D. Wright, "The Economic Development of Washington," *Proceedings of the Washington Academy of Sciences* 1 (December 1899): 180–82; Julian Street, "Wartime Washington," *Saturday Evening Post*, March 2, 1918, 3.

35. *Washington, D.C., with Its Points of Interest*, 50. Also see Washington as a "residence city" in John Addison Porter, *New Standard Guide to the City of Washington and Environs* (Washington, D.C.: Arlington Publishing Co., 1886), 15.

36. Barton, *Historical and Commercial Sketches*, 37; Theodore Noyes, *Newspaper Libels, The National Capital, and Notes of Travel* (Washington, D.C.: Byron S. Adams, 1894), 51, 53; Ainsworth R. Spofford, *The Founding of Washington City* (Baltimore: Maryland Historical Society, 1881), 62.

37. John Silva Meehan Journal, entries for May 20–21, 23, 25–26, 29, 1846, Meehan Papers, Library of Congress; *Report of the Committee of Arrangements of the First National Fair for the Exhibition of American Manufactures* (Washington, D.C.: N.p., 1846).

38. Spofford, *Washington City*, 62; Henry Adams, *The Education of Henry Adams* (New York: Modern Library, 1931), 43.

39. Washington Board of Trade, Thirteenth Annual Report, 1903, 22, Twenty-second Annual Report, November 1912, 8; Anderson, *Greater Washington*, 62; Washington Chamber of Commerce, Annual Report, January 14, 1919, 5.

40. See the map of the proposed fairgrounds in Reps, *Washington on View*, 224.

41. Editorials in *Washington Star*, August 23, September 6, 1889.

42. Reid Badger, *The Great American Fair: The World's Columbian Exposition and American Culture* (Chicago: Nelson-Hall, 1979), 44–51.

43. *Washington Star*, May 13, 1910.

44. William V. Mahoney to *Washington Star*, May 20, 1939, and Bulletins of the World's Fair Development Co., Inc., of the District of Columbia, in clipping file, "World's Fair for District," Historical Society of Washington, D.C.

45. Bryce, *Nation's Capital*, 37–39; Marcossin, "The New Washington," 312; Wendell P. Stafford, "A Capital of Capitals: The Future of Washington," *Speeches of Wendell Phillips Stafford* (St. Johnsbury, Vt.: Arthur F. Stone, 1913), 255–57.

46. *Washington, D.C., with Its Points of Interest*, 5–6; Stafford, "Future of Washington," 255; Charles Mulford Robinson, "New Dreams for Cities," *Architectural Record* 17 (May 1905): 411.

47. See, for example, Howard Gillette Jr., *Between Justice and Beauty: Race, Planning, and the Failure of Urban Policy in Washington, D.C.* (Baltimore: Johns Hopkins University Press, 1995); U.S. National Capital Planning Commission and Frederick Gutheim, *Worthy of the Nation: The History of City Planning for the National Capital* (Washington, D.C.: National Capital Planning Commission, 1977); John Reps, *Monumental Washington: The Planning and Development of the Capital Center* (Princeton, N.J.: Princeton University Press, 1967); Richard Longstreth, ed., *The Mall in Washington, 1791–1991* (Washington, D.C.: Smithsonian Institution Press, 1991).

48. Gillette, *Between Justice and Beauty*, 100.

49. Reps, *Monumental Washington*; Frederick Gutheim and Wilcomb Washburn, *The Federal City: Plans and Realities* (Washington, D.C.: Smithsonian Institution Press, 1967); U.S. National Capital Planning Commission and Gutheim, *Worthy of the Nation*.

50. See, for example, David Rankin Barbee, *Washington: City of Mighty Events* (Richmond, Va.: Garreth and Massie, 1930), and Lewis J. Nesterman, *Washington Complete Guide* (Washington, D.C.: Capitol Souvenir Co., 1942).

51. Tobin ("Shadow of the Capitol") argues convincingly that the monumental city of the twentieth century expressed the agenda of the increasingly powerful executive

branch and ignored an alternative congressional vision that deplored excessive spending for the federal government and more directly reflected sectional differences.

52. Ibid., 146–77.

53. Wilbur Zelinsky, in *Nation into State: The Shifting Symbolic Foundations of American Nationalism* (Chapel Hill: University of North Carolina Press, 1988), has insightful comments on Washington's nationalistic tourism.

54. Edward Rosskam, *Washington: Nerve Center* (New York: Alliance Book Corp., 1939), 15, 140–41.

55. John Dos Passos, *In All Countries* (New York: Harcourt, Brace, 1934), 227; "Washington, D.C.," *Fortune*, December 1934, 54–64, 124–37.

56. See, for example, John Dos Passos, *State of the Nation* (Boston: Houghton Mifflin, 1944); Scott Hart, *Washington at War, 1941–45* (Englewood Cliffs, N.J.: Prentice-Hall, 1970); Alden Stevens, "Washington: Blight on Democracy," *Harper's Magazine*, December 1941, 50–58; David Brinkley, *Washington Goes to War* (New York: Knopf, 1988); *Metropolitan Washington after 150 Years*, Studies in Business and Economics, vol. 4 (College Park: Bureau of Business and Economic Research, University of Maryland, 1950).

57. Gail Garfield Schwartz, *Technology-Oriented Firms in the Washington Area* (Washington, D.C.: Greater Washington Research Center, 1984); Edward J. Malecki, "Science and Technology in the American Metropolitan System," in Stanley Brunn and James O. Wheeler, eds., *The American Metropolitan System: Present and Future* (New York: Wiley, 1980), 134–40; *Washington Star*, November 26, 1974; "Trade Groups Flock to Washington," *Washington Post*, February 14, 1987; Gladstone Associates, *Visitors and Their Contribution to the Washington Economy* (Washington, D.C.: Washington Area Convention and Visitors Bureau, 1975).

58. Jean Gottman, *Megalopolis: The Urbanized Northeastern Seaboard of the United States* (New York: Twentieth-Century Fund, 1961), 588–606; Delbert Miller, *Leadership and Power in the Bos-Wash Megalopolis* (New York: Wiley, 1975), 7–20, 87–91, 350–51.

59. *Who's Who in Black America*, 4th ed. (Lake Forest, Ill.: Educational Communication Inc., 1985).

60. Zook, *The Residence of Students in Universities and Colleges*; Kelly and Patterson, *Residence and Migration of College Students*; Kelly and Eckert, *Residence and Migration of College Students, 1938–39*; Robert Strong, *Residence and Migration of College Students, 1949–50* (Washington, D.C.: Government Printing Office, 1951); Mabel C. Rice and Paul L. Mason, *Residence and Migration of College Students, Fall 1963: State and Regional Data* (Washington, D.C.: Government Printing Office, 1966); George H. Wade, *Residence and Migration of College Students, Fall 1968: Analytic Reports* (Washington, D.C.: Government Printing Office, 1968).

61. For introductions to the gravity model, see Walter Isard, *Introduction to Regional Science* (Englewood Cliffs, N.J.: Prentice-Hall, 1975), 42–50; Gerald A. Carrothers, "Historical Review of the Gravity and Potential Models of Human Interaction," *Journal of the American Institute of Planners* 22 (1956): 94–102; and R. W. Thomas and R. J. Huggett, *Modeling in Geography: A Mathematical Approach* (Totowa, N.J.: Barnes and Noble Books, 1980), 133–52.

62. The proportion of Howard University students from the Northeast gradually but steadily rose from 16 percent in 1945 to 25 percent in 1985, reflecting the participation of northern blacks in the same regional network (data furnished by Howard University registrar). Compare the backgrounds of Washington's black elite in John J. Harrigan, "Negro Leadership in Washington, D.C." (Ph.D. diss., Georgetown University, 1971).

63. Donald Bogue and Calvin Beale, *Economic Areas of the United States* (Glencoe, Ill.: Free Press, 1961), 31–35; James W. Watson, *North America: Its Countries and Regions* (London: Longmans, 1968), 616–18; Wilbur Zelinsky, "Selfward Bound: Personal Preference Patterns and the Changing Map of American Society," *Economic Geography* 50 (May 1974): 144–79.

64. John Fenton, *Politics in the Border States* (New Orleans: Hauser Press, 1957), 204. Also see Constance McLaughlin Green, *The Secret City: A History of Race Relations in the Nation's Capital* (Princeton, N.J.: Princeton University Press, 1967), 297–98; Sam Smith, *Captive Capital: Colonial Life in Modern Washington* (Bloomington: Indiana University Press, 1974), 17, 60–61; Sam P. Wiggins, *The Desegregation Era in Higher Education* (Berkeley: McCutchan Publishing Corp., 1966), 3–6, 18–19; Benjamin Muse, *Virginia's Massive Resistance* (Bloomington: Indiana University Press, 1961), 3, 73, 139, 142, 159.

65. Metropolitan Washington Board of Trade, "Summary of Activities, 1954–1970," in Washington Board of Trade Papers, Gelman Library, George Washington University; Council for Economic and Industry Research, Inc., "Economic Base Survey for the General Development Plan, National Capital Region," 1956 (mimeographed); Hamer and Co. Associates, *Economic Development in the Washington Area: Staff Study for the Joint Congressional Committee on Washington Area Problems, Congress of the United States* (Washington, D.C.: Government Printing Office, 1958).

66. R. B. Armstrong, "National Trends in Office Construction, Employment, and Headquarter Location in U.S. Metropolitan Areas," in P. W. Daniels, ed., *Spatial Patterns of Office Growth and Location* (Chichester, England: Wiley, 1979), 61–93.

67. *State and Metropolitan Area Data Book* (Washington, D.C.: Government Printing Office, 1991). From 1974 to 1985 Washington's 90 percent growth in producer services employment matched such growth in metropolitan Boston, Los Angeles, and San Francisco and far exceeded that in New York. See Ann Markusen and V. Gwiasda,

"Multipolarity and the Layering of Functions in World Cities: New York City's Struggle to Stay on Top," *International Journal of Urban and Regional Research* 18 (June 1994): 167–93.

68. J. Lynch and D. R. Meyer, "Dynamics of the U.S. System of Cities, 1950–1980: The Impact of Large Corporate Law Firms," *Urban Affairs Quarterly* 28 (September 1992): 38–68.

69. David Ricci, *The Transformation of American Politics: The New Washington and the Rise of Think Tanks* (New Haven, Conn.: Yale University Press, 1993); Atlee Shidler, "Local Community and National Government," in Shidler, ed., *Greater Washington in 1980* (Washington, D.C.: Greater Washington Research Center, 1980), 10.

70. Jonathan Daniels, *Frontier on the Potomac* (New York: Macmillan, 1946), 144–45; Stanley Lieberson and I. L. Allen Jr., "Location of National Headquarters of Voluntary Organizations," *Administrative Science Quarterly* 8 (February 1963): 316–38.

71. M. Jordan, "Trade Groups Flock to Region," *Washington Post*, February 19, 1987.

72. Shidler, "Local Community and National Government," 10; Ricci, *Transformation of American Politics*. The Metropolitan Washington Council of Governments, in *An Economic Profile of the Washington Region, 1980* (Washington, D.C.: Metropolitan Washington Council of Governments, 1980), offers counts of 1,500 and 2,500 based on different national lists.

73. The following paragraphs draw on James A. Smith, *The Idea Brokers: Think Tanks and the Rise of the New Policy Elite* (New York: Free Press, 1991), and Ricci, *Transformation of American Politics*.

74. Donald T. Critchlow, *The Brookings Institution, 1916–1952: Expertise and the Public Interest in a Democratic Society* (De Kalb: Northern Illinois University Press, 1985).

75. Ricci, *Transformation of American Politics*, 208.

76. *Portland Oregonian*, September 28, 1993.

77. Institute for Women's Policy Research, *The Status of Women in the District of Columbia* (Washington, D.C.: Institute for Women's Policy Research, 1996).

78. James Bryce, *The American Commonwealth* (New York: Macmillan, 1914), 2:855.

79. Marcossin, "The New Washington," 312; Stafford, "Future of Washington," 254–55; Bryce, *Nation's Capital*, 37.

80. *Washington, D.C., with Its Points of Interest*, 5–6; Theodore W. Noyes, "A Square Deal for Everybody," *Washington Star*, March 14, 1915; Harrison Rhodes, *American Towns and People* (New York: Robert M. McBride and Co., 1920), 103.

81. A keyword search of the Library of Congress Index to Popular Articles found 1 use in 1983, an average of 3 uses in 1984–86, 16 uses in 1987, 95 uses in 1988, and an

average of 60 uses per year from 1989 through 1993. The Library of Congress Index to Articles on Public Policy found the first use in 1986. For efforts to define the term, see William Safire, "Inside the Circumferential Highway," *New York Times Magazine*, March 15, 1992, and Hugh Sidey, "Life in the Capital Cocoon," *Time*, March 4, 1985, 20. A book that turns the negative take into a blistering attack on Washington insiders is Kevin Phillips, *Arrogant Capital: Washington, Wall Street, and the Frustration of American Politics* (Boston: Little, Brown, 1994).

82. Wilbur Zelinsky, "Conventionland USA: The Geography of a Latterday Phenomenon," *Annals of the Association of American Geographers* 84 (March 1994): 68–86.

83. John Evans, unidentified article on Washington, October 11, 1869, in John Evans Papers, Library of Congress; Albert Gallatin Riddle, *Alice Brand: A Romance of the Capital* (Cleveland: Cobb, Anderson and Co., 1875), 123–24; William Oliver Stevens, *Washington: The Cinderella City* (New York: Dodd, Mead, 1943), 313–19.

84. "Zombie" paraphrases Larry McMurtry, *Cadillac Jack* (New York: Simon and Schuster, 1982), 73; Edmund Wilson, "Washington: Glimpses of the New Deal," in *The American Earthquake* (Garden City, N.Y.: Doubleday, 1958), 535. Also see James Morris, *Cities* (New York: Harcourt, Brace, and World, 1963), 366–68, and Martha Derthick, *City Politics in Washington, D.C.* (Cambridge: Harvard-MIT Joint Center for Urban Studies, 1962), 35.

85. Chapin, *American Court Gossip*, 153.

86. Washington metropolitan per capita income of $23,175 in 1990 was the highest in the nation, above both West Palm Beach in second place and San Francisco–Oakland–San Jose in third place.

87. Brad Leithauser, *Seaward* (New York: Knopf, 1993), 185.

LOS ANGELES ON THE POTOMAC

1. Jack Lait and Lee Mortimer, *Washington Confidential* (New York: Crown, 1951), 3.

2. Kevin Phillips, *The Emerging Republican Majority* (New Rochelle, N.Y.: Arlington House, 1969); Kirkpatrick Sale, *Power Shift: The Rise of the Southern Rim and Its Challenge to the Eastern Establishment* (New York: Random House, 1975).

3. For the origins and definition of the Sunbelt, see Richard M. Bernard and Bradley R. Rice, *Sunbelt Cities: Politics and Growth since World War II* (Austin: University of Texas Press, 1983; Carl Abbott, *The New Urban America: Growth and Politics in Sunbelt Cities* (Chapel Hill: University of North Carolina Press, 1987); and Raymond A. Mohl, ed., *Searching for the Sunbelt: Historical Perspectives on a Region* (Knoxville: University of Tennessee Press, 1990). Washington is included in the Snowbelt in Richard Bernard, ed., *Snowbelt Cities: Metropolitan Politics in the Northeast and Midwest since World War II* (Bloomington: Indiana University Press, 1990).

4. Jack Limpert, interview by author, Washington, D.C., April 9, 1987; Joel Garreau, interview by author, Washington, D.C., March 25, 1987; William Wrench, Executive Director, Fairfax County Economic and Industrial Development Committee, in *Washington Metropolitan Area Economic Development*, Hearings before the Joint Committee on Washington Metropolitan Problems, July 8–10, 1858, 85th Cong., 2d sess., p. 64; Greater Washington Board of Trade, 1978 statement regarding business boom, and Kenneth R. Sparks, Federal City Council, to Vincent C. Burke Jr., June 14, 1976, both in Washington Board of Trade Papers, Gelman Library, George Washington University.

5. Gail Garfield Schwartz, *Technology-Oriented Firms in the Washington Area* (Washington, D.C.: Greater Washington Research Center, 1984).

6. Edward Malecki, "Science and Technology in the American Metropolitan System," in Stanley Brunn and James O. Wheeler, eds., *The American Metropolitan System: Present and Future* (New York: Wiley, 1980), 136.

7. Julian Street, "Wartime Washington," *Saturday Evening Post*, March 2, 1918, 3.

8. Carl Abbott, "New West, New South, New Region: The Discovery of the Sunbelt," in Mohl, *Searching for the Sunbelt*, 7–24.

CHAPTER 5

1. C. Dudley and D. Nunes, "Washington: The New International City," *Washington Post*, February 3, 1980; Greater Washington Board of Trade, *A Capital Link* (Washington, D.C.: Greater Washington Board of Trade, 1987).

2. Paul Knox, "The Washington Metropolitan Area," *Cities*, November 1987, 298; Stephen Fuller, "The Internationalization of the Washington, D.C., Area Economy," in Richard V. Knight and Gary Gappert, eds., *Cities in a Global Society* (Newbury Park, Calif.: Sage, 1989), 118–19; Jean Gottman, "What Are Cities Becoming the Centers Of? Sorting Out the Possibilities," in Knight and Gappert, *Cities in a Global Society*, 64; J. Naylor, "Business Favors Washington First," *Washington Times*, November 19, 1992.

3. "Reports Say D.C. Is a Strong Market, World-Class City," *National Real Estate Investor* 31 (November 1989): 32–37.

4. R. B. Cohen, "The New International Division of Labor, Multinational Corporations, and Urban Hierarchy," in Michael Dear and Allan J. Scott, eds., *Urbanization and Urban Planning in Capitalist Society* (New York: Methuen, 1981), 287–315; John Friedmann, "The World City Hypothesis," *Development and Change* 17, no. 1 (1986): 69–83; Manuel Castells, *The Informational City* (Oxford, England: Basil Blackwell, 1989); Saskia Sassen, *The Global City: New York, London, and Tokyo* (Princeton, N.J.: Princeton University Press, 1991).

5. James Bryce, *The Nation's Capital* (Washington, D.C.: Byron S. Adams, 1913).

6. Heidi H. Hobbs, *City Hall Goes Abroad: The Foreign Policy of Local Politics* (Thousand Oaks, Calif.: Sage, 1994).

7. Leslie Sklair, *Sociology of the Global System: Social Change in Global Perspective* (Baltimore: Johns Hopkins University Press, 1991); Sharon Zukin, *Landscapes of Power* (Berkeley: University of California Press, 1991).

8. Friedmann, "World City Hypothesis"; Michael Peter Smith and Joe Feagin, "Cities and the New International Division of Labor," in Smith and Feagin, eds., *The Capitalist City: Global Restructuring and Community Politics* (Oxford, England: Basil Blackwell, 1987), 3–34; Sassen, *Global City*.

9. S. H. Hymer, *The Multinational Corporation: A Radical Approach* (Cambridge, England: Cambridge University Press, 1979); Castells, *Informational City*; Cohen, "New International Division of Labor."

10. Smith and Feagin, "Cities and the New International Division of Labor"; Anthony D. King, *Global Cities: Post Imperialism and the Internationalization of London* (London: Routledge, 1990).

11. Ann Markusen and Vicki Gwiasda, "Multipolarity and the Layering of Functions in World Cities: New York City's Struggle to Stay on Top," *International Journal of Urban and Regional Research* 18 (June 1994): 167–93.

12. Carl Abbott, "Through Flight to Tokyo: Sunbelt Cities in the New World Economy, 1960–1990," in Arnold Hirsch and Ray Mohl, eds., *Urban Policy in Twentieth-Century America* (New Brunswick, N.J.: Rutgers University Press, 1993), 193–212.

13. Roderick D. McKenzie, "The Concept of Dominance and World-Organization," *American Journal of Sociology* 33 (July 1927): 28–42.

14. Hamer and Co. Associates, *Economic Development in the Washington Area: Staff Study for the Joint Committee on Washington Area Problems, Congress of the United States* (Washington, D.C.: Government Printing Office, 1958); Matthew P. Drennan, "Gateway Cities: The Metropolitan Sources of U.S. Producer Services Exports," *Urban Studies* 29 (April 1992): 217–35.

15. Richard Child Hill and K. Fujita, "Osaka's Tokyo Problem," *International Journal of Urban and Regional Research* 19 (March 1995): 181–94.

16. John Friedmann, *Where We Stand: A Decade of World City Research* (Los Angeles: Graduate School of Architecture and Urban Planning, University of California, 1993), 20; Markusen and Gwiasda, "Multipolarity."

17. A. Thomas and A. J. Thomas Jr., *The Organization of American States* (Dallas: Southern Methodist University Press, 1963), 12–15; S. G. Inman, *Inter-American Conferences, 1826–1954: History and Problems* (Washington, D.C.: University Press of Washington, D.C., 1965), 33–59.

18. *Washington, D.C., with Its Points of Interest Illustrated* (New York: Mercantile Illustrating Co., 1894), 6.

19. James Bryce, *The American Commonwealth*, rev. ed. (New York: Macmillan, 1912), 855–61.

20. Harrison Rhodes, *American Towns and People* (New York: Robert McBride, 1920), 124; C. Hurd, *Washington Cavalcade* (New York: Dutton, 1948), 287.

21. Emily Edson Briggs, *The Olivia Letters* (New York: Neale Publishing, 1906), 164; Helen Lombard, *Washington Waltz: Diplomatic People and Policies* (New York: Knopf, 1941), 3–4; David Brinkley, *Washington Goes to War* (New York: Knopf, 1988), 32, 46.

22. Hurd, *Washington Cavalcade*, 263. Also see James Reston, "L'Enfant's Capital—and Boomtown Too," *New York Times Magazine*, June 1, 1941; Alan K. Henrickson, "A Small, Cozy Town, Global in Scope: Washington, D.C.," *Ekistics* 50 (1983): 135–36.

23. W. O. Stevens, *Washington: The Cinderella City* (New York: Dodd, Mead, 1943), 319–23; Brinkley, *Washington Goes to War*, 50.

24. Robert R. Nathan Associates, *Studies of the National Government in the Economy of the National Capital Region: International Activities 1974* (Washington, D.C.: National Capital Planning Commission, 1978). The count of ambassadors, ministers, first secretaries, and other diplomats worthy of special social attention tripled during the same period. See Helen R. Hagner, *Social List of Washington, D.C.* (Washington, D.C.: N.p., 1940); Carolyn Hagner Shaw, *Social List of Washington, D.C.* (Washington, D.C.: N.p., 1956).

25. Alice Rogers Hager, *Washington City of Destiny* (New York: Macmillan, 1949), 6.

26. Hasia R. Diner and Steven J. Diner, "Washington's Jewish Community: Separate but Not Apart," in Francine Curry Cary, ed., *Urban Odyssey: A Multicultural History of Washington, D.C.* (Washington, D.C.: Smithsonian Institution Press, 1996), 145.

27. Eugene Meyer, "Report of Committee on Site," in *International Monetary Fund—Selected Documents*, Board of Governors Inaugural Meeting, Savannah, Georgia, March 8–18, 1946, in Eugene Meyer Papers, Manuscripts Collection, box 86, Library of Congress; "New Bank Pleases Financiers," *Washington Evening Star*, March 15, 1946; John Morton Blum, *From the Morganthau Diaries*, vol. 3: *Years of War, 1941–1945* (Boston: Houghton Mifflin, 1967), 427–36; R. N. Gardner, *Sterling-Dollar Diplomacy* (Oxford, England: Clarendon Press, 1956), 265.

28. Postwar Planning Committee of the Washington Board of Trade and Committee for Economic Development, *Population and Business Prospects for Metropolitan Washington* (Washington, D.C.: Postwar Planning Committee and Committee for Economic Development, 1946), 1, in Eugene Meyer Papers, Manuscripts Collection, box 153, Library of Congress.

29. Gardner, *Sterling-Dollar Diplomacy*, 298–99.

30. "Virginians Seeking UNO Site Find Jim Crow Law Is Barrier," *Washington Star*, January 6, 1946.

31. Bill Moyers, *Listening to America: A Traveler Rediscovers His Country* (New York: Harper and Row, 1971), 326.

32. Statements by Robert E. McLaughlin, Robert Wagner, Robert Moses, John W. Hanes, and Jacob Javits to President's Commission on the World's Fair, 1959, in Washington Board of Trade Papers, Special Collections, box 233, Gelman Library, George Washington University.

33. William Press to Jameson Parker, March 23, 1959, in Washington Board of Trade Papers, ibid.; "A Fair for Washington," *Washington Post*, August 15, 1959.

34. "Washington Takes on a World Flavor," *U.S. News and World Report*, May 5, 1980.

35. Government of the District of Columbia, *Comprehensive Plan for the National Capital* (Washington, D.C.: Government of the District of Columbia, 1983), 81.

36. U.S. House of Representatives, *Development of the Nation's Capital: Hearings before the Committee of the District of Columbia*, 95th Cong., 1st sess., May 24–25, June 15, 18, 29–30, 1977, serial no. 95-10, p. 1. Also see Oliver T. Carr, remarks at inauguration of Mayor Marion Barry, January 3, 1978, in Washington Board of Trade Papers, Special Collections, Gelman Library, George Washington University; J. R. Tydings, "Statement to Metropolitan Washington Savings and Loan League, 27 May 1978," Washington Board of Trade Papers; Atlee Shidler, "Local Community and National Government," in Shidler, ed., *Greater Washington in 1980* (Washington, D.C.: Greater Washington Research Center, 1980), 13–14.

37. S. Goldstein, "Regional Group Upbeat about 'Common' Market," *Washington Times*, May 3, 1989.

38. Union of International Associations, ed., *Yearbook of International Organizations*, 1962–63 (Brussels, Belgium, 1962).

39. Robert R. Nathan Associates, *Studies of the National Government*, 18–41; Fuller, "Internationalization of Washington," 115.

40. Union of International Associations, ed., *Yearbook of International Organizations*, 1985–86, vol. 2: *Geographic Volume* (Munich: K. G. Saur Verlag, 1985).

41. Sidney Blumenthal, "The Ruins of Georgetown," *New Yorker*, October 21, 28, 1996, 221–37.

42. David A. Johnson, "World City/Capital City: New York in the Changing Global Setting," in John Taylor, J. G. Lengelle, and Carolyn Andrew, eds., *Capital Cities: International Perspectives* (Ottawa, Ont.: Carleton University Press, 1993), 385–86; James R.

Kurth, "Between Europe and America: The New York Foreign Policy Elite," in Martin Shefter, ed., *Capital of the American Century: The National and International Influence of New York City* (New York: Russell Sage Foundation, 1993), 71–94; Martin Shefter, "New York's National and International Influence," in Shefter, *Capital of the American Century*, 1–25.

43. David Ricci, *The Transformation of American Politics: The New Washington and the Rise of Think Tanks* (New Haven, Conn.: Yale University Press, 1993).

44. Washington Board of Trade, *News*, 1986, 10–11A.

45. Greater Washington Board of Trade, *A Capital Link*. Also see Greater Washington Board of Trade, "The Case for Washington: International Companies in Greater Washington, A Partial List," November 1979, in Washington Board of Trade Papers, box 123, Gelman Library, George Washington University.

46. D. Isaac, "D.C. Becomes Choice of More European Firms," *Washington Business Journal*, January 15, 1990, 1; "Singapore Ranked Top City for International Head-quarters," *Daily Journal of Commerce* (Portland), September 10, 1990, 5.

47. See comments by business executives at a December 12, 1979, conference on "Doing International Business in Washington," in Washington Board of Trade Papers, box 390, Gelman Library, George Washington University.

48. Hill and Fujita, "Osaka's Tokyo Problem," 181–94; B. H. Lawrence, "Mobil Makes Its Move," *Washington Post*, September 18, 1989; Greater Washington Board of Trade, *A Capital Link*.

49. William F. Avery, "Managing Public Policy Abroad: Foreign Corporate Representation in Washington," *Columbia Journal of World Business* 25 (Fall 1990): 32–41; P. Choate, "Foreign Capital PACs a Punch," *Across the Board* 25 (October 1988): 60–63; P. Fessler, "Targeting Japan: Do Lobbying Dollars Shape the U.S. Trade Debate?," *Congressional Quarterly Weekly* 48 (March 31, 1990): 972–75; D. Sands, "Region Mobilizes for Growth in Coming Year," *Washington Times*, January 25, 1988; J. Weiss, "Lobby Fodder," *Far Eastern Economic Review* 148, no. 17 (1990): 24.

50. Drennan, "Gateway Cities"; Sassen, *Global City*; Saskia Sassen, *Cities in a World Economy* (Thousand Oaks, Calif.: Pine Forge Press, 1994).

51. Frederick J. Kelly and Ruth E. Eckert, *Residence and Migration of College Students, 1938–39* (Washington, D.C.: Government Printing Office, 1945); Robert Strong, *Residence and Migration of College Students, 1949–50* (Washington, D.C.: Government Printing Office, 1951); Mabel C. Rice and Paul L. Mason, *Residence and Migration of College Students, Fall 1963: State and Regional Data* (Washington, D.C.: Government Printing Office, 1966). The numbers I report from these sources are the totals for the District of Columbia plus one-third of the totals for Maryland (as an estimate of foreign students at the main University of Maryland campus at College Park). The figure of

16,000 for the 1990s is derived from data in the *Chronicle of Higher Education*, November 10, 1995, and includes all listed institutions in the metropolitan area.

52. Wilbur Zelinsky, "Coming to America," *American Demographics* 12 (August 1990): 44–47, 56.

53. Washington Convention and Visitors Bureau, *Conventions and Meetings, Washington, D.C., 1972–81* (Washington, D.C.: Washington Convention and Visitors Bureau, 1972); K. N. Goss, *The Market for International Congresses* (Washington, D.C.: U.S. Travel Service, Department of Commerce, 1975); Gary Gappert, "A Management Perspective on Cities in a Changing Global Environment," in Knight and Gappert, *Cities in a Global Society*, 312–25.

54. C. Dudley and D. Nunes, "Washington: The New International City," *Washington Post*, February 3, 1980; Peter McGrath and Howard Means, "How Washington Became a Real City," *Washingtonian*, October 1980, 130–60; *Washington Post Retail Memo and Sales Planner*, February 1984; S. A. Pressley, "Multicultural D.C. Area Becoming Multilingual," *Washington Post*, February 11, 1992; Henrickson, "Small, Cozy Town," 142.

55. Paul Knox, "The Restless Urban Landscape: Economic and Sociocultural Change and the Transformation of Washington, D.C.," *Annals of the Association of American Geographers* 81 (May 1991): 181–209; Dudley and D. Nunes, "D.C. Provides Refuge for World's Rich," *Washington Post*, February 4, 1980; Robert R. Nathan Associates, *Studies of the National Government*, table 20.

56. The 14 percent figure is for the same territory included in the 1980 metropolitan area. By 1990, the addition of three outlying counties led to an overall figure of 13.2 percent within expanded boundaries.

57. U.S. Department of Commerce, *Statistical Abstract of the United States, 1993* (Washington, D.C.: Government Printing Office, 1993); Cary, *Urban Odyssey*, xxi.

58. Metropolitan Washington Airports Authority, "Washington Dulles International Airport Aircraft Operations," Office of Strategic Planning, Metropolitan Washington Airports Authority, Alexandria, Va., 1994; M. Leepson, "Meetings and Travel: Washington's Airports," *Regardie's Magazine*, April–May 1992, 57–74.

59. Wilbur Zelinsky, "North America's Vernacular Regions," *Annals of the Association of American Geographers* 70 (February 1980): 1–16; John Shelton Reed, "The Heart of Dixie: An Essay in Folk Geography," *Social Forces* 54 (November 1976): 925–39.

60. In making comparisons among cities, I have assumed that the various outlets for the International House of Pancakes and similar uses of the terms cancel each other out. More problematic is the fact that the methodology does not pick up national terms that may represent either business-institutional connections (Korea Society) or significant immigrant communities (Korean Methodist Church).

61. Table 5.2 includes the six cities compared by Markusen and Gwiasda ("Multi-polarity") plus three major Sunbelt cities.

62. "The 100 Largest U.S. Multinationals," *Forbes,* July 19, 1993, 182–86; G. Mehl, *U.S. Manufactured Exports and Export-Related Employment: Profiles of the 50 States and 33 Selected Metropolitan Areas for 1983* (Washington, D.C.: International Trade Administration, U.S. Department of Commerce, 1987); Thierry J. Noyelle, *Competition Comes to Town: Financial Services in the Washington Economy* (Washington, D.C.: Greater Washington Research Center, 1985).

63. Liz Spayd, "Its Official: Washington-Baltimore," *Washington Post,* December 29, 1991.

64. Klaus Kunzman and M. Wegener, "The Pattern of Urbanization in Western Europe," *Ekistics* 58 (November–December 1991): 282–91; Michael Parkinson, "The Rise of the Entrepreneurial European City: Strategic Responses to Economic Changes in the 1980s," *Ekistics* 58 (November–December 1991): 299–308; Joe R. Feagin, *Free Enterprise City* (New Brunswick, N.J.: Rutgers University Press, 1988); Saskia Sassen and Alejandro Portes, "Miami: A New Global City?," *Contemporary Sociology* 22 (July 1993): 471–77; Alejandro Portes and Alec Stepick, *City on the Edge: The Transformation of Miami* (Berkeley: University of California Press, 1993); Dana White and Timothy Crimmins, "How Atlanta Grew: Cool Heads, Hot Air, and Hard Work," *Atlanta Economic Review* 28 (January 1978): 7–15.

65. D. A. Heenan, "Global Cities of Tomorrow," *Harvard Business Review* 55 (March 1977): 79–92; R. J. Cattani, "Washington at the Global Frontier," *Christian Science Monitor,* December 19, 1990.

66. King, *Global Cities.*

CHAPTER 6

1. Edward P. Jones, *Lost in the City* (New York: Morrow, 1992), 52–53.

2. Ibid., 50. Cassandra is incorrect, by the way, for the young man later explains that he "came up from South Carolina to learn some things" (p. 53). But he looks country to a sophisticated Washingtonian like Cassandra.

3. Ibid., 247.

4. Programs for annual Shad Bake/Spring Outing in Washington Board of Trade Papers, box 212, Gelman Library, George Washington University.

5. Ibid.

6. Contrast the development patterns in James Albert Wineberger, "Road Map of the District of Columbia" (Washington, D.C., 1880), in Geography and Map Division, Library of Congress, with the U.S. Coast and Geodetic Survey of 1885–86 map, *Maryland-District of Columbia-Virginia Washington Sheet* (Washington, D.C.: U.S. Geological

Survey, 1891), in John W. Reps, *Washington on View: The Nation's Capital since 1790* (Chapel Hill: University of North Carolina Press, 1991), 233. Also see Howard Gillette Jr., *Between Justice and Beauty: Race, Planning, and the Failure of Urban Policy in Washington, D.C.* (Baltimore: Johns Hopkins University Press, 1995), 76; Alan Lessoff, *The Nation and Its City: Politics, "Corruption," and Progress in Washington, D.C., 1861–1902* (Baltimore: Johns Hopkins University Press, 1994), 238–40.

7. Lessoff, *Nation and Its City*, 161–62.

8. Anneli Moucka Levy, "Washington, D.C., and the Growth of Its Early Suburbs" (M.A. thesis, University of Maryland, 1980).

9. See the multiple views by Edward Sachse in the 1850s and 1860s in Reps, *Washington on View*, 132–27.

10. James Keily, *Map of the City of Washington, D.C.* (1851), and Albert Boschke, *Topographical Map of the District of Columbia, Surveyed in the Years 1856–59* (1861), in Reps, *Washington on View*, 125, 139.

11. The following are in the Geography and Map Division, Library of Congress: *Entwistle's Handy Map of Washington and Vicinity, Showing Public Buildings, Churches, Hotels, Places of Amusement, and Lines of Street Rail Roads* (Washington, D.C.: J. C. Entwistle, 1876); *Map of Washington, Georgetown and Vicinity* (Washington, D.C.: W. H. and O. H. Morrison, 1881); Francis R. Fava Jr., "Map of the City of Washington and Surroundings Prepared for Barton L. Walker, Real Estate Broker," 1980; W. Kelsey Schrepf, "Map of the District of Columbia and Adjacent Portions of Maryland and Virginia, Prepared Especially for Thomas J. Fisher and Co., Real Estate Brokers," 1891.

12. *Official Map of Washington: Fifteenth Annual International Christian Endeavour Convention, July 8–13, 1899* (Washington, D.C.: Norris Peters Co., 1896); *The Standard Guide Ready Reference Map of Washington* (Washington, D.C.: Foster and Reynolds, 1901), both in Geography and Map Division, Library of Congress.

13. Map of Washington in *Rand McNally Indexed Atlas of the World* (Chicago: Rand McNally, 1893), in Geography and Map Division, Library of Congress; James T. DuBois, "The Altograph of Washington City, or, Strangers' Guide," 1892, in Reps, *Washington on View*, 227.

14. Theodore R. Davis, "Washington City, D.C.," 1869, and "Our National Capital, Viewed from the South," 1882, in Geography and Map Division, Library of Congress.

15. In Reps, *Washington on View*, 263, see William Olson, *Washington, the Beautiful Capital of the Nation* (Washington, D.C.: A. B. Graham Co., 1921). In Geography and Map Division, Library of Congress, see several aerial photographs: Fairchild Aerial Survey, from *Washington Star*, August 3, 1924; *Washington Star* Graphic Section, March 3, 1929; *Washington Post* Rotogravure Section, August 10, 1930; and Edward Spofford, *Washington, D.C.* (New York: C. S. Hammond and Co., 1933).

16. U.S. Army Corps of Engineers, *Potomac River Basin Report* (Baltimore: U.S. Army Engineer District, 1963); Richard L. Stanton, *Potomac Journey: Fairfax Shore to Tidewater* (Washington, D.C.: Smithsonian Institution Press, 1993); George M. Danko, *Potomac River Basin: An Annotated Bibliography* (Washington, D.C.: Government Printing Office, 1981); *Potomac River Basin: Research, Planning, Development*, Studies in Business and Economics, vol. 11, no. 3 (College Park: Bureau of Business and Economic Research, University of Maryland, 1957).

17. U.S. Department of the Interior, *The Nation's River: A Report on the Potomac from the U.S. Department of the Interior, with Recommendations for Action by the Federal Interdepartmental Task Force on the Potomac* (Washington, D.C.: Government Printing Office, 1968); Timothy John Broedling, "A Study in Program Formulation: Factors Causing Delay in the Development of a Comprehensive Long-Range Plan for the Potomac River Basin" (M.B.A. thesis, George Washington University, 1967); David K. Hartley, *Regional Planning: The Potomac Experience* (Washington, D.C.: Congressional Research Service, 1980).

18. Frederick Gutheim, "The Lower Potomac River," talk at public meeting of Interstate Commission on the Potomac River Basin, February 26, 1965, p. 5, in Gutheim Papers, Special Collections, Gelman Library, George Washington University.

19. *The Potomac Conference: Toward a Potomac Action Strategy* (Baltimore: Maryland Department of State Planning, 1976); *The View from the River, the View from the Hill: Proceedings of the 1976 Fall Public Meeting* (Bethesda, Md.: Interstate Commission on the Potomac River Basin, 1977).

20. Paul D. Barker Jr., "The Chesapeake Bay Preservation Act: The Problem with State Land Regulation of Interstate Resources," *William and Mary Law Review* 31 (Spring 1990): 735–72.

21. National Capital Planning Commission, *The Urban River: A Staff Proposal for Waterfront Development in the District of Columbia* (Washington, D.C.: Government Printing Office, 1972). Also see U.S. Bureau of Outdoor Recreation, *The Potomac: A Model Estuary* (Washington, D.C.: National Capital Planning Commission, 1970); Federal City Council, *Report of the Waterfront Task Force* (Washington, D.C.: Federal City Council, 1982); Keith Brooks, *Anacostia River: An Annotated Bibliography* (Bethesda, Md.: Interstate Commission on the Potomac River Basin, 1987).

22. National Capital Planning Commission, *Extending the Legacy: Planning America's Capital for the Twenty-first Century* (Washington, D.C.: National Capital Planning Commission, 1997).

23. A U.S. National Park Service map and brochure of 1977, *Welcome to Washington: Day Trips*, directs visitors to Antietam, Harper's Ferry, and Baltimore but not the Chesapeake littoral. In contrast, a tidally oriented Washington is depicted in L. Azzinaro, *Washington, D.C.: A View of the World* (Ossining, N.Y.: Harvey Hutter and Co.,

1990), a cartoon-style bird's-eye map of the greater Washington area. The artist puts Chesapeake Bay in the foreground in great detail and the District of Columbia in the middle. One inch suffices for the rest of the United States west to the Pacific and one inch for the northeastern United States, but the map gives four inches for points south and seven inches for Chesapeake Bay with identification of Ocean City, Assateague, Annapolis, Baltimore, Williamsburg, and Virginia Beach.

24. John Barth, *The Tidewater Tales* (New York: Putnam, 1987), 363; U.S. Census of Housing, 1980, vol. 1: *Characteristics of Housing Units*, chap. A: "General Housing Characteristics." Newspaper circulation data are compiled by the Standard Rate and Data Service, *Newspaper Circulation Analysis*.

25. A. Maurice Low, "Washington: The City of Leisure," *Atlantic Monthly*, December 1900, 767. Also see the description of a spring day on the Potomac in Albert Gallatin Riddle, *Alice Brand: A Romance of the Capital* (Cleveland: Cobb, Andrews and Co., 1875), 376–77, and a warm February in Henry Adams, *Democracy* (New York: Henry Holt, 1908), 113. Riddle's spring day arrives "from the southern sea, up the wandering Potomac . . . from over the South it came." Adams's warm spell is "a deceptive gleam of summer. . . . Then men and women are languid; life seems, as in Italy, sensuous and glowing with color . . . the struggle of existence seems to abate."

26. Gary Snyder, "It Pleases," in *Turtle Island* (New York: New Directions Publishing, 1974), 44; Karl Shapiro, "Washington Cathedral," *Collected Poems, 1940–1978* (New York: Random House, 1978), 5.

27. Jean Toomer, *Cane* (New York: Boni and Liveright, 1923), 85.

28. Charles N. Concini, "Washington Then and Now," *Washingtonian*, October 1975, 51–66; Howard Means, "The Northernization of Washington," *Washingtonian*, August 1978, 82–86.

29. Audit Bureau of Circulation data furnished by the several magazines.

30. Nelson Polsby, "The Washington Community, 1960–1980," in Thomas E. Mann and Norman Ornstein, eds., *The New Congress* (Washington, D.C.: American Enterprise Institute, 1981), 20; James J. Haggerty, *Hail to the Redskins* (Washington, D.C.: Seven Seas Publishing, 1974), 102, 128, 134; David Slattery, *The Washington Redskins* (Virginia Beach, Va.: Jordan and Co., 1977), 63.

31. Neil V. Rosenberg, *Bluegrass: A History* (Urbana: University of Illinois Press, 1985), 27, 112–13, 138–39, 147–48, 224–26, 323–30, 354–55.

32. Musicologists distinguish Piedmont blues from the blues styles of the Mississippi Delta and Texas. Leading practitioners included Gary Davis, Josh White, Sonny Terry, and Blind Boy Fuller. See Barry Lee Pearson, *Virginia Piedmont Blues: The Lives and Art of Two Virginia Bluesmen* (Philadelphia: University of Pennsylvania Press, 1990); Bruce Bastin, *Red River Blues: The Blues Tradition in the Southeast* (Urbana: University of

Illinois Press, 1986), 315–17; Glenn Hinson to author, May 30, 1987; Michael Licht to author, April 24, 1987.

33. Polsby, "Washington Community," 19.

34. Migration data for 1955–60 are for state economic areas covering the District of Columbia; Montgomery and Prince Georges Counties, Md.; and Alexandria, Arlington, and Fairfax Counties, Va. For 1975–80, data from the Metropolitan Washington Council of Governments and the Northern Virginia Planning District Commission allowed the construction of a metropolitan region including the District of Columbia; Montgomery, Prince Georges, and Charles City Counties, Md.; and Alexandria, Arlington, Fairfax, Prince William, and Loudoun Counties, Va.

35. Morris Janowitz, *The Professional Soldier: A Social and Political Portrait* (Glencoe, Ill.: Free Press, 1960), 87–89; John Hawkins Napier III, "Military Tradition," in Charles Regan Wilson and William Ferris, eds., *Encyclopedia of Southern Culture* (Chapel Hill: University of North Carolina Press, 1989), 641–43.

36. Alvin Sunseri, "Military and Economy," in Wilson and Ferris, *Encyclopedia of Southern Culture,* 731–32.

37. C. Taylor Barnes and Curtis C. Roseman, "The Effect of Military Retirement on Population Redistribution," *Texas Business Review* 55 (May–June 1981): 100–106.

38. Brett Williams, *Upscaling Downtown: Stalled Gentrification in Washington, D.C.* (Ithaca, N.Y.: Cornell University Press, 1988), "The South in the City," *Journal of Popular Culture* 16 (Winter 1982): 30–41, and interview by author, Washington, D.C., April 10, 1987; John Cromartie and Carol Stack, "Reinterpretation of Black Return and Nonreturn Migration to the South, 1975–1980," *Geographical Review* 79 (July 1989): 297–310.

39. Joseph McGee, *Social and Economic Aspects of the Functional Entity of Washington, D.C.,* Catholic University Studies in Sociology, no. 25 (Washington, D.C., 1947); William Warner, *Beautiful Swimmers: Watermen, Crabs, and the Chesapeake Bay* (Boston: Little, Brown, 1976).

40. See materials in the following folders in the Greater Washington Board of Trade Papers, box 408, Gelman Library, George Washington University: "Baltimore/Washington Marketing Plan 1976," "Baltimore-Washington Regional Association," and "Baltimore/Washington Common Market Materials 1980."

41. Rudolph A. Pyatt Jr., "The Marketing of 'Washimore,'" *Washington Post,* August 21, 1989; Miles Maguire, "Dual Market Builds as Companies Set Up Satellite Operations," *Washington Times,* November 3, 1991; *Regardie's Magazine,* July 1989, 226–45.

42. Liz Spayd, "It's Official: Washington-Baltimore," *Washington Post,* December 29, 1991.

43. Paul Rotherburg, quoted in Liz Spayd, "Region to Become Major U.S. Market," *Washington Post*, September 10, 1991.

44. Janet Naylor, "Business Favors Washington First," *Washington Times*, November 19, 1992, citing Washington demographer George Grier.

45. Susan Pepper, quoted in Duncan Spencer, "Brokers and Developers See Baltimore and Washington as One Big Market," *Regardie's Magazine*, July 1989, 226–30.

46. Carroll Doherty, "The WashBalt Syndrome," *American Spectator*, November 1988, 56; Jeremy Schlosberg, "Welcome to Baltington," *American Demographics* 11 (March 1989): 56–57.

47. Washington Board of Trade, "Marketing Concept for the Baltimore/Washington Common Market" (June 1976) and 1978 statement on business conditions, both in Washington Board of Trade Papers, box 408, Gelman Library, George Washington University; Diane Granat, "Is Washington-Baltimore the Next Silicon Valley?," *Washingtonian*, April 1987, S3–S22; Edwin T. Haefele, "Developing the Region's Economy," in Atlee Shidler, ed., *Greater Washington in 1980* (Washington, D.C.: Greater Washington Research Center, 1980), 149; Stephen Fuller, "Regional Economic Interdependence: The Washington/Baltimore Common Market," paper delivered at the annual meeting of the Association of Collegiate Schools of Planning, Atlanta, November 1985; George Grier and Eunice Grier, *Greater Washington at Mid Decade: Shifting Growth Trends and Their Implications for the Regional Future* (Washington, D.C.: Greater Washington Research Center, 1985).

48. In 1958 Washington's most important telephone "partners," in descending order, were New York, Baltimore, Philadelphia, Norfolk, and Richmond. Baltimore's partners were Washington, Philadelphia, Norfolk, Richmond, and New York. In both cases, the volume of calls to the two Virginia cities was higher than a simple gravity model would predict. Jean Gottman, *Megalopolis: The Urbanized Northeastern Seaboard of the United States* (New York: Twentieth-Century Fund, 1961), 589–92.

49. A study by the University of Virginia defined a "golden crescent" as the eastern third of the state. See "Job Growth in Virginia," *Washington Post*, May 22, 1989.

50. John Shelton Reed, "The Heart of Dixie: An Essay in Folk Geography," *Social Forces* 54 (June 1976): 925–39; Wilbur Zelinsky, "North America's Vernacular Regions," *Annals of the Association of American Geographers* 70 (March 1980): 1–16.

51. The tallies omit two types of regional usage that might confuse the data: (1) Northwest, Northeast, Southeast, and Southwest when they clearly referred to the location of Washington businesses within one of the city's standard street address quadrants, and (2) regional terms that were obviously part of the name of national organizations located in Washington because of the presence of the federal government.

228 NOTES TO PAGES 174–78

52. Carl Abbott, "The End of the Southern City," in *Perspectives on the American South* (New York: Gordon and Breach, 1987), 4:187–218.

53. William S. White, "Public and Personal: Home Town USA," *Harper's Magazine*, June 1960, 95; Haynes Johnson, "The Capital of Success," *Washington Post Magazine*, February 2, 1986, 44; "Washington vs. New York," *Newsweek*, June 20, 1988, 16–24; William Regardie (March 13, 1987), Joel Garreau (March 25, 1987), and Jack Limpert (April 9, 1987), interviews by author, Washington, D.C.

54. Manuel Castells, "Space and Society: Managing the New Historical Relationships," in Michael Peter Smith, *Cities in Transformation: Class, Capital, and the State* (Beverly Hills, Calif.: Sage, 1984), 241–45; Pierre Clavel, *Opposition Planning in Wales and Appalachia* (Philadelphia: Temple University Press, 1983).

55. States of birth of presidents of the Washington Board of Trade from 1940 to 1985 were compiled from information in the Washington Board of Trade Papers, Gelman Library, George Washington University. Also see Atlee Shidler, "Local Community and National Government," in Shidler, *Greater Washington in 1980*, 24, and Robert N. Gray, personal communication, April 23, 1987. Washington thus appears to display the transition from locally oriented to cosmopolitan elites as discussed in Robert K. Merton, *Social Theory and Social Structure*, enlarged ed. (New York: Free Press, 1968), 441–72.

56. Council for Economic and Industry Research, Inc., "Economic Base Survey for the General Development Plan, National Capital Region," Washington, D.C., 1956 (mimeographed); Hamer and Co. Associates, *Economic Development in the Washington Area: Staff Study for the Joint Congressional Committee on Washington Area Problems, Congress of the United States* (Washington, D.C.: Government Printing Office, 1958); Metropolitan Washington Board of Trade, "Summary of Activities, 1954–1970," Washington Board of Trade Papers, Gelman Library, George Washington University.

57. The most thorough studies of intrasuburban differences are Howard Gillette Jr., "A National Workshop for Urban Policy: The Metropolitanization of Washington, 1946–68," *Public Historian* 7 (1985): 6–27, and Dennis Gale, *Washington, D.C.: Inner City Revitalization and Minority Suburbanization* (Philadelphia: Temple University Press, 1987), 11–49, 184–95. Demographics are treated in Stanley K. Bigman, *The Jewish Population of Greater Washington in 1956* (Washington, D.C.: Jewish Community Council of Greater Washington, 1957), and Eunice Grier and George Grier, "The Sorting Out of Washingtonians: Patterns of Residential Movement in the Metropolitan Area," in Shidler, *Greater Washington in 1980*, 49–68. A perceptive popular treatment of social and behavioral differences is Barbara Palmer, "Maryland vs. Virginia," *Washingtonian*, April 1981, 126–33.

58. Jeffrey R. Henig, *Gentrification in Adams Morgan* (Washington, D.C.: Center for Washington Area Studies, George Washington University, 1982); Suzanne Berry

Sherwood, *Foggy Bottom, 1800–1975* (Washington, D.C.: Center for Washington Area Studies, George Washington University, 1978); Brett Williams, "'There Goes the Neighborhood': Gentrification, Displacement, and Homelessness in Washington, D.C.," in Anna Lou Dehavenon, ed., *There's No Place Like Home: Anthropological Perspectives on Housing and Homelessness in the United States* (Westport, Conn.: Bergen and Garvey, 1996), 145–62.

59. Novelist Susan Shreve has taken the measure of Northwest Washington in such books as *Children of Power* (New York: Macmillan, 1979) and *A Woman Like That* (New York: Atheneum, 1974).

60. The inner districts of Arlington, Virginia, which have absorbed large numbers of Asian immigrants, might also be included in this east side sector.

61. Constance McLaughlin Green, *The Secret City: A History of Race Relations in the Nation's Capital* (Princeton, N.J.: Princeton University Press, 1967), 274–312; Benjamin Muse, *Virginia's Massive Resistance* (Bloomington: Indiana University Press, 1961), 3, 73, 139, 142, 159; George H. Callcott, *Maryland and America, 1940 to 1980* (Baltimore: Johns Hopkins University Press, 1985), 152–54, 244; U.S. Commission on Civil Rights, *A Long Day's Journey into Light: School Desegregation in Prince Georges County* (Washington, D.C.: Government Printing Office, 1976), 69–148; Michael S. Mayer, "The Eisenhower Administration and the Desegregation of Washington, D.C.," *Journal of Policy History* 3, no. 1 (1991): 24–41; Dennis John O'Keefe, "Decision-Making in the House Committee on the District of Columbia" (Ph.D. diss., University of Maryland, 1968), 57–62, 71–74.

62. Steven J. Diner, "From Jim Crow to Home Rule," *Wilson Quarterly* 13 (Winter 1989): 90–98.

63. Harry S. Jaffe and Tom Sherwood, *Dream City: Race, Power, and the Decline of Washington, D.C.* (New York: Simon and Schuster, 1994); Jonathan I. Z. Agronsky, *Marion Barry: The Politics of Race* (Latham, Md.: British American Publishing Co., 1991); Gillette, *Between Justice and Beauty.*

64. Wilbur Zelinsky, *The Cultural Geography of the United States* (Englewood Cliffs, N.J.: Prentice-Hall, 1973), 117.

65. John Shelton Reed, *Southerners: The Social-Psychology of Sectionalism* (Chapel Hill: University of North Carolina Press, 1983) and *One South: An Ethnic Approach to Regional Culture* (Baton Rouge: Louisiana State University Press, 1982), 119–26.

Essay on Sources

This study of the regional and transregional character of Washington has been determinedly eclectic. I have tried to read widely in the descriptive literature of guidebooks, directories, travel accounts, and magazine profiles. I have tried to learn what Washington residents thought about their city by reading reminiscences, autobiographies, early histories, and letters in manuscript collections. In part because local politics and planning have been extensively studied by other scholars, I focused much of my own research on the records and publications of business organizations, such as the Board of Trade and the Chamber of Commerce, that have tried to articulate visions and economic development agendas for Washington as a community.

In attempting a fresh look at a familiar city, this book has avoided a detailed retelling of several episodes in Washington's history that have been thoroughly treated by previous historians. Examples are the shaping and implementation of Pierre L'Enfant's plan, the Chesapeake and Ohio Canal, life and society during the Civil War, the rise and fall of Alexander Shepherd, and the work and consequences of the McMillan Commission. Readers wanting more information on these topics can turn to far more knowledgeable scholars.

Where available, I have used quantifiable evidence for judging changes in Washington's characteristics. Census data on population origins and migration patterns are invaluable. So is systematic biographical information on the origins and careers of business and community leaders, for the city's leaders have expressed and projected their own values onto the city. I also tried to quantify the changes in the regional character of names that Washingtonians have applied to their businesses and organizations.

Visual evidence has been an exciting and stimulating part of this study. In maps and pictures Washington has presented different faces to the world. Over the decades, residents and visitors have understood its relationships with site and landscape in differing ways. Where one stands to picture the city or how one centers a map are telling indicators of what the artist, photographer, or cartographer thinks important. The resulting depictions, in turn, shape the ways in which others see and understand the city.

At the intrametropolitan scale, I have tried to be sensitive to contrasts between different parts of Washington. In the antebellum decades, Washington was both similar to and different from Georgetown and Alexandria. In the late twentieth century, the "urban realms" of northern Virginia, eastern Washington and Prince Georges County, and Northwest Washington and Montgomery County contribute substantial differences as well as similarities to the overall character of Greater Washington. Implicit in the regional differentiation of the twentieth century are other, and equally important, differentiations by class and race.

A starting point for all Washington historians is the two-volume urban biography by Constance McLaughlin Green, *Washington: Village and Capital, 1800–1878* (Princeton, N.J.: Princeton University Press, 1962), and *Washington: Capital City, 1879–1950* (Princeton, N.J.: Princeton University Press, 1963). Based on newspapers and published descriptions, the books lack sophisticated interpretation but provide an invaluable summary of institutional development. The most valuable history from the earlier generation of city biographies is Wilhelmus Bogart Bryan, *A History of the National Capital from Its Foundation through the Period of the Adoption of the Organic Act* (New York: Macmillan, 1914–16). Two more recent works also require special mention for comprehensively combining multiple themes. Alan Lessoff, *The Nation and Its City: Politics, "Corruption," and Progress in Washington, D.C., 1861–1902* (Baltimore: Johns Hopkins University Press, 1994), looks at local politics and self-determination in relation to physical development and national politics. Howard Gillette Jr., *Between Justice and Beauty: Race, Planning, and the Failure of Urban Policy in Washington, D.C.* (Baltimore: Johns Hopkins University Press, 1995), traces local politics and physical development in the context of racial conflict and difference.

More commonly, studies of Washington have tended to focus on one of three broad research themes—race, physical development, and the federal presence. The first is especially useful for understanding Washington as a "southern city," the second for understanding it as a "national city," and the third for understanding its evolution as a networked information city.

Washington has been an exemplar and test case for American racial relations, a role exacerbated by its border location. The evolution of the black community from the early decades of the city through Reconstruction is treated in Letitia Woods Brown, *Free Negroes in the District of Columbia, 1790–1846* (New York: Oxford University Press, 1972); Constance McLaughlin Green, *The Secret City: A History of Race Relations in the Nation's Capital* (Princeton, N.J.: Princeton University Press, 1967); and Allan Johnston, *Surviving Freedom: The Black Community of Wash-*

ington, D.C., 1860–1880 (New York: Garland Publishing, 1993). Blacks and European immigrant groups are covered in Francine Curro Cary, ed., *Urban Odyssey: A Multicultural History of Washington, D.C.* (Washington, D.C.: Smithsonian Institution Press, 1996). Studies of contrasting segments of black Washington in the late nineteenth and early twentieth centuries are Willard Gatewood, *Aristocrats of Color: The Black Elite, 1880–1920* (Bloomington: Indiana University Press, 1990); Rayford W. Logan, *Howard University: The First Hundred Years* (New York: New York University Press, 1969); James Borchert, *Alley Life in Washington: Family, Community, and Folklife in the City, 1850–1970* (Urbana: University of Illinois Press, 1980); and Elizabeth Clark-Lewis, *Living In, Living Out: African-American Domestics in Washington, D.C., 1910–1940* (Washington, D.C.: Smithsonian Institution Press, 1994).

Isolation and interaction among different groups of white and black Washingtonians in recent decades are the subjects of a number of community-based social science studies: Ulf Hannerz, *Soulside: Inquiries into Ghetto Culture and Community* (New York: Columbia University Press, 1969); Joseph Howell, *Hard Living on Clay Street: Portraits of Blue Collar Families* (Garden City, N.Y.: Doubleday, 1973); Eliott Liebow, *Tally's Corner* (Boston: Little, Brown, 1967); Brett Williams, *Upscaling Downtown: Stalled Gentrification in Washington, D.C.* (Ithaca, N.Y.: Cornell University Press, 1988); Jeffrey R. Henig, *Gentrification in Adams Morgan* (Washington, D.C.: Center for Washington Area Studies, George Washington University, 1982); and Dennis Gale, *Washington, D.C.: Inner City Revitalization and Minority Suburbanization* (Philadelphia: Temple University Press, 1987).

Since the 1790s local and national leaders have struggled with the challenge of planning and building a city "worthy of the nation." A number of students of Washington's built environment have looked at formal planning, architecture, neighborhood evolution, and the framing issues of local and national politics.

The starting points for understanding Washington's very first decade are Kenneth Bowling, *The Creation of Washington, D.C.: The Idea and Location of the American Capital* (Fairfax, Va.: George Mason University Press, 1991), and John W. Reps, *Washington on View: The Nation's Capital since 1790* (Chapel Hill: University of North Carolina Press, 1991), which interweaves discussion of the city's physical growth with a fascinating inventory of maps and pictorial descriptions. Frederick Gutheim, *The Potomac* (New York: Rinehart, 1949), puts the city into its regional context, with attention to social, economic, and environmental issues.

The evolution of the public city is treated in John Reps, *Monumental Washington: The Planning and Development of the Capital Center* (Princeton, N.J.: Princeton University Press, 1967); U.S. National Capital Planning Commission and Frederick Gutheim, *Worthy of the Nation: The History of Planning for the National Capital* (Washington, D.C.: National Capital Planning Commission, 1977); Frederick

Gutheim and Wilcomb Washburn, *The Federal City: Plans and Realities* (Washington, D.C.: Smithsonian Institution Press, 1967); Vivien Green Fryd, *Art and Empire: The Politics of Ethnicity in the United States Capitol, 1815–1860* (New Haven, Conn.: Yale University Press, 1992); and Richard Longstreth, ed., *The Mall in Washington* (Washington, D.C.: Smithsonian Institution Press, 1991). Also available are a number of neighborhood studies on such areas as Georgetown, Foggy Bottom, Brookland, Anacostia, and Capitol Hill.

One of the reasons we seek to understand Washington as a physical place is to judge how its built environment has influenced local and national politics. James Sterling Young, *The Washington Community, 1800–1828* (New York: Columbia University Press, 1966), addresses this question directly by examining the living arrangements and social interactions of early members of Congress. Kathryn Allamong Jacob, *Capital Elites: High Society in Washington, D.C., after the Civil War* (Washington, D.C.: Smithsonian Institution Press, 1995), explores the social context of postbellum politics, and Jessica Ivy Elfenbein, *Civics, Commerce, and Community: The History of the Greater Washington Board of Trade, 1889–1989* (Dubuque, Iowa: Kendall-Hunt Publishing Co., 1990), examines the institutional context. The politics themselves are considered in detail in William M. Maury, *Alexander "Boss" Shepherd and the Board of Public Works* (Washington, D.C.: Center for Washington Area Studies, George Washington University, 1975), and in the books by Gillette and Lessoff.

Washington as an information center is the subject of James Kirkpatrick Flack, *Desideratum in Washington: The Intellectual Community in the Capital City, 1870–1900* (Cambridge, Mass.: Schenkman, 1975), and David Ricci, *The Transformation of American Politics: The New Washington and the Rise of Think Tanks* (New Haven, Conn.: Yale University Press, 1993). Also see John Tracy Ellis, *The Formative Years of the Catholic University of America* (Washington, D.C.: American Catholic Historical Society, 1946); C. Joseph Nuesse, *The Catholic University of America: A Centennial History* (Washington, D.C.: Catholic University of America Press, 1990); and Elmer L. Kayser, *Bricks without Straw: The Evolution of George Washington University* (New York: Appleton-Century-Crofts, 1970).

Recent politics are the subject of Martha Derthick, *City Politics in Washington, D.C.* (Cambridge: Harvard-MIT Joint Center for Urban Studies, 1962); Sam Smith, *Captive Capital: Colonial Life in Modern Washington* (Bloomington: Indiana University Press, 1974); Harry S. Jaffe and Tom Sherwood, *Dream City: Race, Power, and the Decline of Washington, D.C.* (New York: Simon and Schuster, 1994); and Jonathan I. Z. Agronsky, *Marion Barry: The Politics of Race* (Latham, Md.: British American Publishing Co., 1991).

Deserving special mention outside the three broad categories of social, physical, and political history are several portraits of Washington during wartime:

Margaret Leech, *Reveille in Washington, 1860–1865* (New York: Harper and Brothers, 1941), deservedly won a Pulitzer Prize. Mary Mitchell, *Divided Town* (Barre, Mass.: Barre Publishing, 1968), also covers the Civil War years, and David Brinkley, *Washington Goes to War* (New York: Knopf, 1988), considers World War II.

These books are just a starting point for Washington history. Persons interested in the capital city can also be grateful that the Center for Washington Area Studies at George Washington University in the early 1980s published two valuable guides to historical literature and information sources. Perry G. Fisher and Linda J. Lear, *A Selected Bibliography for Washington Studies and a Description of Major Local Collections* (1981), includes useful annotations by knowledgeable Washington historians. Rita A. Calvan, *Selected Theses and Dissertations on the Washington, D.C., Region* (1983), is unannotated but thorough.

INDEX